**OUR GREATEST PASSION
IS ENABLING YOUR BUSINESS
TO GROW.**

**WE ARE A GLOBAL BANKING GROUP,
ACTIVE IN 40 COUNTRIES AROUND THE WORLD.**

A leader in Italy in all business areas, we are passionate about our clients' work
and fully committed to their success. We create financial services and products for them everywhere they are.
And solutions as unique as their needs and ambitions.

INTESA SANPAOLO

www.group.intesasanpaolo.com

The energy to see and the energy to do.

Our energy has been traveling around 5 continents for over 60 years. Thanks to the work of all our hands.

eni

eni.com

GREAT DECISIONS 2017

About the cover

A weather-beaten, torn European Union flag flies in Hastings, a town on England's southeast coast best known for the 1066 Battle of Hastings.

Photo Credit:
Paul Mansfield/Getty Images

GREAT DECISIONS IS A TRADEMARK OF THE FOREIGN POLICY ASSOCIATION.

© COPYRIGHT 2017 BY FOREIGN POLICY ASSOCIATION, INC., 470 PARK AVENUE SOUTH, NEW YORK, NEW YORK 10016.

PRINTED IN THE UNITED STATES OF AMERICA BY DARTMOUTH PRINTING COMPANY, HANOVER, NH.

LIBRARY OF CONGRESS CONTROL NUMBER: 2015915676

ISBN: 978-0-87124-256-3

The *2016 Opinion Ballot Report*, Global Discussion Questions and the Index to Great Decisions topics can now be found online in the Resources section at **www.greatdecisions.org**

Researched as of November 25, 2016.

The authors are responsible for factual accuracy and for the views expressed.

FPA itself takes no position on issues of U.S. foreign policy.

"*Civilization* is in a race

between education and catastrophe." Was H.G. Wells indulging in hyperbole when he made that observation? I think not. In the Age of Globalization, education has never counted for more.

Consider, for a moment, higher education. The university is one of America's bedrock civic institutions. It is here that many learn to shed ancient prejudices. It is here that many learn to transcend parochialism—the self-absorbed kind of parochialism that Shakespeare alluded to when he said, "There is no world without Verona's walls." It is here that many are prepared to become what Aristotle called "genuine citizens"—capable and disposed to participate in public affairs. And it is here that many develop portable skills to pursue complex endeavors. Universities grow the economic pie. They enable their graduates to overcome trivialization—to look back on their lives and say, "I made a difference."

In *The Future of Higher Education in the Age of Globalization*, I note that "The prospects for peace and prosperity are greatly enhanced by institutions of higher learning that prepare open-minded world citizens." Strobe Talbott, president of the Brookings Institution, elaborates: "A phrase briefly fashionable in the mid-20th century—'citizen of the world'—will have assumed real meaning by the end of the 21st." This perception is confirmed by the Center for International Business Education and Research (CIBER). After surveying over 800 American CEOs, CIBER found that an overwhelming majority of them (85%) believe that a global perspective is vital for their workforce at both the management and entry levels.

According to the Association of International Educators, while 81% of American students express a strong interest in pursuing their education abroad, only 1% actually study abroad annually. In contrast, 1,043,839 international students are currently enrolled in American institutions of higher learning. They contribute $32.8 billion to the U.S. economy and over 400,000 jobs are created or supported by their presence. California draws the most international students (149,328) followed by New York (114,316).

These students are drawn to the United States by the quality of education. But they are also attracted by the American way of life. Many, for the first time, can express themselves freely and observe first hand government of, by and for the people.

However, in a recent speech to the World Affairs Councils of America, Carl Gershman, president of the National Endowment for Democracy, warned of "a crisis of democracy." He cited the loss of geopolitical power by the United States and its allies, and the corresponding increase in the influence of authoritarian countries. This weakening of "hard power," he observed, has been paralleled by a deterioration of "soft power," as authoritarian governments use sophisticated techniques to undermine global norms enshrined in the Universal Declaration of Human Rights and strive to confer primacy on unlimited state sovereignty.

"Of greatest concern," said Gershman, "is the third dimension of the problem, which is the crisis of democratic values and will in the established democracies of the West." He traces the origins of this crisis to the financial collapse of 2008 and to the economic stagnation that followed. Dysfunctional government and a backlash against globalization have given rise to populism and illiberal politics in Europe and the United States.

Gershman continues:

> Since it is the democratic West that has built the security, political, and economic institutions that constitute the liberal world order and that have produced unprecedented peace and prosperity over the past seven decades, this crisis of legitimacy now threatens to shake the foundations of contemporary global civilization.

> We have grown complacent about our democracy, assuming that its survival is inevitable and that it doesn't need constant care and civic engagement. Last July, NED published an article in its Journal of Democracy by Roberto Stefan Foa and Yascha Mounk that was ominously entitled "The Danger of the Deconsolidation." It contains some very alarming statistics about the attitudes of young people towards democracy that show that democratic commitment declines with age. Young people, in other words, show less commitment to democracy than their parents and grandparents.

> For example, only 30 percent of millennials think it's "essential" to live in a democracy, compared to 72 percent of those born before World War II. Twenty-four percent of millennials think that democracy is a bad way to run the country. Among all age cohorts, the share of Americans who thinks it's best to have "a strong leader" who doesn't have to bother with a parliament or elections has steadily risen, from 24 percent in 1995 to 32 percent in 2011. In 1995 one in sixteen respondents felt that it would be a good thing for the army to rule. Today that figure is one in six. Citing the declining trust in government in our country, Foa and Mounki write that democratic breakdown is "extremely unlikely" in a world where citizens fervently support democracy, but that "is no longer certain…that this is the world we live in" today.

While the 2016 presidential election exposed fault lines in our political economy, there is more that binds us as a people than divides us. We must not let our allies down and we must not let ourselves down. We must strengthen our democracy at home and promote democracy abroad. The United States has always been the voice that inspires democracy in the world. If that voice is muffled or divided, the entire world will lose a beacon of hope.

Democracy, the rule of law, education and economic development are bulwarks of freedom and peace. In my book, *In Pursuit of Peace: Conflict Prevention and World Order,* I stress that we should not take a stable world order for granted. Peace is not the default state of international relations. American leadership will be necessary to ensure global stability and security.

Noel V. Lateef
President and CEO
Foreign Policy Association

Continuity and change in American foreign policy

by Robert P. Haffa, Jr.

The 2016 Presidential election will usher in a new administration with an opportunity to continue on the foreign policy path that the Obama administration has traveled over the last eight years, or to change the objectives and adjust the instruments of that policy. That choice can be informed through an understanding of American foreign policies during the Cold War (1947–91) and afterward. Since the end of World War II, when the United States abandoned past policies of isolationism to assume leadership in the international political system, two themes have dominated. The first was the containment of the Soviet Union during the Cold War. Although various administrations adopted different strategies to achieve that objective, they remained faithful to the overall goal. After the Cold War ended, American foreign policies appeared less consistent in purpose and implementation, lacking a bipartisan consensus on objectives and strategies. Following the terrorist attacks of September 11, 2001, however, the United States once again focused on a singular foreign threat, albeit a less than existential one. Similar to the varied strategies of containment, the George W. Bush and Barack Obama administrations adopted contrasting approaches to countering terrorism and waging war against its practitioners and sponsors. Within a range of foreign policy issues, the next President will also decide how much the United States should concentrate on the threat of international terrorism, and how to conduct that policy.

Strategies of containment: Continuity in American foreign policy during the Cold War

Although it may seem counterintuitive, the fact is that continuity and change can affect American foreign policy nearly simultaneously. This seems particularly true when there is broad agreement on the objectives of that policy through various Presidential administrations but differences in the perception of resources available to pursue those goals and the proper instruments to pursue them. One of the better historical developments of this concept is John Lewis Gaddis' book *Strategies of Containment*. In that work, Gaddis argued that the overarching objective of American foreign policy during the Cold War was the containment of the Soviet Union, and that successive administrations of differing political parties adopted that goal. However, owing largely to the perceived health of the domestic economy, as well as to pressing domestic priorities, these administrations adopted either *symmetric* means (matching the adversary at every level) or *asymmetrical* approaches (applying American strengths against the opponents' weaknesses). Thus Eisenhower, prizing a stable economy and balanced budget over other national objectives, sought more "bang for the buck." His administration emphasized the atomic superiority the U.S. enjoyed over the Soviet Union and adopted an asymmetrical policy of "massive retaliation" in response to any

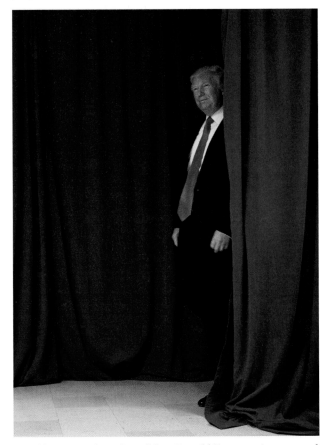

Republican presidential candidate Donald Trump arrives to speak on Sept. 8, 2016, at Cleveland Arts and Social Sciences Academy in Cleveland. (EVAN VUCCI/AP PHOTO)

ROBERT P. HAFFA, JR., *is an adjunct professor of political science at John Hopkins University and a non-resident senior fellow at the Center for Strategic and Budgetary Assessments in Washington, DC. He leads a Great Decisions group in Naples, Florida.*

For an annotated bibliography of the works referenced in this article, please go to the Resources section at www.greatdecisions.org

TIMELINE: American Foreign Policy after 1945

HARRY S TRUMAN LIBRARY AND MUSEUM

1947–53 Truman-doctrine: The policy of containment was launched by Harry Truman in 1947 with his speech before Congress arguing that the U.S. must come to the aid of countries threatened by totalitarian regimes. Aid to Greece and Turkey, the Marshall Plan, the Berlin airlift and NATO formed foundations of the Doctrine, as did the "militarization" of containment through the Korean War.

1953–61 Eisenhower's New Look: Responding to an unpopular, drawn out, and costly conventional war in Korea, the Eisenhower Administration chose to leverage America's advantage in atomic weapons by declaring that communist aggression anywhere might be met with "massive retaliation."

1961–68 Kennedy-Johnson's Flexible Response: With Soviet nuclear weapons making "massive retaliation" less credible, and with fiscal constraints removed from the Defense budget, the Kennedy administration shifted to a strategy of "flexible response," emphasizing conventional military capabilities to deter U.S. adversaries and to defend America's interests and allies.

1969–77 Nixon-Kissinger Détente: Détente originated in the aftermath of the Vietnam War, as the U.S. recognized its limits as a "global policeman" and confronted military parity with the Soviet Union. The approach prioritized diplomatic relations between the U.S. and the USSR to pursue U.S. foreign policy objectives at lower levels of tension and cost.

1977–81 The Carter Doctrine: Following Watergate and Nixon's resignation, Jimmy Carter emphasized moral commitments and human rights in foreign policy-making. Following the Soviet invasion of Afghanistan in 1979, however, his Doctrine declared the Persian Gulf and its oil resources to be of vital interest to the United States.

1981–93 The Reagan doctrine: Ronald Reagan advocated "peace through strength" and sought to roll back Soviet gains, rebutting the Brezhnev doctrine that such gains were irreversible. George H.W. Bush maintained this emphasis on idealism and moral principles as he sought to create a post-Cold War "new world order."

1993–2001 Bill Clinton's foreign policy: The Cold War over, Bill Clinton's foreign policy was guided by the concept of "selective engagement," focused on the domestic economy, and advocated a policy of "engagement and enlargement" to capitalize on the U.S. victory in the Cold War and promote democracy worldwide.

2001–2008 George W. Bush doctrine: George W. Bush's foreign policy, forged by the 9/11 attacks and their aftermath, idealistically championed a balance of power that favors human freedom and justified preemptive war against America's enemies in a "War on Terror."

2008–2016 The Obama doctrine: Burdened by the Great Recession of 2008, Barack Obama attempted to retreat from the war on terror in Iraq and Afghanistan and focus on "nation building at home." However, Obama was incapable of escaping from the footprints of his predecessors in foreign policy, and a perceived retrenchment in U.S. foreign engagement has been accompanied by challenges from Russia, ISIS, China, North Korea, and other state and non-state actors.

U.S. President Barack Obama speaks about his decision to increase U.S. troop levels in Afghanistan by about 30,000 during a speech at the U.S. Military Academy at West Point, New York, on December 1, 2009. (ROGER L. WOLLENBERG/POOL/CORBIS VIA GETTY IMAGES)

Soviet encroachment. In contrast, although the Kennedy-Johnson administrations shared a similar "zero-sum" perspective of competition with the Soviets for the allegiance of the "third world," they adopted a more symmetrical approach. This strategy of containment known as "flexible response" was applied across the spectrum of foreign policy instruments: a conventional and unconventional military build-up; an expanding economy to support the attendant costs of these new capabilities; renewed emphasis on non-military measures including reenergized public diplomacy and negotiations; and, the strengthening of alliances.

Despite changes in method and means, however, the continuity in American foreign policy was demonstrated by its dedication to containing the U.S.S.R., a goal that was ultimately achieved with the Soviet Union's demise.

To illustrate these shifts in strategy—with the understanding that strategy is a means of fitting together objectives and resources—Gaddis pointed to what he termed an administration's "strategic code" guiding American foreign policy. Those guidelines included assumptions about American interests in the world, potential threats to them, and desirable, feasible, and acceptable responses to those threats. Of interest to those of us considering prospects for continuity and change in U. S. foreign policy in 2017, Gaddis joined Henry Kissinger in concluding that barring unforeseen events (9/11 or the Soviet invasion of Afghanistan come to mind) these perspectives were formed before the administration's accession to office, and tended not to change over the years. Gaddis enumerated five of these strategic guidelines used to pursue containment during the Cold War. George Kennan's original strategy implemented by the Truman administration stressed the long-term nature of the competition and advocated employing America's industrial might to moderate Soviet behavior. Paul Nitze' s NSC-68, validated by the invasion of South Korea by the North in June 1950, led to a "militarization" of containment. Eisenhower's nuclear-intensive "New Look" of the 1950s sought to leverage the American nuclear advantage, relying less on expensive conventional forces after an unpopular and costly limited war in Korea. The Kennedy-Johnson strategy of "flexible response" moved away from the "massive retaliation" doctrine of the "New Look" to a more symmetric approach to deterrence and defense. The Nixon-Kissinger policy of détente revived Kennan's realist concept of containment, emphasizing negotiation and compromise while awaiting the Soviet Union's internal collapse. Updating that list would include the Carter doctrine declaring vital U.S. interests in the Persian Gulf region (an alteration in the administration's view following the 1979 Soviet invasion of Afghanistan) and the Reagan-George H.W. Bush doctrines of global, multi-layered, long-term competition with the Soviets that contributed to the undoing of the "evil empire."

It is beyond our scope here to deal in detail with these varied foreign policies, but they provide us a useful analytical framework as we ponder the future.

As history has recorded, each of these macro-approaches

President John F. Kennedy and First Lady Jacqueline Kennedy stand in an open car to greet members of the 2506 Cuban Invasion Brigade at the Orange Bowl Stadium in Miami, Florida, in December 1962. The Brigade was comprised of Cuban exiles who participated in the Bay of Pigs invasion of April 1961. (CECIL STOUGHTON. WHITE HOUSE PHOTOGRAPHS. JOHN F. KENNEDY PRESIDENTIAL LIBRARY AND MUSEUM, BOSTON)

to foreign policy formulation and implementation had their limits. As Gaddis explains, symmetry responds to all threats, peripheral and central, and provides the policymaker an extensive menu of options to counter them. But a strategy of symmetry adopts a defensive crouch while demanding nearly unlimited resources to meet all thrusts with a matching parry. On the other hand, a strategy of asymmetry encourages the decision-maker to distinguish between vital and less important interests, allocate scarce resources accordingly, and seek opportunities to leverage the nation's strengths against an opponent's weakness. Could the best elements of each strategy be combined to form a more effective course of action? Gaddis thinks not. Despite the thread of continuity in the objective of containment, institutional amnesia, domestic politics, and a reassessment of resources and priorities in each new administration weigh against constancy in practice, as each new administration attempts to create a distinctive identity and coin a new strategic concept. Frequently, as Gaddis concludes, it was the dominance of economic factors and campaign promises to restore or expand the American economy that led to these shifts in strategies of containment.

After the Cold War: Continuity without consensus

The abrupt end of the Cold War surprised many a political scientist and foreign policy professional, and no one was quite sure what to do about it. Certainly the continuing objective of containment had been reached—thus offering an

A Red Army base along the supply route near Pul-e-Khumri during the invasion of Afghanistan by the Russians, January 1980. (PHOTO BY ROMANO CAGNONI/GETTY IMAGES)

opportunity for change—as scholars and politicians deliberated a "unipolar moment," the "end of history," and a "new world order." Clearly there was a call for a "peace dividend" and Bill Clinton, setting aside the foreign policy successes of the George H.W. Bush administration, pointed out to the electorate that it was the domestic economy that mattered. As Gaddis argued, the perception of the limited resources available to pursue symmetric military responses and the priority of domestic programs influenced foreign policy choices in the post-Cold War era, as well.

Yet, without an overriding objective such as containment to guide the direction of foreign policy, America's path in international politics appeared uncertain. Indeed, policy choices offered both continuity and change. In an influential article in the Winter 1996 issue of *International Security*, Barry Posen and Andrew Ross suggested four post-Cold War foreign policy models or "grand strategies:" a retreat from global leadership; a campaign of liberal internationalism; an effort to maintain U.S. primacy; or an *ad hoc* policy of "selective engagement." As Steven Hook and John Spanier point out in their book, *American Foreign Policy since World War II*, the first two strategies represented continuity with pre-war idealistic thrusts in U.S. foreign policy, while the second two incorporated a realist perspective appealing now to an America occupying the commanding heights of international politics.

None of those candidate strategies were adopted in totality by post-Cold War administrations. Hook and Spanier suggest the foreign policy of the Clinton administration closely followed the spirit of George H. W. Bush's "new world order" in adopting a policy of "assertive multilateralism" and declaring a course of action described as "engagement and enlargement" as a successor to containment. Both administrations sought to strengthen the liberal international order within a new global landscape. However, owing to the Clinton administration's focus on the domestic economy, we can characterize its strategy as an "asymmetric" one,

owing to the belief that, without an expanding economy, the United States could not afford to play an influential role in the international political system. With that expanding economy, Clinton was able to choose, Chinese-menu like, from the four grand strategies proposed. "Enlargement" was interpreted as spreading democratic forms of government in a new twist on Wilsonian idealism. Bolstered by Congressional additions to the President's defense budget, the American military was able to maintain its primacy and selectively engage in the Balkans and elsewhere. But there were other international crises, notably the plight of failed states in Africa, where America chose to retreat, or to remain aloof. Thus some of the policy approaches of the G.H.W. Bush administration based on a realist perspective were continued through Bill Clinton's two terms. Somewhat surprisingly, Henry Kissinger agreed with this multi-faceted approach. In his 2001 book *Does America Need a Foreign Policy?* Kissinger advocated a policy blending interests and values, idealism and realism.

If George W. Bush had read the Kissinger book before September 11, 2001, he might have agreed with most of it. Like Bill Clinton and unlike his father, George W. Bush lacked familiarity with issues in foreign affairs, and relied primarily on his advisers to bring him policy options. When he was running for President, Mr. Bush made the case for continuity in American foreign policy based on Cold War policies emphasizing international alliances and a strong military dedicated to deterring state actors, but not engaging in irregular warfare or nation building. In a debate with Vice President Al Gore during the 2000 Presidential campaign, Bush rejected the proposition that the United States should be exporting American ideals and dictating a path to democracy. His views changed a year later.

Nevertheless, as Ivo Daalder and James Lindsay argued in their 2005 book *America Unbound: The Bush Revolution in Foreign Policy,* it was not a change in U.S. foreign policy *goals*, but *how those goals should be achieved* that sparked the revolution. The oceans that had long protected U.S. borders were unable to defend against the terrorist attacks of 9/11, and the Bush Administration responded with a "war on terror" resulting in intervention in Afghanistan to topple the Taliban regime allowing sanctuary to America's new enemies, and a preventive war against Saddam's pro-terrorist and WMD-capable regime in Iraq. Eschewing the reactive strategies of containment and traditional reliance on allies, the Bush administration championed regime change and preemptive attack in pursuit of national security. However, the Bush administration also returned to the idealistic goals of promoting freedom and democracy reminiscent of the Clinton foreign policy agenda; the 2006 *National Security Strategy* document linked the war on terror with the spread of democracy. Achieving a more democratic and peaceful world would not be pursued through multilateral initiatives and international organizations, but rather with the preemptive use of military force to overthrow tyrannical autocracies—with a "coalition of the willing" if available, unilaterally if necessary. The strategy declared it was "idealistic about our national goals, and realistic about the means to achieve them." Buoyed by a booming economy, the Bush administration advocated a symmetric strategy of assertive conventional and irregular military action against terrorist networks and their supporters. Yet the 2006 security strategy coupled defeating terrorism with spreading democracy and increasing human freedom.

As we trace continuity and change in American foreign policy, Hook and Spanier's point that swings in post-war American foreign policy may have been pushed by citizens in the voting booth is relevant and timely. Barack Obama steered a campaign and was elected to the Presidency partially on a platform seeking an alternative to the Bush Doctrine and its war on terror. Mr. Obama pledged to appease the international community that he claimed the U.S. had alienated, championed "soft power" over military might, and emphasized diplomacy as the primary instrument of American foreign policy. As appealing as these might have been to the attentive public, the Obama administration was also shackled by the economics of the time—the "Great Recession" of 2008 clearly influenced the administration's decisions as to what could be done internationally and what resources needed to be redirected to "nation building at home." Nevertheless, Mr. Obama reiterated a George Bush pre-election pledge—to adhere to the liberal international order and to reinforce the modalities guiding American foreign policy since World War II. The Obama administration reflected policy continuity in other ways, as well, following his predecessor's goal of achieving U.S. primacy in the international political system, and retaining Robert Gates as Secretary of Defense to oversee America's military retrenchment from Iraq and Afghanistan.

Despite his change agenda, however, President Obama was unable to keep his promise to retreat from the periphery to the core, retrench from foreign wars, and pivot away from the Middle East to regions he considered more important to America's future. As he directed the withdrawal of U.S. ground forces from Afghanistan and Iraq, President Obama was forced to bolster U.S. counter-terrorist and counter-insurgency capabilities with special operations forces, clandestine CIA operations, and lethal drones, a strategy Professor Gaddis might categorize as "asymmetric." The objective of defeating terrorist groups and their supporters remained, but the strategies had changed. President Obama, in an interview in the April 2016 *Atlantic*, characterized his foreign policy as one of selective engagement, "doubling down where success is plausible, and limiting American exposure to the rest."

In an article in the September/October 2015 issue of *Foreign Affairs*, Gideon Rose suggests one should judge a President's handling of foreign policy as that of a member of a track relay team or a middle relief pitcher in baseball: taking over from his predecessor, working hard, and passing on policies that worked—or didn't— to his successor. That sounds like a case for continuity. Yet, as Rose admits, the

U.S. President Ronald Reagan, commemorating the 750th anniversary of Berlin, addresses on June 12, 1987, the people of West Berlin at the base of the Brandenburg Gate, near the Berlin Wall. Due to the amplification system being used, the President's words could also be heard on the Eastern (Communist-controlled) side of the wall. "Tear down this wall!" was the famous command from President Reagan to Soviet leader Mikhail Gorbachev to destroy the Berlin Wall. The address Reagan delivered that day is considered by many to have affirmed the beginning of the end of the Cold War and the fall of communism. On Nov. 9–11, 1989, the people of a free Berlin tore down that wall. (DIETER KLAR/PICTURE-ALLIANCE/DPA/AP IMAGESS)

retrenchment from peripheral interests to core values and its emphasis on asymmetric military means, sanctions, and negotiations left the Obama administration's foreign policies subject to calls for change. Specifically, Bret Stephens' rebuttal to Rose in the same *Foreign Affairs* issue contends that President Obama's retreat from foreign interventions created power vacuums filled by newly aggressive state actors and newly formed violent extremist organizations. Stephens also raises the issue of domestic economics influencing foreign policy, arguing that these priorities need not be seen as zero-sum, but rather that a country's prosperity depends on international security and stability. It remains to be seen if the United States will return to a more expansive use of American power in the continued pursuit and defense of the liberal international order, or will retrench and shy away from international obligations and commitments. Observ-

The twin towers of the World Trade Center billow smoke after hijacked airliners crashed into them early 11 September 11, 2001.(HENNY RAY ABRAMS/AFP/GETTY IMAGES)

ing this dichotomy, Richard Haas, president of the Council on Foreign Relations, posited that the United States is now engaged in a great foreign policy debate "between a besieged traditional internationalism and an energized new isolationism." Which will dominate: the momentum of continuity or the push for change?

American foreign policy 2017: The momentum of continuity

What factors might push American foreign policy in essentially the same direction as that of the Obama administration? The election of Hillary Clinton, from the same Democratic Party and the Secretary of State during Mr. Obama's first term, would have suggested a desire for continuity. Indeed, some party activists promoted Mrs. Clinton's nomination as a step toward Mr. Obama's "third term," and, with her election, an extension of his relatively cautious, asymmetric, big-picture, long-game orientation and nurturing of the liberal international order.

However, additional factors sustain the momentum of continuity, even with the election of Mr. Trump. The "war on terror," although the Obama-Clinton State Department chose not to call it that, will persist and very likely occupy center stage in the next President's first term and perhaps much longer than that. Just as Mr. Obama has been unable to break away from the war on violent extremist organiza-

tions as proposed and practiced by George W. Bush, so the next President will have to determine the weight of military action the United States should bear and how prudently and effectively some of that burden can be shouldered by U.S. allies and friends. Here the limits placed by public opinion and the role of Congress acting as a brake on policy change will come into play. The September 2013 Congressional vote against U.S. military action in Syria, despite the regime's use of poison gas on civilians that crossed President Obama's "red line," suggests a non-interventionist mood in the body politic trending toward isolationism. Such a policy of restraint, if either forced on a new administration or adopted by it, would certainly push for change. But public opinion limits on further intervention, while keeping the war on terror on course, suggests continuity.

Finally, despite campaign rhetoric on both sides, there is the orthodoxy of American foreign policy over the decades since World War II that, despite isolationist flirtations after Korea and Vietnam calling for America to "come home," positions America as the indispensable nation providing global leadership to keep the liberal international order intact. This position champions continuity: seeking reconciliation and a cessation of hostilities in the Middle East; ensuring stability in NATO Europe and beyond in the face of Russian mischief making, aggression and annexation; and, keeping the sea lanes in the South China Sea—and more broadly, the global commons—open for business. Within that globalized economy, the U.S. must continue its underwriting and stewardship of the global economic system.

American foreign policy 2017: The push for change

If continuity has momentum on its side, what are the factors suggesting change in America's foreign policy in the next administration? As Richard Haas explains, a rising tide of public dissatisfaction with foreign entanglements coupled with economic frustration at home has strengthened isolationist impulses. Recent polls taken by Pew and other sampling organizations suggest a majority of Americans are content to let our allies and friends fend for themselves, while a plurality believes that the United States is too heavily committed abroad. Political science models based on recent GDP growth, the incumbent President's approval rating, and the public's desire for new leadership in the White House after eight years forecast that it's "time for a change." A recent poll taken by the Chicago Council on World Affairs found that "defending our allies' security" ranked near the bottom of foreign policy priorities. These isolationist views have been voiced by both the political left and right: Bernie Sanders waged a nearly successful presidential campaign railing against international trade and conflict; Donald Trump won the election, preaching a new brand of isolationism, questioning the utility and affordability of America's alliances, and adopting a slogan of "America First."

If there is one principal factor that indicates a desire for change in American foreign policy in 2017, it would be the victory of Donald Trump. Building on the growing gap between the foreign policy elite on K-Street and the *hoi polloi* on Main Street, Mr. Trump pledged to abandon the "Washington playbook," force allies to pay their fair share for American protection and support, retrench from overseas bases, and renegotiate trade deals with friends and spheres of interests with competitors.

Other factors could also change the vectors of American foreign policy. Although Richard Neustadt's classic book, *Presidential Power* emphasized the use of persuasion, Arthur Schlesinger's *Imperial Presidency* may be closer to the truth these days. As reported in the *Washington Post* of July 31, 2016, presidential scholars now warn that so many powers have been added to the Presidency—primarily through the use of Executive orders by George W. Bush and Barrack Obama—that a new President might be able to quickly push his foreign policy agenda through a gridlocked and passive Congress.

Finally, to recall an often referenced but unreliably authenticated statement on continuity or change in foreign policy, British Prime Minister Harold MacMillan, when once asked what troubled him most in the future responded, "Events, dear boy, events." The Soviet invasion of Afghanistan changed Jimmy Carter's view of how to maintain

A Kurdish marksman stands atop a building as he looks at the destroyed Syrian town of Kobane, also known as Ain al-Arab, on January 30, 2015. Kurdish forces recaptured the town on the Turkish frontier on January 26, in a symbolic blow to the jihadists who have seized large swathes of territory in their onslaught across Syria and Iraq. (BULENT KILIC/AFP/GETTY IMAGES)

international security. The terrorist attacks of 9/11 altered George W. Bush's mindset, coupling his idealistic doctrine of spreading democracy with his realistic response of preemptive war. Events such as another severe economic recession, a North Korean or Iranian use of nuclear weapons, a Russian assault on a NATO ally, or an ISIS-inspired attack within the continental United States are plausible events that could change the course of American foreign policy.

Will continuity or change characterize future American foreign policy? In looking at past policies, and in considering future choices, one might conclude, "a little bit of both." In his classic work *Democracy in America* Alexis de Tocqueville concluded that the conduct of foreign policy in a democracy is a particularly difficult undertaking. A more modern historical review, agreeing with that assessment, suggests that continued well-defined objectives combined with changing resource-dependent strategies can lead to a successful American foreign policy.

Great Decisions 2017: Continuity and Change

As we deliberate the topics prepared for our consideration in this year's Great Decisions program, we may want to speculate on the probability of continuity or the chances of change in American foreign policy in these issue areas. As we do, consider U.S. foreign policy objectives over time, the strategies that have been declared and practiced, and the instruments employed—successfully or not. Also keep in mind that in volatile regions and issues such as these, American foreign policy may be required to be reactive, rather than proactive.

■ **The European Union.** The Brexit vote requiring the United Kingdom to exit the European Union clearly will lead to change in American policies toward its closest allies. Added to that, Europe finds itself in the throes of what has been termed "its worst political crisis since World War II," facing problems of immigration, a newly aggressive Russia, the fear of terrorist attacks, and a battered Euro. Some have suggested that the tide of European integration has turned, and that a new era of "re-nationalization" is emerging. If so, the U.S. may be forced to abandon its long-term policy encouraging European union, to seek better partners in Europe than the EU, and to emphasize NATO as its principal means of wielding influence.

■ **Trade, jobs and politics.** Here we find a close link between domestic and foreign policy. Deep-seated frustrations regarding American job losses and slow rates of economic growth have been tied to international trade. Taking these criticisms into account, Mr. Trump has threatened to "tear up" previous deals and impose tariffs on China. We noted above how Congress can place constraints on the Executive branch in foreign policy but, as reported recently in the *New York Times*, Presidents have surprising power to end international trade agreements. If the U.S. were to change its international trade policy, it might feel some economic pain resulting from being cut out of global markets, and its leadership in global trade might be lost.

■ **China and the South China Sea.** A case study in China's attempt to achieve some degree of regional hegemony is illustrated by its maritime claims of sovereignty and right-of-way in the South China Sea. The recent decision by the Permanent Court of Arbitration at the Hague rejecting China's claims provides the U.S. with solid ground for continuing its foreign policies in the region: freedom of navigation, a code of conduct to lower chances of a military miscalculation in the waterways, adherence to the rule of law, and confidence-building measures to avoid the appearance of great-power conflict in the region.

■ **Saudi Arabia.** There is no doubt that the pillars that once formed the foundation of U.S.-Saudi relations have started to crumble. The Cold War is over, and with it the Soviet threat to Saudi oil fields. Iraq similarly no longer threatens those fields. And America's dependence on Saudi oil has lessened. Given those changes, as well as Saudi domestic policies and foreign priorities that the U.S. finds objectionable, many question whether Saudi Arabia is worth the trouble, and if America should move away from this troubled partnership. Common interests—containing Iran, defeating radical Islamic terrorist organizations, and relying on the Saudis for regional leadership and influence --may call for continuing the relationship as it now exists, but also acknowledging its limits, and seeking productive change.

■ **Petroleum.** Change is afoot here. Predictions of American dependency on costly natural gas imports, as the world's oil supply peaked, have been proven wrong. The twin revolutions of horizontal drilling and hydraulic fracturing have resulted in a significant increase in U.S. energy production. The U.S. is now an energy superpower, having a major impact on energy supply and oil prices. Such an energy advantage can provide U.S. foreign policy new leverage: reassuring allies, imposing sanctions, strengthening trade negotiations. Armed with this new instrument, America will be faced with opportunities for energy collaboration, rather than competition.

■ **Latin America.** Given the diversity of this region, there is ample opportunity for both continuity and change in U.S. foreign policy. Relations between the U.S. and various Latin American states and governments have experienced cyclical ups and downs over the last decades. Now, as many of those states appear to be moving toward more centrist forms of governments—with added opportunities for change in Cuba, Colombia and Venezuela--the U.S. may be able to foster improved relations with its neighbors to the south. Transnational organized crime, drug trafficking, and immigration problems should be placed high on an agreed-upon agenda.

■ **Afghanistan and Pakistan.** America's longest war in Afghanistan has not been aided by the distrust existing between the U.S. and Pakistan over Afghanistan's political composition and its role in regional security. To maintain stability in Afghanistan, the U.S. has been required to extend its military presence there, and a new administration will be faced with a choice between continuity and change. The change in that region, one still seen as important to negate any return of Afghanistan to its role as a host for international terrorism, may require a more robust American political strategy in support of the Afghan government, continued economic aid, a settlement among the varied political and military actors outside the elected government—including some elements of the Taliban—and a regional agreement acceptable to Pakistan. A tall order.

■ **Nuclear security.** Change has occurred in the world's balance of nuclear weapons. The bipolar competition of the Cold War has been replaced by what has been termed the "second nuclear age," meaning a multipolar competition among existing and emerging nuclear powers. This shift has implications for America's nuclear umbrella shielding its allies, crisis stability, missile defense, multilateral arms control, and other scenarios of nuclear proliferation and provocation. Whether in the hands of North Korea, Iran, or a violent extremist organization, nuclear weapons pose new challenges of continuity and change to American defense and foreign policy.

The future of Europe: coping with crisis
by Andrew Moravcsik

British Prime Minister Theresa May (center left) kisses President of the European Commission Jean-Claude Juncker during a group photo at the Council of the European Union on the first day of a two day summit on October 20, 2016, in Brussels, Belgium. Theresa May is here attending her first EU Council meeting after becoming prime minister following the Brexit vote. (JACK TAYLOR/GETTY IMAGES)

Since 2008, the European Union (EU) has wrestled with a set of severe and overlapping crises. Jean-Claude Juncker, president of the European Commission, has coined a French technocratic neologism to describe this difficult situation: The EU faces a "polycrise." Many pessimists now openly assert that one or more of these crises may prove fatal for Europe, in that it could trigger a dissolution or collapse of the EU.

Yet the EU is far stronger and more stable than these doom and gloom scenarios would have us believe. It has been around so long and is so deeply embedded in the lives of contemporary Europeans that there is no chance it will disappear anytime soon. Integration has been underway for over 65 years, longer than most of the world's countries have been independent nations. Its major purpose is to institutionalize the management of regional interdependence in Europe, which is mostly economic in nature but extends also to political, legal and cultural matters. Today, roughly 10% of European national laws originate, at least in significant part, in Brussels. Most of what the EU does, such as assuring free trade

ANDREW MORAVCSIK, *is a professor of politics and the director of the EU Program at Princeton University. He has authored over 125 scholarly publications on European integration and many other topics. A similar number of his policy analyses have appeared in many publications, including Foreign Affairs, where he is the book review editor (Europe). He has served as a U.S. government trade negotiator, special assistant to Korea's deputy prime minister, press assistant at the European Commission, editor of a Washington foreign policy journal, and a nonresident senior fellow of the Brookings Institution.*

and investment within a Single Market, establishing common regulations, permitting free movement of people, coordinating homeland security, and undertaking many types of collective foreign and defense action, remain essentially untouched by these crises. The EU remains the most ambitious and successful example of voluntary international political cooperation in human history.

Today's headlines do not record these quiet successes. They focus instead on four sensational crises that threaten the EU. The first is a conventional geopolitical crisis. Many view Europe as a continent in decline, a process that is sped up by internal fragmentation and disagreement. On its borders, from Russia to Turkey to Libya, the EU is surrounded by increasingly bold and authoritarian opponents, as well as violent terrorist groups—all of which appear to be exploiting Europe's military weakness. The second crisis is one of democratic governance. British Euroskeptics, the National Front in France and many other right-wing nationalist politicians and parties play an ever

more important role in European politics. To these groups, the EU appears a suspiciously cosmopolitan and technocratic institution that lacks democratic legitimacy—and they vocally oppose it. The third crisis stems from millions of migrants who are landing on Europe's shores and crossing its borders. Many are from neighboring Mediterranean countries, but some come from other EU member states. This influx seems to be swamping the ability of individual governments and Europe as a whole to respond. The fourth and final crisis centers on the EU's single currency, the euro. Those countries that use the euro (the so-called "Eurozone" countries) have remained mired in low growth, unemployment, high debt and austerity for almost a decade. Modest reforms to the Euro system have treated the symptoms but not restored Europe to economic health.

Even if these crises are not potentially fatal for the EU, they are serious. This article seeks to assess just how worried we should be, and how each crisis is likely to unfold in the future. It concludes that the first three—the

geopolitical, democratic and migrant crises—have been greatly exaggerated. There is no geopolitical crisis. Europe remains a superpower, not just in military terms, but in economic and cultural ones. It remains remarkably successful at projecting its geopolitical influence, not least in critical zones of conflict, such as Ukraine, Iran and Libya. The crisis of democratic legitimacy is real, but it is not specific to the EU, which actually enjoys more popular trust and support than national governments. The migration crisis has battered European society and politics over the past 18 months. Yet it can be, and to a surprising degree already has been, reduced to manageable proportions. This leaves the fourth crisis, that of the euro. In contrast to the three others, this crisis is real, persistent and troubling. External financial tensions continue to generate austerity and low growth a decade after the financial shock of 2008. It may also affect the other policies, because robust economic growth is the ultimate source of geopolitical influence, democratic legitimacy and an ability to cope with migration. ∎

Geopolitical influence

The conventional wisdom is that Europe today is a weak geopolitical actor, overshadowed by the two dominant global hegemons of the 21st century: the U.S. and China. Europe's power—particularly its military power—remains underfinanced and fragmented. Slow economic and demographic growth are inexorably leading to decline, which is exacerbated by the EU's disunity. Europe was unable to agree on how to act in the former Yugoslavia in the 1990s or in Iraq in the 2000s, nor was it able to act alone in Libya in the 2010s. President Vladimir Putin's Russia acts as it

Ukrainians living in Italy attend a demonstration to mark the second anniversary of the annexation of Crimea by the Russian Federation, in Rome, February 28, 2016. (RICCARDO DE LUCA/ANADOLU AGENCY/GETTY IMAGES)

wishes on Europe's eastern frontier, invading and annexing its neighbors and violating norms of the "post-Cold War" legal order.

These apparently anemic responses convince many observers that Europe is a geopolitical has-been. Yet nothing could be further from the truth. In assessing relative global influence, policy analysts conventionally distinguish three dimensions: military ("hard") power, economic power, and persuasive cultural and institutional ("soft") power. In each area, Europe remains one of the two most influential political actors in contemporary world politics, alongside the United States. In most respects, its global and regional reach far surpasses that of China and Russia—and even, in some areas, the U.S. On most issues, Europe remains as unified as it needs to be to project power. Overall, Europe is the world's

! Before you read, download the companion **Glossary** that includes definitions and a guide to acronyms and abbreviations used in the article. Go to **www.greatdecisions.org** and select a topic in the Resources section on the right-hand side of the page.

"second superpower"—the only political entity able to project dominant military, economic and cultural influence trans-continentally. It will be decades, even generations, before Europe loses this status.

Europe's military might

First consider the projection of military force. While the U.S. is clearly the world's preeminent military power, responsible for 36% of global military spending, the EU (at 12.2%) is in second place, spending 20% more than China and over three times more than Russia. Europe's arsenals of military aircraft, ships and nuclear weapons are larger and more sophisticated than China's. Moreover, this current military spending underestimates Europe's relative clout greatly. Since military materiel, technology and experience are acquired over decades or even generations, trends in overall military capability lag many decades behind trends in annual spending. Thus, even if it eventually starts outspending Europe on an annual basis, China will require an additional 25–50 years to come close to Europe's role.

Among observers in Washington, Beijing, and Moscow, as well as many EU officials, the conventional wisdom states that while its overall military spending may be large, fragmentation condemns Europe to impotence. The existence of 28 separate and "compartmentalized national defense markets," rather than one centralized EU institution, is said to create "needless multiplication in the cost of…maintaining and operating military forces," to dampen competition among defense firms, to shrink operative economies of scale for the procurement of military equipment, and to generate the "lack of a common strategic view" and "a clear vision for the future."

Yet we need only track real military activity across the globe to see that this conventional wisdom is misleading. Europe in fact behaves much like a unified superpower. Besides the U.S., only Europeans consistently project military force transcontinentally: They have deployed 25–50,000 combat troops into conflict areas nearly every year since the end of the Cold War. They lead operations in Africa, the Red Sea, sectors of Afghanistan, and the Middle East—and they maintain military bases in dozens of countries.

No other single country, save the U.S., can match Europe's record of action. China and Russia, for example, hardly project any effective military force outside their immediate backyards, and almost never against organized opposition. Russia's military activity outside the former Soviet Union is limited to Syria, its sole remaining Middle East ally, plus a base in Vietnam. Setting aside small, contested atolls in the South China Sea, a few hundred miles off its shoreline, China is only now constructing its very first foreign base in Djibouti, a country that makes a profitable business of renting space, and already hosts a much larger presence of U.S., French, Japanese, Italian and other Western forces. China's modest world posture is unsurprising, since it has one formal ally (North Korea) and enjoys close political-military relations with only a few other countries. The last time China waged war was in 1979, when it fought Vietnam and lost.

Why can Europe project military force globally and regionally as if it were a powerful single unit? First, EU member states face no significant internal threats, so they can direct all of their military potential toward external missions. Unlike China or Russia, they are stable democracies, maintain no internal border controls, pose no military challenge to one another, have no outstanding border disputes, and are all NATO or EU members.

Second, even though the EU is not a unitary state, its member states tend to agree in principle on military deployments, rather than blocking and limiting one another. While coalitions of the willing are the norm—rather than universal participation in missions—fundamental intra-European disagreements are rare. Since the end of the Cold War, there have been only two: one 25 years ago concerning the former Yugoslavia, which was quickly overcome; and the second war in Iraq, which involved only half of European countries. In all the rest of the dozens of Western military interventions since the end of the Cold War, European countries have agreed and sent adequate troops to support missions.

Third, while fragmentation does create operational and procurement inefficiencies, the best estimate is that this wastage totals only about 13–14% of European military spending. This is not notably worse than estimated wastage in U.S. or Russian procurement policy.

Soldiers belonging to the EU's military training mission in Mali stand guard outside the mission's headquarters in Bamako during the visit of the Malian president after an attack by gunmen on March 21, 2016. (HABIBOU KOUYATE/AFP/GETTY IMAGES)

Finally, while in some cases European militaries still can conduct operations only with U.S. support, as they did in Libya, this hardly imposes any real-world limitation, because the U.S. and Europe have been on the same side of all but one major Western military operation of the last quarter century. The only exception is the U.S. war in Iraq—and even that was supported by most European states.

Europe's military power is globally significant, yet projecting coercive force is not its strong suit. European countries prefer to avoid and solve regional and global problems by non-military means. They have therefore specialized in the second and third dimensions of global power: economic and cultural/institutional influence. Most contemporary global problems—from postwar reconstruction to climate change—are better addressed through such instruments.

Europe's economic power

Without a doubt, Europe is the world's preeminent non-military power, surpassing even the U.S. This influence begins with the economy. Even in bad times, Europe's nominal gross domestic product (GDP) remains nearly 50% larger than that of China and nearly 13 times larger than that of Russia. Often overlooked, but just as important, Europe's per capita nominal GDP remains four to five times higher than China's or Russia's, which frees a larger surplus for international activity. Furthermore, the EU is the world's largest trading bloc and investor. This trade is far less vulnerable to disruption than that of other countries because Europe lies at the center of stable high value-added networks of economic activity, many of them intra-European. By contrast, China remains highly dependent on exports and foreign investment, in particular low value-added processing of goods and components designed, produced and consumed outside of the country. Russia remains highly and asymmetrically dependent on exports to and investment from Europe.

Europe leverages its economic clout in many ways. Three examples illustrate the range of its influence. First is the offer of membership in and association with the EU. Over the past 20 years, Europe has expanded from 12 to 28 members—and this enlargement remains the most cost-effective means to spread democracy, free markets and rule of law pursued by any post-Cold War Western government. EU enlargement has placed new democracies on a more stable track, despite some recent slippage in countries like Hungary and Poland. European influence on neighborhood states such as Morocco, Serbia, Tunisia and others has been appreciable. The second example is foreign assistance. Europe supplies more than 50% of all (public and private) foreign aid to developing countries—about three times more than the U.S. or China. Third is sanctions. Europe is the critical link in recent Western restrictions. It is the largest economic partner of nearly every Middle Eastern country, with more than ten times more regional trade and investment than the U.S. enjoys. After 30 years of ineffective U.S. sanctions, Europe's decision in 2012 to join the U.S. in boycotting Iran halved Iranian exports and swiftly brought about a nuclear deal.

A recent example of the effectiveness of Europe's civilian power is its decisive response to Russian aggression in Ukraine. From the start of the crisis, Western governments unanimously ruled out any direct military engagement in favor of economic and diplomatic responses. Europe has led these efforts, which rely almost entirely on Europe's role as a predominant civilian power. In most areas it is about ten times more influential than the U.S.

The principal policy response has been the provision of economic assistance to Ukraine—without which the country would have collapsed long ago. Europe gives about $9 billion in annual aid, and the U.S. about $1 billion. Europe backed its aid with trade liberalization: European trade with Ukraine is 13 times larger than that of the U.S., which renders U.S. sanctions largely meaningless. Europe has also borne almost all the cost of imposing sanctions on Russia because European trade and investment with Russia are also more than ten times greater than those of the U.S. Given Europe's decisive influence vis-à-vis Russia, it is hardly surprising that Western diplomatic discussions with Moscow have been led by German Chancellor Angela Merkel and other Europeans, who have met over ten times more often with Kremlin officials than their American counterparts. While of course it would be unrealistic to expect ideal outcomes, the major result three years on is that Ukraine, a large country of

German Chancellor Angela Merkel (right) meets with Russian President Vladimir Putin for a "Normandy Four" meeting that also included France and Ukraine, October 19, 2016, at the Chancellery in Berlin, Germany. Under discussion were the conflicts in Ukraine and Syria. (MAURIZIO GAMBARINI/ANADOLU AGENCY/GETTY IMAGES)

great geographical, cultural, economic and military importance to Russia, has turned irreversibly toward to the West.

Europe's soft power

Europe wields a powerful persuasive and cultural influence on its region and the globe. The ideal of Europe has spread far beyond the EU: It is not by chance that the protesters in Maidan Square, the center of the 2014 Ukrainian revolution, waved EU flags. Europe's support for international law, organization and civil society is unmatched anywhere on the globe. When democratic countries draft new constitutions, they draw on European constitutional values of parliamentary government, global human rights and social democracy more often than corresponding U.S. or Chinese political values. Europe wins more Olympic medals than any other political unit, and more than all others combined in the winter games. It enjoys a preeminent position in the top ten global spectator sports, including soccer, tennis, cricket and volleyball. Europe hosts more foreign university students (not including intra-EU exchanges) than any region or country. Its languages are more widely spoken than any others. Neither Russia, nor China, nor in many respects the U.S., can match Europe's cultural clout. ■

Right-wing radicalism and Brexit

Over the last two decades, the EU and its policies have faced various types of political criticism and opposition. Trust in the EU, as measured by polls, has declined since 2008. Euroskeptic parties have prospered in direct elections to the European Parliament and on the extreme right of the political spectrum in some countries. A politician of one such party recently came close to winning the (ceremonial) post of president of Austria, and some fear that the National Front's Marine Le Pen might soon win the (powerful) presidency of France. If she succeeds, she has threatened to call a referendum on French membership in the EU. Referenda on European issues have failed in France, Ireland, Denmark, Greece, and the Netherlands—culminating in the "Brexit" referendum of June 23, 2016, in which the British voted narrowly to leave the EU.

Many attribute these problems to the EU's so-called "democratic deficit." In this view, widely held on the extremes of the European political spectrum, as well as among many who comment on Brussels politics, the EU is democratically illegitimate because it lacks a directly elected executive, parliamentary sovereignty, transnational public deliberation and other institutions to assure the electoral accountability characteristic of most advanced industrial democracies. As a result, some critics insist, unelected EU technocrats run rampant over individual rights and interests, while citizens across European countries respond with rising mistrust and antipathy toward the EU. This, in turn, fosters nationalism, xenophobia, and higher vote totals for extremist and Euroskeptic parties. The only solution, critics maintain, is to "democratize" EU institutions by establishing direct elections for the European Commission, granting greater formal oversight for national parliaments, and fostering pan-European deliberation and debate.

Giving individuals an incentive to participate might involve expanding EU powers to include new issues: Migration, social welfare and generational equality are sometimes mentioned.

The myth of Europe's democratic deficit

Yet the EU's crisis of democratic legitimacy is largely a myth. In a formal sense, there is no democratic deficit. The EU is actually quite accountable to national voters. The two dominant EU decision-making institutions, the

Members of the European Parliament take part in a voting session at headquarters in Strasbourg, November 22, 2016. (FREDERICK FLORIN/AFP/GETTY IMAGES)

(Left) Leader of the United Kingdom Independence Party (UKIP), Nigel Farage (center), speaks during a press conference near the Houses of Parliament in central London on June 24, 2016, after Britain voted to leave the EU. (GLYN KIRK/AFP/GETTY IMAGES) (Right) David Cameron, then-UK prime minister and leader of the Conservative Party, delivers his resignation speech in Downing Street following the Brexit vote, London, UK, June 24, 2016. (CHRIS RATCLIFFE/BLOOMBERG/GETTY IMAGES)

European Parliament and the European Council, are entirely comprised of directly elected parliamentarians, national ministers and chief executives. (The European Central Bank, even more than most central banks, is an exception, to which we shall return below.) When asked, absolute majorities of the public in every European country except Cyprus and Greece believe the EU can be described as "democratic"—more than believe it can be described as "technocratic." Over the past 40 years, the EU's trust and popularity among the public has changed relatively little. The percentage of Europeans expressing the opinion that "my country's membership in the EU is a bad thing" has fluctuated between 10% and 18%, and is now 17%. By contrast, over half of Europeans report the belief that "my country's membership in the EU is a good thing"—a percentage that has recently risen sharply in the wake of the Brexit vote. Indeed, for 40 years public trust in the EU's political institutions has been continuously higher than trust in national ones—and it remains so today, even in Britain, where more people trust the EU Commission than the British Parliament. A slight decline in recent years is not specific to the EU: Trust and confidence in national governments have declined in parallel.

At heart, the belief that Europeans are alienated by a distant and undemocratic EU rests on the false intuition that rendering institutions more directly democratic—political scientists call this "input legitimacy"—usually generates greater public trust and popularity. In fact, the citizens of almost all modern democracies have greater trust in more distant and insulated political institutions—the army, police, courts, bureaucracies, and international institutions like the EU and the UN—than they do in their own nationally elected politicians and parliaments. Thus, the European countries where publics are most pessimistic about the future of the EU are not those in which citizens feel most disenfranchised, but those in which citizens most believe that "voice" counts in EU policymaking.

Pessimists about Europe point to the British vote for Brexit, arguing that it may serve as a model for many similar efforts to dismantle the EU. Yet this is unlikely. In some other European countries, referenda are not permitted, and in many others it would require a consensus among ruling politicians to authorize it. This seems unlikely, since Continental politicians would be hesitant to follow the British lead. They can see clearly that the government in London is delaying the beginning of the negotiations over Brexit because it is unsure of what to do. As part of the

world's most economically interdependent continent, it is simply not viable for Britain to withdraw entirely from long-standing arrangements with Europe that guarantee open trade, investment, free movement of people, common regulations, homeland security coordination, collaborative research and university exchanges, and foreign and defense policy coordination. Insofar as the British government has formulated a position, it is to attempt to negotiate something very similar to current EU policies—with the exception of inward immigration—outside the EU. Simply negotiating new trade and investment arrangements is estimated to require 30,000 new government officials that Britain does not have. Few, if any, governments are likely to wish this situation on themselves. This is what the historical record shows us: All previous negative national referendum results on EU issues—in Greece, the Netherlands, France, Denmark and Ireland— were quickly reversed.

If criticisms of the EU do not actually stem from dissatisfaction with its democratic procedures, perhaps they stem from dissatisfaction with Europe's concrete policies. When polled, Europeans report economic growth and immigration (along with terrorism) to be their most salient political concern. Europe faces crises in both areas, to which we now turn. ■

Policing Europe's borders

The migration crisis hit Europe hard in 2015. Over one million migrants entered the EU, compared with just 280,000 the year before. About 80% came from three war-torn countries—Syria, Afghanistan and Iraq—mostly by crossing the Mediterranean Sea and Southern Europe. Of these, most were men, but 25% were children, and 17% women. The great majority arrived by sea, a process in which almost 4,000 lost their lives. Nearly 1.3 million individuals applied for asylum, double the number during the preceding year. Germany, with almost a half-million asylum applications, was the leading destination. Chancellor Merkel spoke inspiringly about Europe's humanitarian duty, while many Germans shared their time, money and homes to help refugees. Yet less enthusiastic countries—Hungary (with 177,130 migrants), Sweden, Austria, Norway, Finland—received more asylum-seekers per capita. Together with Germany, these countries accounted for well over two thirds of Europe's asylum applications.

The migration crisis of 2015 posed two major challenges to Europe. The first was a political threat to ruling governments. National electorates in every country have a limited tolerance for inward migration. This opposition, research suggests, does not arise primarily from immigration's direct economic effects on individual wages or tax burdens, but from native prejudice against immigrants and a desire to defend national cultures. One result is that opposition is often strongest not in big cities like London or Paris, with many migrants, but in regions where immigrants are less numerous. Over the longer-term, the level of migration Europe experienced in 2015 is politically unacceptable in every EU member state, including Germany. Today, most large Western countries hovered around the world average of about 13% foreign-born residents, and the trend since 2008 has been toward lower levels of net immigration. Those who arrive face stricter legal barriers, labor market discrimination, violence and other hostile actions, as well as declining economic opportunities—often encouraged or condoned by European politicians, particularly on the right. In this context, sudden increases in migration flows into Europe, and even across Europe, simply serve to fuel political extremism.

A second challenge is that mass migration threatens the EU's "Schengen zone" of passport-free movement. Europeans value free movement across internal frontiers more than any other everyday achievement of the EU. Migrants place strain on this system of open borders because they move in response to employment opportunities, family links, and ethnic or cultural ties. This can place uneven burdens on countries, and those most concerned about internal security, economic welfare or political stability are tempted to re-impose border controls. Over the past year, the European Council has authorized temporary checks at Germany's land border with Austria, Austria's land border with Slovenia and Hungary, some French border crossings, and a few Scandinavian ferry terminals and bridges. These controls are largely directed at non-EU nationals with Schengen visas, some of whom who are now subject to identity checks within the zone. Former French President Nicolas Sarkozy has argued for such internal border controls on non-Europeans to be generalized. EU citizens will soon have their identity checked against police databases at the EU's external borders, as has always been the case for non-EU citizens.

National quotas for distributing migrants: a political sideshow

In assessing the EU's response, commentators and journalists have paid most attention to proposals for distributing a high proportion of asylum applicants to different governments through centralized national quotas set in Brussels. The inability to do so is often seen as a major EU policy failure. Yet quo-

Volunteers and rescuers help refugees disembark safely from the inflatable boats they used to cross from Turkey. More than 300 refugees landed on the shores of Lesbos, Greece, March 13, 2016. (NIKOLAS GEORGIOU/ZUMA WIRE/ALAMY LIVE NEWS)

Pro-refugee demonstrators stand in front of riot police as they shout against French far-right National Front supporters in Marseille, southern France, on November 5, 2016.
(BERTRAND LANGLOIS/AFP/GETTY IMAGES)

tas are neither mandated by European law, nor are they a realistic objective, because they do not take account of domestic political pressure and the interests of migrants themselves. There is no overriding technocratic reason why migrants should be evenly distributed across Europe. Instead, the whole issue of quotas is a political sideshow that national politicians exploit to help manage domestic pressures resulting from migration.

Only slightly more realistic is the EU's current formal migration regime—called the "Dublin Regulation." It seeks to prevent multiple asylum applications ("asylum shopping") and situations where no member state takes responsibility at all ("asylum orbiting"). The Dublin system, which dates back from agreements imposed on new and peripheral member states immediately after the end of the Cold War, stipulates that the first member state an asylum seeker enters remains legally responsible for them. Yet it is unrealistic for border countries like Greece, Italy or Hungary to bear the brunt of nearly 2 million migrants—and, in practice, they do not. Instead, most migrants move on to Germany, Austria and the Nordic countries, where there is more employment and a high tolerance of immigration.

In this context, the German government proposed last year that the EU manage migrant flows through quotas, and the European Commission backed the idea. Yet no plan is ever likely to be accepted if, as European Commissioner for Migration Dimitris Avramopoulos stated, it invites national politicians to ignore "the political cost" and stop worrying about reelection. Accordingly, national interior ministers offered no more than symbolic support for a token quota system that applies to only 66,000 migrants (under 5% of more than a million new refugees who crossed into Europe in 2015) and contains no enforcement provisions. For example, the plan obliges Hungary to take 1,294 asylum seekers—a meaningless dictate for a country that is already hosting over 175,000 refugees. The European Council also established ad hoc measures to assist the governments of Italy, Hungary and Greece, which received financial aid and the option for the EU to organize relocation of about a quarter of their current refugee population elsewhere in Europe. Four governments, including Hungary, voted against even this modest proposal, and currently refuse to implement it. Even among those governments that supported it, opposition

from the public, politicians and refugees themselves means that only 7,000 refugees have actually been relocated.

Quotas do not, in fact, serve as practical instruments of refugee management. Instead, they are tools that national leaders manipulate to deflect domestic political pressure. Leaders do so in diverse, and even contradictory, ways, thereby increasing the chaos for migrants. In ideologically pro-European countries that are relatively open to asylum-seekers, such as Germany, centrist politicians support EU schemes because they may help muster domestic public support for a generous asylum policy. In pro-European countries with more migrants than they can handle, such as Italy, quotas are a potential means to share the burden. In countries with low tolerance for migration and right-wing nationalist governments, politicians exploit the EU to deflect blame onto Brussels and Berlin for domestic refugee management policy they would have to adopt anyway. For example, Hungarian Prime Minister Viktor Orbán bolstered his popularity by calling a referendum against EU quotas, even though formal quotas were insignificant and informal ones would have reduced the number

EU Commissioner for Migration Dimitris Avramopoulos gives a press conference in Brussels on April 6, 2016, after launching a drive to overhaul the EU's asylum rules.
(JOHN THYS/AFP/GETTY IMAGES)

of migrants in Hungary by one third. He won a 98% majority—even though a boycott meant that participation fell below the 50% formally required for passage—and a boost in public support.

European governments are now discussing more modest and practical intergovernmental proposals to distribute migrants. According to these, the Dublin Regulation would remain in force during normal times. If flows increase, governments could engage in "effective solidarity," whereby each EU state would "pick and choose" how to comply, whether by making financial contributions, relocating refugees elsewhere, or accommodating asylum seekers themselves. In "extraordinary circumstances," governments would simply bypass the EU Commission and Parliament, and strike intergovernmental deals in the European Council. This deal is far more likely to work, because it is more sensitive to domestic political pressures.

Blocking migration: Europe's wall

In responding to the migration crisis, the most important medium-term policy issue facing national politicians is not how to allocate existing refugees, but how to reduce the overall number who enter in the first place. Europe's, and particularly Germany's, willingness to accept over a million migrants has been an impressive display of humanitarian solidarity. Yet right-wing politicians like Nicolas Sarkozy are not wrong to point out that continued open migration at 2015 levels would be politically unsustainable, no matter how migrants were allocated. Thus European borders are likely to remain closed in the future. Critics will complain that Europe is neglecting its humanitarian and international legal obligations, and substantial numbers of desperate migrants will continue to perish in the Mediterranean Sea, yet restricting immigration is now an unavoidable political necessity.

For a decade, the EU has quietly been raising the barriers to inward migration. These policies render it harder for migrants to reach Europe and less pleasant once they arrive. Beginning in 2007, the EU's border protection agency (FRONTEX) began upgrading land border controls with Turkey, culminating in the construction of a fence along the border. Bulgaria followed suit in 2015. Europe developed and strengthened rules placing financial responsibility for repatriation on commercial carriers that transport refugees. Most importantly, Europe has established repatriation arrangements with external states. In 2008, Italian Prime Minister Silvio Berlusconi signed a treaty with Libya providing for cooperation against immigration and the forcible repatriation of some in Italy—though this agreement has lapsed due to the Libyan Civil War. In March 2016, on the basis of unilateral efforts led by German Chancellor Merkel, Europe signed a similar agreement with Turkey. Now the only migrants who can enter from Turkey are those placed on a list and processed there. Migrants that seek to circumvent this procedure by traveling directly to Greece are returned and replaced with those on the list—up to a total of 72,000 per year. Finally, humanitarian concerns have led the EU to strengthen support for search and rescue missions in the Mediterranean, which have become too expensive for countries like Italy to conduct alone.

While many commentators assume that migration into Europe is uncontrollable (or undesirable), in fact, recent efforts to limit it have been strikingly successful. In the summer and fall of 2015, over 200,000 refugees per month entered Europe through Greece. A year later, that number had been reduced 40-fold to less than 5,000 per month.

To be sure, this policy is not without political difficulties. The Turkish government has demanded major quid pro quos, including visa-free travel to the EU, an acceleration of membership negotiations and large cash transfers. The European Parliament is now raising objections, and Turkey is threatening retaliation if the EU abrogates the agreement. On top of that, the problem of migration from Libya toward Italy remains. Although it may heat up in the future, these flows from Libya are ten times smaller than previous flows through Greece. Still, Europe has succeeded for the moment in reducing the pressure of migration to a tolerable level. ∎

A Hungarian soldier looks down on migrants queueing for food being distributed from a doorway in the border fence close to the E75 Horgas border crossing between Serbia and Hungary on July 16, 2016 in Horgos, Serbia. (MATT CARDY/GETTY IMAGES)

1

Slow growth and inequality

The fourth and most serious crisis facing Europe centers on its single currency, the euro. More than 15 years ago, when the EU agreed to establish the euro, European leaders promised higher growth, greater equality, enhanced domestic political legitimacy and a triumphant capstone for federalism. Yet for nearly a decade now, the results have included anemic economic growth, rising inequality, simmering political radicalism, and raging Euroskepticism.

Even in economic good times, growth under the euro was unexceptional, but in 2008 the global financial crisis revealed the system's true costs and underlying weaknesses. Since then, inflation-adjusted GDP in the Eurozone has shrunk by 8%, compared to a 5% expansion in European countries that remain outside. Neither Greece nor Italy has seen economic growth in ten years—and the Italian financial system may be the next to collapse. This loss of output totals trillions of euros. While losses from short recessions are often offset by higher-than-average growth thereafter, losses from prolonged depressions such as this are not.

The euro has also exacerbated inequality within and among nations. Since 2007, Germany has grown by about 5%, while France, the Netherlands and Belgium have remained stagnant, and Greece, Spain, Italy, Ireland, Finland and Portugal have all suffered contractions greater than what they experienced during the Great Depression. Inequality has also sharpened within countries—stunningly in countries like Greece, but also in Germany—and it is reflected in the shattered lives of unemployed youth, bankrupt business-owners and vulnerable citizens who may never regain their previous standard of living. In many European countries, a lost decade is becoming a lost generation.

Prolonged depression has spawned right-wing nationalists and Euroskeptics. In Austria, France, the Netherlands, Italy, Greece, Finland, Germany and elsewhere, radical right-wing parties are enjoying more electoral success than at any time since the 1930s. In Spain and Italy, left-wing anti-system parties are prospering. Support for and trust in EU institutions, traditionally higher than the popularity of

national political institutions (even in Britain), fell through the floor. Anti-European radicalism is spreading. A catastrophic collapse of the system may yet lie ahead.

Causes of the crisis

How did Europe fall into this trap of low growth, high inequality and political discontent? The German-led euro single currency arrangement has played an important role, because it eliminated independent national monetary and exchange rate policies. Absent currency appreciation, German productivity, wage restraint and technical excellence reduced the real price of exports. Meanwhile, many of Germany's Southern neighbors, absent currency depreciation, experienced easy credit and increasing demand for German goods. Rising German exports of goods and services were balanced by rising credit to the state or private actors, or through financing of construction booms, as in Spain and Ireland. Some countries, such as Greece, fell into this trap in part due to their own unwise and profligate fiscal policy, but others, such as Spain, fell into it despite model fiscal policies. External imbalances and low growth in response to fixed exchange-rate systems are hardly unique to the EU: Similar problems arose under the 19th and early 20th century gold standard system; in the U.S. during the 1970s, leading to the collapse of the Bretton Woods system; and more recently in Argentina, which experimented with a currency peg in the 1990s.

Currency pegs often suppress growth because, in order for every country and region to benefit equally, their underlying macroeconomic fundamentals—wage and price inflation, public and private deficits, external shocks, and relative competitiveness—must converge. This convergence is essential to sustained macro-

Greek pensioners try to pass a police blockade to go toward the prime minister's office during an anti-austerity demonstration in Athens on October 3, 2016.
(LOUISA GOULIAMAKI/AFP/GETTY IMAGES)

economic growth because a currency peg eliminates the national policies that deficit governments normally employ to adjust to external disequilibria and adapt their economy to a diverse international system. For example, when a country is beset by economic recession, a negative external shock or eroding competitiveness, its government normally loosens domestic monetary policy (thereby lowering interest rates and stimulating investment), lets the currency depreciate (thereby boosting exports, reducing imports and transferring income to the tradeable sector of the economy), and increases spending (which stimulates consumption and investment). None of these are possible under the euro. Those who created the euro expected convergence among diverse domestic institutions and international market positions to follow European monetary union, yet it has not.

This leaves deficit countries in southern Europe with only one tool to restore external balance. It is "internal devaluation," the politically-correct term in Europe for a semi-permanent state of austerity: cutting wages, government spending, consumer demand, corporate investment, imports and, ultimately, growth. This may eventually restore external balance, but as Joseph Stiglitz, Paul Krugman and other Nobel-Prize winning economists have argued, it exacts an enormous cost in lost growth. Deficit countries and their creditors, like individuals and firms in the domestic economy, would be better off in the long term if they could adjust, but they cannot.

Even for a surplus country like Germany, the costs of a flawed monetary system may eventually boomerang back to lower exports, induce financial instability and create political tensions. Depression also undermines the political legitimacy of domestic governments and the international organization responsible for the rules—in this case the EU. Low or negative growth and rising inequality within a system that seems to deny them any control leads national publics to grasp at radical alternatives. In the interim,

deficit countries are to a greater or lesser degree in receivership, being managed by the EU. Decisions are increasingly driven by capital markets, European rules, and dictates from Paris and Berlin.

What can Europe do about it?

The fact that deficit and surplus countries in Europe both ultimately suffer from macroeconomic disequilibria induced by the Euro system suggests that perhaps they could cooperate to reform or change that system. Yet nearly a decade into the financial crisis, little has been done. Three alternatives exist, of which two—structural reform to render the system more symmetrical or permitting some countries to leave the system—offer the hope of fundamental long-term improvement. Yet Europe has chosen the remaining option—the worst of the three, from a long-term perspective—namely, to "muddle through" by imposing general austerity on deficit countries and managing the symptoms. Let's review these options.

One option for Europe would be to enact fundamental structural reforms to make the euro system more symmetrical—that is, to generate more growth and distribute it more equally.

This would require encouraging not just convergence to lower wage and price inflation, different education systems, tax reform, investment targeted at exports, and similar corporate governance on deficit countries, but also to encourage opposite trends in Germany and other surplus countries. Stiglitz and others have detailed how the EU might rewrite tax laws, loosen monetary policy, change corporate governance rules, and boost wage growth, consumer spending and investment. The EU could discourage trade surpluses, for example by taxing countries that run them. The German government could unilaterally engineer an increase in domestic wages (for example, through stronger union bargaining rights) or expand deficit spending. Countries should be permitted to declare bankruptcy and start over, just as most countries permit firms to do. Over time, all this might help deficit countries stimulate growth and restore export competitiveness, both vis-à-vis Germany (by increasing German demand and raising the relative price of German goods) and also vis-à-vis the rest of the world (by lowering the real exchange rate of the Euro).

Another part of this structural reform agenda could be to encourage

The euro sign sculpture stands illuminated outside the former European Central Bank headquarters at dusk in Frankfurt, Germany, October 20, 2016. (KRISZTIAN BOCSI/BLOOMBERG VIA GETTY IMAGES)

Leader of France's far-right National Front party, Marine Le Pen, delivers a speech during a political rally on September 3, 2016 in Brachay, France. Marine Le Pen has vowed to hold a referendum on whether France stays in or leaves the European Union if she wins the 2017 presidential election. (CHESNOT/GETTY IMAGES)

large fiscal transfers, migration and other factor movements that can offset Euro-induced distortions and inequities. Such policies might replicate the compensating factor flows that make single currencies viable within large sovereign states, such as the U.S. American federal government programs like unemployment insurance, welfare payments, infrastructure spending, progressive taxation and industry bailouts add up to sizable fiscal transfers from richer and more economically vibrant regions to poorer and depressed ones. The EU might establish a similar system of fiscal transfers from creditor countries like Germany to deficit countries like Greece and Italy. Former Greek Minister of Finance Yanis Varoufakis proposes massive European investment and anti-poverty programs. An even more significant compensating inter-regional factor flow in the U.S. is internal migration. When some states suffer long-term sectoral decline—as have farms in the Midwest or industries in the Rust Belt—people move out to economically more buoyant states. Europe, Germany and other surplus countries might accept continuous migration flows from deficit countries. Germany might benefit

from such policies, since its growth has slowed as well, in large part due to its dependence on exports to other countries in Europe that are suffering under austerity.

In theory, deep structural reform seems an optimal choice. For this reason, the phrase "monetary union requires fiscal union" has become commonplace among European federalists. Yet such reforms stand little chance of adoption. Germans are unlikely to renounce the export-led growth that has stemmed from its 60-year tradition of high savings, low inflation, modest wage settlements and export promotion through an undervalued exchange rate. They are even less likely to accept massive fiscal transfers to other countries. Varoufakis estimates that EU fiscal capacity, now about 1% of GDP and 2% of European public spending, would have to increase at least ten-fold to have an impact resembling that of a national government. Germans also protest, with some justification, that this could simply encourage irresponsible behavior by debtors—a so-called "moral hazard" problem. Even if the German government were inclined to support such policies, its own electorate and business elites would surely

block them. Even less likely are large increases in northward migration. To be sure, a few percent of the Greek labor force has already fled, mostly to locations outside the Eurozone. Yet for migration to have a significant macroeconomic effect, many millions of Italians, Spanish, Greeks and Portuguese would have to move to Germany. In the current political climate, this is impossible.

This leads us to a second alternative, which is to break up the euro as we know it. Stiglitz believes that such a "friendly separation" could be achieved at a reasonable cost—preferably by separating the Eurozone into macro-economically compatible subgroups, each with its own currency. Electronic banking, credit auctions, capital controls, a system of trade chits for exports and new management of debt make such changes feasible without speculators gaming the system, short-circuiting any change or triggering catastrophic bank runs. Rendering European integration more compatible with prosperity and a measure of national autonomy would not weaken the EU; it would strengthen it.

Yet, even though it would likely be to their long-term advantage, almost all European politicians publicly reject this option. So do publics within Eurozone countries, which support the maintenance of the euro. To be sure, throughout the crisis, eliminating the euro as we know it has been closer to the surface than many are aware. We know that the Greek, Spanish and Italian governments all thought seriously about this option. Yet they backed away because surplus governments like Germany threatened to withdraw support, the short-term costs could be extremely high and public opinion firmly supports the euro. This leaves European governments in an ironic situation. The euro was initially sold to governments as being difficult and costly in the short-term, but good for European economies in the long term. Now, most analysts concede that it is a costly and inappropriate policy in the long term, but concede that large short-term costs preclude countries from leaving.

If fundamentally reforming the euro and eliminating the euro as we know it are both unlikely, the only remaining option is to "muddle through" with current policies, as Europe has done for nearly a decade now. This is not to say the EU has done nothing. It has enacted policies that strengthen the EU's short-term crisis management capability and address some of the symptoms and risks of the current euro system. Eurozone member states created various funds and processes—the European Financial Stability Fund and European Stability Mechanism, for example—to help stabilize debt crisis. They have encouraged the International Monetary Fund to join the effort. They have quietly approved monetary easing by the European Central Bank (ECB) and its aggressive rhetorical defense of the euro—for ex-

ample, President Mario Draghi's celebrated promise that "the ECB is ready to do whatever it takes to preserve the euro." In addition, first steps toward "banking union"—central oversight, regulation and insurance of European banks—have been put in place. Banking reform could continue by offering EU financial guarantees that decouple banks from national governments. It would be necessary to restructure or mutualize debt, perhaps using GNP-indexed bonds that reward investors if the country grows, or creating Eurobonds that make all European governments responsible for national debts.

These steps are insufficient to make the euro system work fairly and efficiently. The underlying macroeconomic divergences based on persistent differences in national systems of wage-setting, corporate governance and fi-

nancial intermediation remain. Eliminating austerity and low growth, and the disproportionate costs of the current system on deficit countries, which will ultimately cycle back to Germany, requires far more serious reform. In the absence of convergence, Germany and other European creditor governments resist more intensive means of muddling through, because these involve accepting financial responsibility for the future consequences of policies adopted in debtor countries. To avoid risk, and even moral hazard, such policies would also require a large increase in the EU's oversight, control and intervention in national financial systems, which are rejected by every EU member state—Germany no less than Italy or Greece, where governments have developed unique relationships with banks. ∎

The virtues of muddling through

We have seen that the conventional wisdom about the EU's weakness and fragility exaggerates the severity of crises and problems Europe faces. The geopolitical, democratic legitimacy and migration crises are modest and manageable. That leaves the euro crisis, which remains untreated. Modest reforms to the euro system have addressed the symptoms, but have failed to restore Europe to economic health. Ultimately robust economic growth is what underlies Europe's geopolitical influence, democratic support and ability to manage migration. Europe is not out of the woods.

Why do commentators tend to exaggerate the EU's failures? There are many reasons, but one important one is simple and banal: Most of what occurs in the EU is deadly dull and thus of little interest to the public. EU decision-making processes are slow, technocratic and legalistic. It rarely handles issues that are of primary importance to

voters. One consequence is to induce a bias among journalists, policy analysts and even scholars toward sensationalist reporting of crises. Excitement attracts readers, which leads these commentators to report European challenges, difficulties, and failures. By contrast, success, stability and incremental change managed by technocrats are rarely acknowledged. 250,000 refugees a month arrive in Europe and it is front-page news. That number falls to 5,000, and only specialists are aware.

The EU's intrinsic banality also leads, ironically, to ideological polarization. Because the EU's pragmatic issues are of little inherent interest to anyone, even elites, those who do pay close attention to Europe tend to be highly ideological. They are either Euroskeptics and Euro-enthusiasts. Both have an incentive to highlight crises and failures in the EU—though for opposite reasons. Euroskeptics seek to show that the integration is mis-

guided and must be reversed at once, whereas Euro-enthusiasts seek to show that we need more centralized and powerful EU institutions.

Yet Euroskeptics and Euro-federalists both miss the true source of the EU's success. Europe does not specialize in highly centralized institutions devoted to grand institutional schemes. When it embarks on such efforts, as with the euro, it runs the greatest risks. Instead, it is at its best when it simply "muddles through," creating decentralized solutions to common problems. As Brexiteers are learning to their surprise, if the EU did not exist, it would have to be invented, because the pragmatic tasks it carries out are essential to maintaining peace and prosperity on the world's most interdependent continent. An optimistic future depends in large part on finding solutions to the euro crisis that are consistent with the EU's successful political tradition. ∎

discussion questions

1. German Chancellor Angela Merkel has been the central figure in Europe's management of the migration crisis. To what extent do you agree with Merkel's open-door policy for refugees? Can she successfully manage the integration of refugees within Germany? What about throughout Europe?

2. The euro and migration crises, as well as the Brexit vote, have shaken European unity. To what extent do you believe in the premise of European integration? Can the European project prevail, or is the EU simply too diverse?

3. What are the prospects for the "special relationship" between the U.S. and the UK in light of Brexit? How does the American public view the UK in comparison to other European countries and the EU as a whole?

4. To what extent is the perception that the EU suffers from a "democratic deficit" justified or unjustified?

5. Russia's recent actions in Ukraine and Crimea, as well as its support for Syrian President Bashar al-Assad, have raised concerns about the security of Eastern Europe. How might Russian, European and American calculations here be impacted by the arrival of the new U.S. administration?

Don't forget: Ballots start on page 115!

suggested readings

Archick, Kristin, "The European Union: Current Challenges and Future Prospects." **Congressional Research Service**, June 21, 2016. 16 pp. Available free online: <https://www.fas.org/sgp/crs/row/R44249.pdf>. This report examines the history of the EU, its major challenges going forward, and the implications of those challenges for EU-U.S. relations.

McDonald-Gibson, Charlotte, **Cast Away: True Stories of Survival from Europe's Refugee Crisis**. New York: The New Press, 2016. 256 pp. This book compiles first-hand accounts of refugees who crossed the Mediterranean, painting a personal picture of the crisis.

Saunders, Doug, **The Myth of the Muslim Tide: Do Immigrants Threaten the West?** New York: Vintage, 2012. 208 pp. This book rejects fears that Muslim immigrants pose an inherent threat to the West, and concludes instead that societies must create economic and political opportunities for newcomers.

Speck, Ulrich, "The West's Response to the Ukraine Conflict: A Transatlantic Success Story." **Transatlantic Academy**. 2015–16 series, no. 4. 23 pp. Available free online: < http://www.transatlan-ticacademy.org/sites/default/files/publications/Speck_WestResponseUkraine_Apr16_web.pdf>. This report assesses the response of European countries, the U.S. and partners like Canada and Japan in addressing Russian aggression in Ukraine.

Soros, George, **The Tragedy of the European Union: Disintegration or Revival?** New York: PublicAffairs, 2014. 208 pp. Soros analyzes the euro crisis, offering a penetrating critique of the single currency from the perspective of a former supporter of the project.

Stiglitz, Joseph, **The Euro: How a Common Currency Threatens the Future of Europe**. New York: W.W. Norton & Company, 2016. 448 pp. Nobel Prize-winning economist Joseph Stiglitz argues that the euro was flawed from its beginning, and presents possible ways forward for the Eurozone.

Tsoukalis, Loukas, **In Defense of Europe: Can the European Project Be Saved?** Oxford: Oxford University Press, 2016. 280 pp. Tsoukalis discusses how the international financial crisis evolved into an existential crisis for the EU, and contemplates the circumstances under which Europe might hold together or divide.

To access web links to these readings, as well as links to additional, shorter readings and suggested web sites,
GO TO www.greatdecisions.org
and click on the topic under Resources, on the right-hand side of the page

Trade, jobs and politics

by Jeremy Haft

Starbucks coffee shop by Chinese streetsigns in the Yu Garden Bazaar Market, Shanghai, China (PHOTO BY TIM GRAHAM/GETTY IMAGES)

Before your morning cup of coffee had to crisscross the planet on its way to your mug, before your shirt and your car and your aspirin were fabricated all over the world, before the onset of globalization, if a label said something was "Made in the USA" or "Made in China," it usually was. These days, it almost never is. Most of the products we consume are not produced by just one country. They're "Made in the World," a collaboration of many countries.

Modern manufacturing looks very little like the classic economic theory advanced by David Ricardo in 1817. The father of free trade argued that if one country is better at making wine, and another is better at making cloth, then both countries become wealthier by focusing on what they're good at and trading with one another. Today, the wine and cloth once produced by countries A and B are now produced in collaboration by countries A, B, C, D and E.

But our economic metrics haven't kept up. Globalization has transformed the way we make things so rapidly, we're still using statistics to describe David Ricardo's wine-for-cloth world. Astonishingly, U.S. trade numbers consider our imports as made entirely by the last country that shipped them to us, ignoring the value contributed by all the countries that helped design and manufacture these products—including the United States.

So your shirt label may say China, but its content was probably made in the USA, a leading global exporter of cotton. Your iPhone label may say China, but America made the software and many critical components. China's share,

JEREMY HAFT, *entrepreneur, Georgetown University adjunct professor, and author, has founded and run trading companies in China for nearly 20 years in a wide variety of industries. Haft's current start-up is an export management firm that sells U.S. hides, pork, and other agricultural products to China. He is the author of* All the Tea in China, *a primer on how to do business in China, and the recent* Unmade in China, *which examines America's enduring competitive advantages over China in the coming century. Haft lectures at Georgetown University's School of Foreign Service and McDonough School of Business.*

Street scenes from the historical steel mill town of Braddock, Pennsylvania on October 13, 2016. Braddock was once a thriving center of America's steel industry but once the mills closed, it suffered severe economic decline and depopulation. Efforts are being made to repurpose many of the abandoned buildings for art projects and community development, and U.S. Steel's Edgar Thomson mill is still operational. (PHOTO BY ANDREW LICHTENSTEIN/ CORBIS VIA GETTY IMAGES)

from assembly and some non-critical components, is just a tiny fraction of the overall value of the phone. Yet our trade statistics assign 100% of the value of these imports to China, the last country that shipped them to us.

Misleading numbers promote a myopic view of ourselves in the world. Like looking through the wrong end of a telescope, these metrics show a shrunken image of America's true economic size and competitiveness. We seem on the decline, while developing economies like China seem all the more menacing. What's worse, our out-of-date economic numbers rationalize policies that kill jobs instead of saving them and support political rhetoric that mobilizes voters to act against their own economic interests.

Consider the 2016 presidential contest, which perhaps more than any other election in the last 30 years, was dominated by talk of trade. Donald Trump and Bernie Sanders shared a common economic message: that trade has deci-

mated the middle class. Fix trade, and you bring back jobs from overseas. Like the rallying cry for Britain's vote to leave the largest free trade zone in the world, Trump and Sanders blamed globalization and bad trade deals for killing millions of jobs. The anti-trade message resonated broadly and deeply, helping to motivate more than 25 million Republicans and Democrats to support Trump and Sanders in the primaries and more than 61 million Americans to vote for Donald Trump in the general election.

At the core of this economic argument are two sets of numbers—gross domestic product (GDP) and the balance of trade—both of which were developed in an era long before globalization. As such, they severely distort today's economic realities, painting a false picture of the relationship between trade and jobs and distracting our attention from the true causes of our economic challenges. To separate fact from fiction and to determine whether the policy proposals advanced by the President-elect are sound, we must go beyond the usual analysis of economic conclusions to critique the underlying numbers themselves.

An especially clear articulation of the case against trade can be found in Don-

ald Trump's speech on June 28, 2016, that was billed as his jobs plan, remarks *The Atlantic* would later call "shockingly specific." It was the week after the Republican convention in Cleveland. The calamitous Brexit vote had happened just four days earlier on the 24th. At a metal recycling plant in western Pennsylvania, the candidate stood behind a teleprompter in front of a wall of scrap. It was a perfect opportunity to talk about America's export strength and how for many years, scrap metal was a leading U.S. export to China, which lacks a robust recycling industry. Your Chinese-made doorknob or faucet or air conditioner vent were probably fabricated from U.S. recycled steel, supporting jobs in small and midsized firms across America at recycling plants like the one Trump was speaking at.

Who better than the self-styled "Blue Collar Billionaire" to talk about the economic resilience of the Rust Belt? How Pennsylvania was one of 30 states to export more than $1 billion worth of goods to China in 2015—up from just 17 states in 2006. And having nearly doubled the value of its goods exports to China in that time period, how Pennsylvania was a hair's breadth away from joining the 31 states that have seen triple digit export growth to China since 2006. Or how the other Rust Belt states have also seen their goods exports to China surge—how in 2015, Indiana exported $2.1 billion worth of manufactured goods to China, up 178% since 2006; Ohio: $3.3 billion, up 124%; Michigan: $3.5 billion, up 220%; and Illinois: $5.5 billion, up 201%. For a supposedly depressed region, laid low by Mighty China, the Rust Belt was selling goods to China hand over fist, a clear sign of abiding competitiveness.

Instead, the candidate painted a picture of economic decline. "Many Pennsylvania towns once thriving and humming are now in a state of despair," he said. "This wave of globalization has wiped out totally, totally our middle class." Trade was the culprit and smart trade the solution. "To understand why trade reform creates jobs, and it creates a lot of them," he said, "we need

Before you read, download the companion **Glossary** that includes definitions and a guide to acronyms and abbreviations used in the article. Go to **www.great decisions.org** and select a topic in the Resources section on the right-hand side of the page.

to understand how all nations grow and prosper. Massive trade deficits subtract directly from our gross domestic product." Slower growth rates lead to fewer jobs created.

Trump put his finger on the two underlying metrics that correlate trade and jobs: gross domestic product and trade balances. But like so many others who cite these metrics, he did not define them. GDP is widely used and widely misunderstood. A relic from the distant past, GDP was invented during the Great Depression as an effort to capture the entire output of our economy in one number. In 1944, it became the standard measurement to gauge economic size by the World Bank and International Monetary Fund. GDP is such a ubiquitous number today that you typically hear "GDP" and "the economy" used interchangeably, such as, "the U.S. economy grew 1% in the first quarter," when what's meant is that "our GDP grew 1%."

Although there are a few different ways to calculate GDP, the most common methodology, and the one typically employed by the World Bank, is to tally up the spending in an economy, plus the value of exports and minus the value of imports. The claim we've been hearing for years that China is the world's second largest economy, and now the world's largest, is based on World Bank GDP calculations, adjusted for "purchasing power parity" (PPP). Here is a typical example, from Nobel-laureate economist, Joseph Stiglitz, writing in *Vanity Fair*: "2014 was the last year in which the United States could claim to be the world's largest economic power. China enters 2015 in the top position, where it will likely remain for a very long time, if not forever."

Stiglitz proclaims China's new status citing recently published World Bank GDP figures. Ironic, as Stiglitz himself famously called for an end to "GDP fetishism" in 2009 because gross domestic product, a relic from the Great Depression, does not accurately reflect modern, globalized economic systems. Nor does it tell you much about a country's true economic size. Suppose you wanted to compare your

family's wealth to the Jones's. Would you start on January 1 and add up everything you spent through December 31? So if you spent $200,000 over 12 months on food, mortgage, school and other expenses, then the value of your household wealth would be $200,000? And if the Jones's spent $300,000, then they'd be the richer family? No, to compare your family's wealth, you'd want to look at your assets and liabilities. What you own minus what you owe. That number would be a much more accurate picture of your net worth, not how much you spent in a given year.

It's the same with national economies. GDP tries to capture one year's economic output through measuring expenditures. But knowing how much China and America spent in a given year tells us very little about our relative economic size. A much more appropriate metric than GDP to size an economy is "national wealth": how much a country's government, households and firms own minus what they owe—or, what a business would call its balance sheet of assets and liabilities. Comparing China and America's national wealth reveals a very different picture from GDP.

According to analysis by Credit Suisse and the U.S. Federal Reserve, China's total household wealth in 2015 was about $21 trillion, and the United States' was between $79 to 83 trillion— that's around a $60 trillion delta, which

is widening fast, not converging; over $20 trillion in the delta appeared just in the past few years. If we factor in the assets and liabilities of government and industry, which in China includes giant state-owned corporations, a conservative estimate still puts the U.S. more than $40 trillion ahead.

This is not a picture of a Rising China that has overtaken the United States economically. In fact, China is falling faster and faster behind, not catching up or beating us. So when Donald Trump said in his jobs speech that, "today I'm going to talk about how to make America wealthy again," the data on national wealth demonstrate that America already *is* much wealthier than China, or any other country, and is getting more so each year.

Adjusting GDP to factor in purchasing power parity, as is customary at the World Bank, further distorts an already misleading metric. PPP tries to make apples to apples comparisons between two economies—so that a unit of currency spent in, say, Manhattan would equal a unit of currency spent in Beijing. But, prices tend to vary widely within a single country, as well as over time. And, PPP numbers for China rarely take into account a key metric in pricing: inflation, which is a closely guarded, politically sensitive issue in China. The new World Bank statistics that Joseph Stiglitz cited in *Vanity Fair*

Republican presidential candidate Donald Trump speaking at Alumisource, a steel industry firm, in Monessen, PA, June 28, 2016. (HILARY SWIFT/THE NEW YORK TIMES/REDUX)

are no exception. An independent, comprehensive survey of Chinese housing prices was not conducted, so a critical data point was overlooked.

The finer points of defining GDP, of course, do not make for scintillating politics, and Trump, unsurprisingly, glossed over them. In laying out his case, he linked job losses to GDP and trade imbalances, arguing that slower GDP growth rates due to trade deficits lead to fewer jobs created. "From 1947 to 2001," he said, "gross domestic product grew at a rate of 3.5%. However, since 2002, the year after we fully opened our markets to Chinese imports, the GDP growth rate has been cut in half.... For every 1% of GDP growth, we failed to generate in any given year, we failed to create over one million jobs." Correlating employment to GDP growth squares with mainstream economic theory. Okun's Law of 1962, another numeric fossil from a pre-globalized era, states that each three percentage point increase in GDP will decrease unemployment by 1%. While this theory

has informed monetary policy over the years, the law's durability has come into question by the Federal Reserve during the recovery from the Great Recession.

The Cleveland Fed pointed out that, "the unemployment rate fell from 9.1% to 8.3% in 2011, but real GDP grew only 1.6%. That growth rate is roughly half of what our rule of thumb would suggest we need just to hold the unemployment rate constant." Since the Great Recession, America's GDP growth has not exceeded 2.5% , yet unemployment in the United States has fallen from 9.1% to 4.9%, a rate considerably faster than what Okun's Law would have predicted. The Fed concluded that Okun's Law is not a reliable rule of thumb and that the relationship between GDP and employment is "dynamic."

That's in part because GDP, created to reflect a 1937 America, does not accurately represent how jobs are supported in today's globalized supply chain. GDP is a tally of expenditures, plus exports and *minus* imports. Embedded in the math is an assumption that

exports add economic output and jobs to the economy, while imports subtract output and jobs. Yet, imports support millions of workers across America, usually at the beginning and end of the global supply chain: at the beginning, with design, engineering and the production and export of critical components; and at the end, after imported goods arrive on American soil, with transportation, warehousing, retail and service, which support jobs in trucking, rail, air, storage, marketing, construction, law, finance and customer service, among others. This often overlooked fact accounts for part of the reason why the relationship between GDP and employment is dynamic: as imports rise, jobs are created. Since 1981, imports have been increasing steadily, while unemployment has been trending down, except during the Great Recession of 2008, which slowed trade and caused significant job losses. Looking at the last 30 years, there is no correlation between imports and job losses in the employment data. ∎

Outsourcing

Jobs lost to overseas competition was a highly politicized issue in 2016, in part because of a lack of reliable numbers. According to the Congressional Research Service, "No comprehensive data exist on the number of production and services workers" whose jobs have been moved overseas. "The only regularly collected statistics… come from the BLS [Bureau of Labor Statistics] series on extended mass layoffs."

While they provide a good baseline, however, the data are based on unemployment insurance claims that typically don't reflect part-time or seasonal labor—a growing segment in the new "gig economy." Nor do the data represent companies who choose to open facilities in other countries instead of the U.S., without laying off existing workers. So to extrapolate broader outsourcing numbers, economists employ additional data, such as the levels of U.S. direct investment abroad and imported

intermediate goods. But, just because a business is investing in another country does not necessarily mean it is firing domestic employees and shipping those jobs overseas. Nor does the import of intermediate goods, which make up 75% of global trade, necessarily spell the loss of jobs here at home, as many workers are required to transform those components into final products. For example, the Mercedes Benz factory in South Carolina imports components from the E.U., China and Mexico, where they are assembled by U.S. workers into cars.

Because measuring outsourcing is highly conjectural, it's easily politicized. For decades, both Democrats and Republicans have claimed China is stealing our jobs *en masse*. The Romney and Obama campaigns portrayed China as a giant job killer in the 2012 election, in which nearly $50 million was spent on television ads that cast the other candidate as soft on outsourcing to China. Some 4,700 of those

ads were aired in Cleveland alone, the site of the future 2016 Republican presidential convention.

But just because we lose jobs, doesn't necessarily mean trade is killing them. In America, millions of jobs are created and lost every year; four to six million jobs are lost each month as part of normal turnover. In 2008, an especially bad year for American employment amid a severe economic retraction, the U.S. lost 30.8 million jobs, but created 25.3 million jobs. A major cause of job losses in the manufacturing sector is technology. Today, U.S. manufacturing produces three and a half times more output per worker hour than in 1979, when manufacturing was at peak employment. From 2009-2011, U.S. manufacturing output rose 20% but employment increased only 4%. As we get better at making things more efficiently, workers are laid off.

The notion, then, of "bringing our jobs back" from other countries—a cornerstone of the Trump and Sanders economic message—overstates how many jobs have been lost to foreign competi-

ARCTIC OCEAN

Queen Elizabeth Islands

Ellesmere Island

GREENLAND (DENMARK)

Beaufort Sea

Victoria Island

Baffin Bay

Baffin Island

Denmark Strait

Davis Strait

Reykjavík

ARCTIC CIRCLE (66°33')

ALASKA (U.S.)

Great Bear Lake

Gulf of Alaska

Anchorage

Juneau

Great Slave Lake

Churchill

Hudson Bay

Labrador Sea

Aleutian Islands

Vancouver

Seattle

CANADA

NORTH AMERICA

Lake Winnipeg

Great Lakes

Montréal

Québec

Ottawa

Toronto

New York

NORTH ATLANTIC OCEAN

NORTH PACIFIC OCEAN

UNITED STATES

Chicago

Denver

St. Louis

Washington, D.C.

AZORES (PORTUGAL)

San Francisco

Los Angeles

Dallas

Atlanta

BERMUDA (U.K.)

CANARY ISLANDS (SPAIN)

WESTERN SAHA (ADMINISTER BY MOROC

TROPIC OF CANCER (23°27')

Monterrey

Gulf of Mexico

Miami

Nassau

THE BAHAMAS

MEXICO

Havana

CUBA

VIRGIN ISLS. (U.S.)

BRITISH VIRGIN ISLS. (U.K.)

ANGUILLA (U.K.)

ST. KITTS AND NEVIS

ANTIGUA AND BARBUDA

GUADELOUPE (FR.)

DOMINICA

MARTINIQUE (FR.)

ST. LUCIA

BARBADOS

ST. VINCENT AND THE GRENADINES

GRENADA

Nouakchott

HAWAII (U.S.)

Honolulu

Mexico City

Veracruz

HAITI

DOMINICAN REPUBLIC

Port-au-Prince

Santo Domingo (U.S.)

PUERTO RICO

CAPE VERDE

Dakar

Praia

SEN

Banjul

THE GAMBIA

N ATOLL

Belmopan

GUATEMALA

BELIZE

JAMAICA

Kingston

Caribbean Sea

MONTSERRAT (U.K.)

GUINEA-BISSAU

Bissau

Conakry

Freetow

SIERRA LEON

Mo

PALMYRA ATOLL (U.S.)

Guatemala City

HONDURAS

Tegucigalpa

San Salvador

EL SALVADOR

Managua

NICARAGUA

ARUBA (NETH.)

NETHERLANDS ANTILLES (NETH.)

TRINIDAD AND TOBAGO

Port-of-Spain

N REEF S.)

KIRITIMATI (CHRISTMAS ISLAND)

COSTA RICA

San José

PANAMA

Panama

Medellín

Caracas

VENEZUELA

Georgetown

GUYANA

Paramaribo

SURINAME

Cayenne

FRENCH GUIANA (FR.)

RVIS ISLAND (U.S.)

EQUATOR

Bogotá

Cali

COLOMBIA

Quito

GALAPAGOS ISLANDS (ECUADOR)

ECUADOR

Manaus

Belém

ATI

Iquitos

PERU

BRAZIL

Recife

MARQUESAS ISLAND (FR. POLYNESIA)

SOUTH AMERICA

FRENCH POLYNESIA (FRANCE)

Lima

Cusco

La Paz

BOLIVIA

Brasília

ISLANDS Z.)

TUAMOTU ARCHIPELAGO (FR. POLYNESIA)

Sucre

Rio de Janeiro

SOCIETY ISLANDS (FR. POLYNESIA)

TROPIC OF CAPRICORN (23°27')

Antofagasta

PARAGUAY

Asunción

São Paulo

SOUTH ATLANTIC OCEAN

TUBUAI ISLANDS (FR. POLYNESIA)

PITCAIRN ISLANDS (U.K.)

EASTER ISLAND (CHILE)

ISLA SALA Y GÓMEZ (CHILE)

CHILE

Santiago

URUGUAY

Buenos Aires

La Plata

Montevideo

ARGENTINA

Bahía Blanca

JUAN FERNÁNDEZ ISLANDS (CHILE)

FALKLAND ISLANDS (ADMINISTERED BY U.K. CLAIMED BY ARGENTINA)

SOUTH GEORGIA AND THE SOUTH SANDWICH ISLANDS (ADMINISTERED BY U.K., CLAIMED BY ARGENTINA)

SOUTH PACIFIC OCEAN

Punta Arenas

Stanley

Scotia Sea

SOUTH ORKNEY ISLANDS (B.A.T.)

Drake Passage

SOUTHERN OCEAN

Amundsen Sea

Bellingshausen Sea

Weddell Sea

Ross Sea

Ross Ice Shelf

Ronne Ice Shelf

VENEZUELA	Independent state
GUADELOUPE (FRANCE)	Dependent territory
Ottawa ⊛	Capital
Bangalore ●	Major city

Scale 1:35,000,000

Robinson Projection with standard parallels 38°N and 38°S
Source: CIA World Factbook

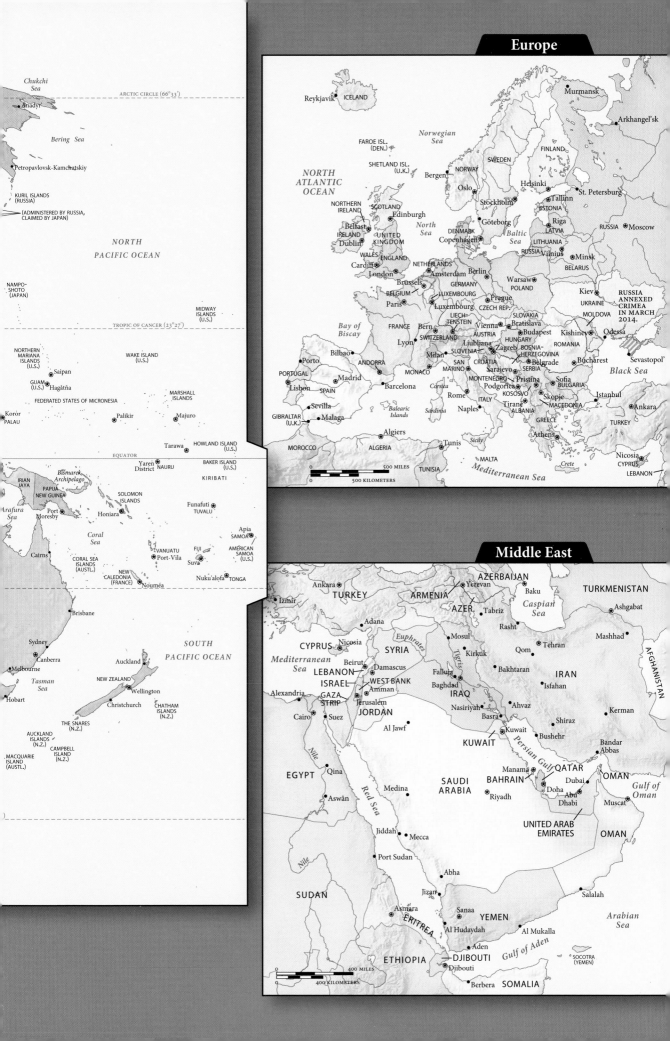

Europe

Reykjavik • ICELAND

Murmansk

Arkhangel'sk

Norwegian Sea

NORTH
ATLANTIC
OCEAN

FAROE ISL.
(DEN.)

SHETLAND ISL.
(U.K.)

Bergen

NORWAY

Oslo

SWEDEN

FINLAND

Helsinki

St. Petersburg

Stockholm

Tallinn

ESTONIA

NORTHERN
IRELAND

SCOTLAND

Edinburgh

DENMARK

Göteborg

Copenhagen

Baltic
Sea

Riga

LATVIA

RUSSIA

Moscow

Belfast

IRELAND

Dublin

UNITED
KINGDOM

WALES

ENGLAND

Cardiff

London

North
Sea

NETHERLANDS

Amsterdam

Berlin

LITHUANIA

Vilnius

Minsk

RUSSIA

BELARUS

Brussels

BELGIUM

GERMANY

Warsaw

POLAND

Kiev

UKRAINE

RUSSIA
ANNEXED
CRIMEA
IN MARCH
2014.

Paris

LUXEMBOURG

Luxembourg

Prague

CZECH REP.

SLOVAKIA

MOLDOVA

Kishinev

Odessa

Bay of
Biscay

FRANCE

Bern

LIECH-
TENSTEIN

Vienna

AUSTRIA

Bratislava

Budapest

HUNGARY

Bucharest

Sevastopol'

Lyon

SWITZERLAND

Ljubljana

SLOVENIA

Zagreb

BOSNIA-
HERZEGOVINA

ROMANIA

Black
Sea

Porto

Bilbao

Milan

SAN
MARINO

CROATIA

Belgrade

SERBIA

Sofia

BULGARIA

Istanbul

PORTUGAL

Madrid

ANDORRA

MONACO

MONTENEGRO

Pristina

Podgorica

KOSOVO

Skopje

Ankara

Lisbon

SPAIN

Barcelona

Corsica

Rome

ITALY

Tirane

ALBANIA

MACEDONIA

TURKEY

Sevilla

*Balearic
Islands*

Sardinia

Naples

GREECE

Athens

GIBRALTAR
(U.K.)

Malaga

Algiers

MOROCCO

ALGERIA

Tunis

Sicily

Crete

Nicosia

CYPRUS

LEBANON

TUNISIA

MALTA

Mediterranean Sea

500 MILES

500 KILOMETERS

Middle East

Ankara

TURKEY

ARMENIA

AZERBAIJAN

Yerevan

Baku

*Caspian
Sea*

TURKMENISTAN

Ashgabat

Izmir

Adana

AZER.

Tabriz

Rasht

Mashhad

CYPRUS

Nicosia

SYRIA

Euphrates

Mosul

Qom

Tehran

*Mediterranean
Sea*

Beirut

Tigris

Kirkuk

Bakhtaran

IRAN

AFGHANISTAN

LEBANON

Damascus

Falluja

Isfahan

ISRAEL

WEST BANK

Baghdad

Alexandria

GAZA
STRIP

Amman

Jerusalem

IRAQ

Nasiriyah

Ahvaz

Kerman

Cairo

Suez

JORDAN

Basra

Shiraz

Kuwait

Bushehr

Bandar
Abbas

Al Jawf

KUWAIT

Persian Gulf

QATAR

OMAN

EGYPT

Qina

Manama

Dubai

*Gulf of
Oman*

Nile

Medina

SAUDI
ARABIA

BAHRAIN

Doha

Abu
Dhabi

Muscat

Red Sea

Aswân

Riyadh

UNITED ARAB
EMIRATES

OMAN

Jiddah

Mecca

Nile

Port Sudan

Abha

SUDAN

Jizan

Salalah

Asmara

Sanaa

YEMEN

*Arabian
Sea*

ERITREA

Al Hudaydah

Al Mukalla

ETHIOPIA

DJIBOUTI

Aden

Gulf of Aden

SOCOTRA
(YEMEN)

Djibouti

Berbera

SOMALIA

400 MILES

400 KILOMETERS

---

*Chukchi
Sea*

ARCTIC CIRCLE (66°33')

Anadyr

Bering Sea

Petropavlovsk-Kamchatskiy

KURIL ISLANDS
(RUSSIA)

(ADMINISTERED BY RUSSIA,
CLAIMED BY JAPAN)

NORTH
PACIFIC OCEAN

NAMPO-
SHOTO
(JAPAN)

MIDWAY
ISLANDS
(U.S.)

TROPIC OF CANCER (23°27')

NORTHERN
MARIANA
ISLANDS
(U.S.)

WAKE ISLAND
(U.S.)

Saipan

GUAM
(U.S.)

Hagåtña

MARSHALL
ISLANDS

FEDERATED STATES OF MICRONESIA

Koror

PALAU

Palikir

Majuro

Tarawa

HOWLAND ISLAND
(U.S.)

EQUATOR

Yaren
District

NAURU

BAKER ISLAND
(U.S.)

IRIAN
JAYA

*Bismarck
Archipelago*

PAPUA
NEW GUINEA

KIRIBATI

*Arafura
Sea*

Port
Moresby

SOLOMON
ISLANDS

Honiara

Funafuti
TUVALU

Apia
SAMOA

*Coral
Sea*

VANUATU

Port-Vila

FIJI

Suva

AMERICAN
SAMOA
(U.S.)

Cairns

CORAL SEA
ISLANDS
(AUSTL.)

NEW
CALEDONIA
(FRANCE)

Nouméa

Nuku'alofa

TONGA

Brisbane

SOUTH
PACIFIC OCEAN

Sydney

Canberra

Auckland

Melbourne

NEW ZEALAND

*Tasman
Sea*

Wellington

Hobart

Christchurch

CHATHAM
ISLANDS
(N.Z.)

THE SNARES
(N.Z.)

AUCKLAND
ISLANDS
(N.Z.)

CAMPBELL
ISLAND
(N.Z.)

MACQUARIE
ISLAND
(AUSTL.)

tion and is a misunderstanding of how trade and jobs interrelate. Because we import more manufactured goods than we export from countries like Mexico and China, trade deficits are seen as a chief reason for unemployment in the United States. As Bernie Sanders wrote in his book, *Outsider In the House*, "Our current trade deficit is causing the loss of over 2 million jobs." It was a refrain we heard a lot during the election season. At the Republican convention in Cleveland, Senator Jeff Sessions (R-AL) said, "The deficit with China has increased five-fold and the deficit with Korea doubled. These are job-killing numbers....Bad trade deals close factories, and end high paying jobs." Bernie Sanders also frequently blamed trade imbalances for the loss of millions of American manufacturing jobs. To a lesser extent, Hillary Clinton did, too.

But, like GDP, the way we measure trade harkens back to David Ricardo's world. Based on "gross," not "value-added," measurements, we attribute 100% of the value of imports to the last country that shipped them to us. Gross trade balances ignore how products are actually manufactured today and severely skew our understanding of trade and jobs.

Consider the iPhone. This campaign season, Apple was frequently touted as an example of a company that relocates jobs overseas, the sort of company that both Donald Trump and Hillary Clinton promised to penalize financially. iPhones, however, aren't actually "Made in China." An iPhone 6 costs about $236 dollars to produce, and China's share is less than 5%. The value that China contributes comes from assembly and the production of some low-value, non-critical components. The design and programming of the iPhone's software is done in America, and its higher-value components are manufactured mostly in Japan, South Korea, Germany and the United States before the phone is assembled in China (by a Taiwanese-owned factory). But because China is the last country to export the iPhone to the United States, our trade statistics consider it as 100% Chinese-made.

This methodology severely distorts

*A worker supervises the production of molten iron at a furnace in the production area of the Zhong Tian (Zenith) Steel Group Corporation on May 12, 2016, in Changzhou, Jiangsu, China. (*PHOTO BY KEVIN FRAYER/GETTY IMAGES)

the true balances of trade, and it makes China seem much more mighty than it is. In 2009, for example, iPhones contributed just under $2 billion to America's trade deficit with China. But if we accounted for the actual value that China adds to the making of an iPhone, that deficit would shrink to just $73.45 million. Considering the totality of Chinese imports in this way, our trade deficit with China would probably be more than halved, according to Pascal Lamy, a recent head of the World Trade Organization. And, Lamy was referring only to the imbalance in traded manufactured goods. America runs surpluses with China in the trade of services and agriculture.

Our antique trade numbers not only make China seem much bigger than it is, they also hide America's significant contribution to the global supply chain. Most of the products that the United States imports from China actually contain a significant amount of American-made content: the cotton in your khakis, the cardboard in your Amazon.com box, the recycled steel in your faucet, the leather in your shoes, the software and processor in your iPhone, to mention just a few. When you are buying "Made in China" goods, you are supporting the American ranchers, farmers and factory workers who made the ingredients that went into the imports, plus all the jobs

connected with bringing the products to market once they arrive here.

This evidence of American export strength and competitiveness rarely gets mentioned in the political arena. Both Hillary Clinton and Senator Sherrod Brown (D-OH) jabbed Donald Trump in their convention speeches for outsourcing his Trump-branded products to China, India and Turkey. "Donald Trump says he wants to make America great again," Clinton remarked. "Well, he could start by actually making things in America again." It's an argument that may score political points, but it misconstrues how modern trade really works. Though these products were "made" overseas, they most likely contained a lot of U.S. content. And then there are all the jobs associated with distributing and retailing them. To imply that Trump is somehow not supporting U.S. jobs by sourcing these finished products in other countries is not entirely factual.

Yet misinterpreted trade imbalances are the basis for claims that imports kill U.S. jobs. Here is Sanders in an op-ed for the *Huffington Post*: "Since 2001 [when China joined the World Trade Organization]...we have lost over 4.7 million decent paying manufacturing jobs. NAFTA [the North American Free Trade Agreement] has led to the loss of nearly 700,000 jobs. PNTR [Permanent

Normal Trade Relations] with China has led to the loss of 2.7 million jobs." These numbers are based on the correlation of jobs to gross trade deficits, and they come from a single source, the Economic Policy Institute (EPI), a left-leaning Washington, D.C., think-tank. Trump also cited EPI studies when claiming that trade imbalances cause job losses. In his March 2016 op-ed in *USA Today,* Trump wrote: "An Economic Policy Institute analysis found that Ohio has already lost more than 100,000 jobs to TPP [Trans-Pacific Partnership] countries." And here is Donald Trump again in his August 8, 2016, speech at the Detroit Economic Club, laying out his vision for the economy: "Instead of creating 70,000 jobs, [our trade agreement with South Korea] has killed nearly 100,000, according to the Economic Policy Institute." And later in the same speech: "According to the Economic Policy Institute, the U.S. trade deficit with the proposed TPP member countries cost over 1 million manufacturing jobs in 2015."

EPI specializes in studies that link employment to trade imbalances, so its findings tend to be cited when politicians and media assert that imports kill jobs. Yet these widely cited EPI studies have been discredited by economists at the Bureau of Labor Statistics; by Carl Bialik, *The Wall Street Journal*'s "Num-

bers Guy"; and by many others. BLS's criticism is especially significant, as the Economic Policy Institute uses a BLS input-output model to arrive at its conclusions. This model, however, was originally intended to predict how many jobs would be created from activities like construction projects. "It wasn't meant to hypothesize about job displacement because of imports," said James Franklin, Chief of the Division of Industry Employment Projections at the BLS. Franklin went on to characterize EPI's methodology as, "a common misuse of the data…[which] doesn't square with standard trade theory."

Essentially, these EPI studies assume that a dollar spent on imports from China or South Korea or Mexico is a dollar *not* spent on U.S. goods and services. So as imports rise, jobs are lost. This claim, however, assumes gross, not value-added, trade measurements, overlooking the value of American-made inputs, as well as all the steps involved in bringing an imported product to the consumer. As the San Francisco Federal Reserve Bank said, "If a pair of sneakers made in China costs $70 in the United States…the bulk of the retail price pays for transportation of the sneakers in the United States, rent for the store where they are sold, profits for shareholders of the U.S. retailer, and the cost of marketing the sneakers.

These costs include salaries, wages and benefits paid to the U.S. workers and managers who staff these operations." The Fed estimates that for every dollar spent on imports from China, about 55 cents pays for U.S. services.

There are millions of U.S. jobs associated with the services that support Chinese imports. And counter to conventional wisdom, even the lower value Chinese imports of apparel and toys support over half a million American jobs. What's more, the Fed's 55 cents does not include the value of any U.S.-made content in the imported products. Since most Chinese imports contain a high degree of U.S.-made inputs, a dollar spent on Chinese imported products *is* often much more than 55 cents spent on U.S. goods and services. In other words, the more we import from China, the more American jobs we support.

Trade balances are not scorecards, where exports are good and imports bad, an assumption embedded in GDP math and the EPI studies. Nor are trade deficits akin to liabilities. The trade deficit merely measures the difference between gross imports and exports. And because our trade balances obscure where value is actually added along the supply chain, the gross trade deficit with Mexico, for example, hides the fact that over 40% of Mexican imports consists of U.S.-made content. ∎

Tariffs

Closely tied to the argument that trade imbalances kill jobs is the belief that China's currency manipulation makes trade imbalances worse. As Donald Trump said in his jobs speech in western Pennsylvania, "Hillary Clinton stood by idly while China cheated on its currency [and] added another trillion dollars to the trade deficit." To varying degrees, Sanders, Trump and Clinton all said they would seek to claw back jobs that have been lost through trade by punishing China for currency manipulation, and Trump went so far as to call for a 45% tariff on all Chinese imports.

We've heard this song before. In the 2012 presidential election, Mitt Rom-

ney often said that he would label China a currency manipulator "on day one" of his administration so he could retaliate by raising tariffs on a broad set of imports, and he frequently referred to China's currency policies as "cheating" at campaign rallies and in the town hall debate with Obama—a taunt Trump repeated innumerable times, as well: "We will stand up to trade cheating. Cheating. Cheaters, that's what they are. Cheaters. We will stand up to trade cheating anywhere and everywhere it threatens the American job," he said in his jobs speech.

China's currency policies have been the source of criticism for decades, and again, have been widely misunderstood. Since China has a closed financial system, its currency, the remnimbi or yuan,

is managed, and China's long-standing policy has been to peg its exchange rate to that of the U.S. dollar. When the yuan is cheap, Chinese goods supposedly achieve an unfair pricing advantage—making them more competitive than domestically produced American goods, exacerbating trade imbalances and killing jobs.

But compare China's currency value with U.S. unemployment over the past 25 years. Going back to 1991, except for the Great Recession of 2008 and a blip in 2003, unemployment has been trending down, regardless of whether the yuan is rising or falling in value. The sharp decline in value of the yuan in 1993–94, for example, should have triggered U.S. job losses. But if you look at U.S. unemployment levels for that

(Left): A factory worker produces tires at the Pirelli & C SpA tire factory in Jining, Shandong Province, China on Feb. 24, 2011. (PHOTOGRAPHER: KEITH BEDFORD/BLOOMBERG VIA GETTY IMAGES) *(Right): Workers construct a solar power field in Qinhuangdao, north China's Hebei Province, Oct. 28, 2015.* (YANG SHIYAO/XINHUA/EYEVINE/REDUX)

period, they continued on their downward trend—in other words, America keeps adding jobs despite China's relative exchange rates.

What's more, China's central bank for many months has been trying to prop its currency up. As much as $1 trillion of capital flowed out of China in 2015, putting pressure on the value of the yuan to drop. China has been spending hundreds of billions of dollars worth of its foreign currency reserve to shore up the yuan and prevent further depreciation, which destabilized global markets twice in 2015.

Yet even though China's exchange rate has no discernable impact on our job market, and the fact that China is struggling to keep its value high, not low, candidates from both parties kept harping on currency manipulation. In his jobs speech, Trump provided a list of policies he would pursue if elected, saying he would direct his Treasury Secretary to designate China a currency manipulator, which would trigger an increase in tariffs on Chinese imports. By making it more expensive for China to sell us their goods, Chinese imports would decrease. But since most of the goods that America imports from China *contain* U.S. inputs, then demand for U.S. exports across a number of categories would also decrease, ultimately killing jobs. A sharp decline in Chinese imports would also eliminate jobs in all the industries that help bring those imported products to market, once they arrive in America.

The solar panel industry is a good example of how raising tariffs to protect jobs achieves the opposite result. The Obama administration levied tariffs on imported Chinese solar panels by up to 239%. Politically, this move may have played well to those wanting Obama to "get tough on China," but ultimately, it was a policy misfire because it caused a net job loss to the solar industry.

Solar panel fabrication is just one node in a long, global value chain, in which the United States is a net exporter to China. Our top export is the expensive capital equipment used to make the panels; our second is PV polysilicon, the active element that converts sunlight into energy. China imports these items to fabricate and assemble the panels, relatively lower value functions in the chain, and then exports them back to us. Once they arrive, they must be transported, the site must be prepared, permits must be filed for, and the system must be installed and maintained. Even when the solar panels have been imported, three quarters of the financial value in an installed photovoltaic system flows to America, not China.

However, when tariffs were raised on just one node of the solar supply chain, a vicious circle ensued. After the Commerce Department levied higher tariffs on Chinese imported panels, China responded in kind, raising its tariffs on U.S.-made PV polysilicon to 57%. As a direct result of this tit-for-tat, a major PV polysilicon producer had to cease operations at its plant in Washington state, because of low Chinese demand for its exports.

Tires provide another example. Raising tariffs on tires, as Obama did in 2008, may have helped one part of the value chain, but it hurt others. According to a study from the Peterson Institute of International Economics, Obama's tire tariffs could have saved about 1,200 jobs in tire manufacturing. But the tariffs, in dampening Chinese imports, raised tire retail prices by $1.1 billion in 2011. Higher prices slowed consumer demand, which cost about 3,700 retail jobs, causing a net job loss to the tire industry as a whole.

When Trump defended his proposed 45% tariff on all Chinese imports by saying, "we're already in a trade war with China, and we're losing badly," raising tariffs would have the opposite of the intended effect. Instead of protecting jobs, it would eliminate them. But this kind of reasoned argument is difficult to get across when iconic industries like steel are considered.

Donald Trump often touted steel as a victim of job-killing imports, such as in his jobs speech: "When subsidized foreign steel is dumped into our markets, threatening our factories, the politicians have proven, folks, have proven they do nothing." Far from doing nothing, more than half of the many hundreds of anti-dumping tariffs since 1970 have been levied on imported steel—during both Republican and Democratic administrations, including those of George W. Bush and Barack Obama.

And while employment in the steel industry has declined since 1970, it's debatable to what extent imports were the cause. It took just one quarter of the workers to make nearly 10% more steel in 2011 than in 1980. Advances in productivity and innovation have significantly slimmed the workforce. Today, there are about 130,000–153,000 employees in the steel industry. But downstream, in the industries that consume steel, there are many more jobs, such as about 1.8 million workers at companies that make cars and auto parts. Each job saved by steel tariffs costs three jobs in steel-consuming industries downstream, according to N. Gregory Mankiw, Harvard professor and former Chair of the Council of Economic Advisers writing in *Foreign Affairs*. Higher input costs cut into the profitability of steel consumers, causing layoffs.

Tariffs not only kill jobs in downstream industries, they promote outsourcing. Making imported steel more expensive allows domestic producers to raise prices. In 1991, tariffs of 62.7% on flat panel displays triggered higher domestic input costs, which prompted Toshiba and Apple to move production out of the United States to Japan and Ireland. Using tariffs to bring back jobs from overseas, as promoted by both Trump and Sanders, would threaten millions of jobs, especially at the beginning and end of the global supply chain, and would encourage outsourcing, not defend against it. ∎

Trade deals

The call for widespread import tariffs had broad emotional appeal in the presidential election, as did the portrayal of trade deals as giant job killers. During his prime-time speech at the Democratic convention in Philadelphia, Sanders said that because of his efforts, the party platform now included "strong opposition to job-killing trade agreements like the TPP." Hundreds of delegates waved #StopTPP signs and roared "No TPP," prompting Sanders to veer off script saying, "We have got to make sure that TPP does not get to the floor of the Congress in the lame-duck session." Donald Trump often reminded his listeners that he and Sanders were united against Hillary Clinton's pro-trade stance, as in his jobs speech: "As Bernie Sanders said, Hillary Clinton voted for virtually every trade agreement that has cost the workers of this country millions, millions of jobs." And not to be seen as ignoring what was obviously a widespread hostility to trade in the electorate, Hillary Clinton attacked trade deals in her convention speech, as well: "If you believe that we should say no to unfair trade deals, that we should stand up to China, that we should support our steelworkers and autoworkers and homegrown manufacturers, then join us." Clinton, who had been a major proponent of the TPP as Secretary of State, later doubled down: "I oppose it now, I'll oppose it after the election, and I'll oppose it as president."

Though the candidates often blamed trade deals for hollowing out America's middle class, U.S. manufacturing employment began its sharp decline in 1979, 14 years before NAFTA and 22 years before China's accession to the WTO. All the while, the total value of U.S. manufacturing has been trending upwards. Because of productivity gains—driven by advances in manufacturing technology, supply chain integration and process streamlining—we are making more with fewer workers.

The notion that when we lose manufacturing jobs, they're being shipping overseas is a fallacy. On the whole, the U.S. and China have starkly different capabilities. America's sweet spot is innovation, design and advanced manufacturing; China's is lower value production and assembly. From 1995 to 2002, U.S. factories shed two million jobs, or 11% of manufacturing employment. But during the same period, China lost 16 million manufacturing jobs—15% of its manufacturing employment—part of a global dip in factory employment of about 22 million jobs. Yet, according to a study by Alliance Capital Management, global industrial output rose sharply during that time by 30%.

China is usually shedding more jobs in manufacturing than we are. Today, it is trying to curb excess production capacity in steel, aluminum and coal and has promised to fire five to six million workers. In the meantime, our manufacturing sector has been adding an average of about 152,000 jobs per month since 2010, making up approximately 30% of the 2.8 million jobs lost from 2005–2008. In fact, America created millions of manufacturing jobs in the years after NAFTA was put into place. And from 1993–2001, U.S. manufacturing output increased by one third. The "giant sucking sound" of job losses and de-industrialization from NAFTA, predicted by third-party presidential candidate Ross Perot in 1992, did not happen.

What did happen was a surge in trade among Mexico, Canada and the United States. Since the passage of NAFTA, Canada and Mexico have risen to become our first and second top export markets. (China is ranked third.) And our total trade with Mexico has tripled. In 1993, the year before NAFTA was put into effect, we conducted $90 billion worth of trade with Mexico. In 2015, we traded over half a trillion dollars worth of goods.

Estimates vary on how many U.S. jobs this trade supports. The Wilson Center's Mexico Institute puts the number at around 6 million jobs, while the U.S. Chamber of Commerce estimates 14 million. However you figure, there are millions of American jobs supported by trade with Mexico. Increasing tariffs on Mexican imports, proposed by both Sanders and Trump, would dampen trade, threatening all of the American jobs associated with the beginning and end of the U.S.-Mexico shared supply chain.

Another often-overlooked aspect of NAFTA is foreign policy. There's considerable evidence that increased trade has helped develop Mexico's political economy. Since NAFTA, we've witnessed an evolution to an increasingly market-based, open system in Mexico, led by more democratically inclined governments, such as those of Vincente Fox and Enrique Peña Nieto. That's good for the United States.

Indeed, the Trans-Pacific Partnership was designed with this double-sided economics/foreign policy goal in mind. Though TPP is often characterized as a boon to China, such as in the Fox News Debate when Trump said, "It's a deal that was designed for China to come in as they always do through the back door and totally take advantage of everyone," it's worth noting that China would not be a party to this agreement. TPP was intended to check China's growing influence in the region by economically and politically bolstering China's neighbors, including Japan, Malaysia, Vietnam, Singapore, Brunei, New Zealand and Australia.

TPP was also intended to be a "next generation" trade deal—going farther than NAFTA went on lowering barriers to trade and strengthening environmental, worker and intellectual property protections. Our trading partners, Canada and Mexico, are a party to the TPP, and these new provisions amount to a renegotiation and improvement of NAFTA, which both Trump and Sanders often said they wanted. Economically, the deal would eliminate or reduce nearly 18,000 individual tariffs on American-made manufactured and agricultural goods to TPP countries, making our exports more competitive. It would also put into place enforceable provisions on labor and environment. The deal would require for the first time that workers in member countries have the right to bargain collectively and form unions. It would also ban slave and child labor, require safe workplaces, and set maximum work hours and minimum wages. Environmentally, it would prevent illegal logging, fishing and wildlife trafficking.

TPP would also be the first major trade deal to help small and mid-sized businesses. We heard a lot of talk this campaign season about how TPP is a boondoggle for multinational corporations. But 98% of all U.S. exporters are small-to-midsized enterprises. TPP

Members of a U.S. civic group march in Atlanta on Oct. 1, 2015, to express opposition to the Trans-Pacific Partnership initiative, near the hotel where ministers from 12 countries continue talks on concluding the sweeping Pacific free trade pact. (KYODO/AP PHOTO)

would assist these firms by eliminating or streamlining those aspects of exporting that discourage smaller companies by simplifying export documentation, improving in-country logistics that make it prohibitively expensive to ship smaller orders, and shining a light on corruption or "tea money," as it's sometimes called.

Of course, TPP is not a perfect trade deal. It's a complex agreement of over 5,500 pages, the result of painstaking multilateral negotiations among 12 countries. But it represents a significant improvement over NAFTA in several areas, and to characterize it simply as a boon to big business, as Trump and Sanders did, is to misread the deal. To be sure, though 98% of U.S. exporters are small-to-midsized firms, they represent just 30% of the value of our total exports. Yet multinational firms sit at the top of long supply chains, inhabited by scores of smaller companies. When exports at a multinational company increase, earnings rise for the many firms that sell goods and services to the multinational.

U.S. policy options

The rising tide of trade lifts many boats. Not all, however. Dislocations caused by trade, though vastly overstated, are real. Donald Trump's campaign resonated with voters who believe the government hasn't done enough to protect workers from globalization. Their dis-

content is real and must be addressed by the incoming administration. Attention should be paid to shoring up programs that help workers who have lost their jobs to foreign competition. The Trade Adjustment Assistance (TAA) program of 1962, which reimburses some of the costs of worker retraining, needs an expansion of mandate. Among many shortcomings, the program does not compensate for lower wages when re-entering the workforce, a widespread problem. In considering the shortcomings of TAA, it's worth noting that the U.S. spends less on retraining than any other advanced economy. A national industrial policy would also go a long way toward aligning education and investment in states that need help diversifying their industries and labor force. And as long as we continue to subsidize the carbon emissions produced from transporting inputs and outputs around the world, the prices of traded goods will remain distortedly low. Finally, we must invest in the modernization of our economic statistics, so we have a clearer understanding of our contribution to the global supply chain and its impact on employment. America certainly has its share of problems, such as wage stagnation and inequality. But to blame these issues entirely on trade deflects our attention from their true causes and hinders our ability to pursue helpful policies. ∎

discussion questions

1. Which are the more compelling arguments for and against globalization: arguments about cultural impact, or arguments about economic impact?

2. The tide of public and political opinion has turned against trade deals like TTP, TTIP and even NAFTA. What constitutes a trade deal that is "good" for America versus one that is "bad" for the country?

3. Is the portrayal of China as a "job killer" fair? Why or why not?

4. Can the Brexit vote and the election of Donald Trump be seen as responses to the same economic concerns, or do they differ? How are these two events likely to impact the trading landscape between the U.S. and Europe?

5. What would be the consequences of the U.S. waging a trade war with China? How would the U.S. economy be affected? How might the economies of other countries that trade with the U.S. and China feel the impact?

6. How accurate are current metrics for gauging economic prosperity? In what ways are they misleading or inadequate? How can a maximally accurate picture of national wealth be obtained?

Don't forget: Ballots start on page 115!

suggested readings

Dolin, Eric Jay, **When America First Met China**. New York: Liveright, 2012. 432 pp. Dolin recounts U.S.-China trade relations from their origins to the present.

Dollar, David, "The future of U.S.-China trade ties." **Brookings Institution**, October 4, 2016. Available free online: <https://www.brookings.edu/research/the-future-of-u-s-china-trade-ties/>. Dollar describes the prospects for trade relations between China and the U.S. in the context of a new American administration.

Goodman, Peter S., "More Wealth, More Jobs, but Not for Everyone: What Fuels the Backlash on Trade." **New York Times**, September 28, 2016. Available free online: <http://www.nytimes.com/2016/09/29/business/economy/more-wealth-more-jobs-but-not-for-everyone-what-fuels-the-backlash-on-trade.html>. Goodman offers an extensive critical analysis of free trade across continents.

Hale, Galina and Hobijn, Bart, "The U.S. Content of 'Made In China.'" **Federal Reserve Bank of San Francisco**, August 8, 2011. Available free online: <http://www.frbsf.org/economic-research/publications/economic-letter/2011/august/us-made-in-china/>. Hale and Hobijn assess the extent to which consumer prices of goods and services with the "Made in China" label actually reflect services produced in the United States.

Irwin, Douglas A., **Against the Tide: An Intellectual History of Free Trade**. Princeton: Princeton University Press, 1996. 274 pp. This intellectual history traces free trade from Adam Smith to the present.

Levine, Linda, "Offshoring (or Offshore Outsourcing) and Job Loss Among U.S. Workers." **Congressional Research Service**, December 17, 2012. 12 pp. Available free online: <http://fas.org/sgp/crs/misc/RL32292.pdf>. This report examines the impact of offshore outsourcing on the number of American jobs.

Mankiw, N. Gregory and Swagel, Phillip L., "Antidumping: The Third Rail of Trade Policy." **Foreign Affairs**, vol. 84 no. 4, 2005. pp. 107–119. Available free online: <https://dash.harvard.edu/bitstream/handle/1/2961701/Mankiw_Antidumping.pdf?sequence=2>. Mankiw and Swagel argue that antidumping policy has veered from its intended purpose and now serves to shield powerful industries from competition, to the detriment of American consumers and business.

Stiglitz, Joseph E., **Globalization and Its Discontents**. New York: Norton, 2003. 304 pp. This seminal text in the globalization debate by Nobel prize-winning economist Joseph Stiglitz critiques the institutions of globalization and offers a reform agenda.

To access web links to these readings, as well as links to additional, shorter readings and suggested web sites,

GO TO www.greatdecisions.org

and click on the topic under Resources, on the right-hand side of the page

Conflict in the South China Sea
by Bernard D. Cole

A Chinese coast guard ship (top) and a Philippine supply boat engage in a stand off as the Philippine boat attempts to reach the Second Thomas Shoal, a remote South China Sea reef claimed by both countries, on March 29, 2014. (JAY DIRECTO/AFP/GETTY IMAGES)

The South China Sea is one of the world's most important waterways. It is also the scene of intense international competition. The Straits of Malacca and Singapore, which form its southwestern entry, are some of the world's busiest seaways, serving as the primary link between the Pacific and Indian Oceans. The sea contains lines of communication vital to the economies of China, Japan and South Korea. Approximately one third of the world's commerce passes through its waters. Significant estimated reserves of oil and natural gas are located here, as well as fisheries that accounted for as much as 12% of the global catch in 2016.

The South China Sea is also the scene of the most contentious issues in Asia—territorial disputes between China, Brunei, Indonesia, Malaysia, the Philippines and Vietnam. Taiwan is a disputant, but agrees in general with China's claims.

The U.S., for its part, has important economic, political and military interests in the sea. The U.S. presence here dates to the late 18th century, when the new country's merchant ships ventured into these waters. Vital sea lines of communication, relations with treaty allies and historic friends, and access to the Indian Ocean and beyond have been safeguarded by the U.S. Navy (USN) since the early 19th century.

China's historic claims to the sea date to the Han Dynasty, years before the Common Era. Meanwhile, Beijing's extreme sensitivity to sovereignty issues, here and elsewhere, can be traced to the so-called "100 Years of Humiliation"—the period approximately 1839–1949, when inter-

BERNARD D. COLE *served as a professor of maritime strategy at the National War College from 1995 to 2015. He previously served 30 years in the Navy as a surface warfare officer. Cole has written many articles, book chapters, and eight books, most recently* China's Quest for Great Power: Ships, Oil, and Foreign Policy in China, *published in November 2016. He was named U.S. Naval Institute Press "Author of the Year" for 2014.*

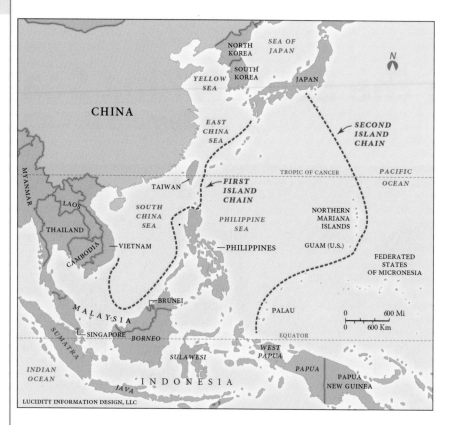

LUCIDITY INFORMATION DESIGN, LLC

nal political, military and economic weakness allowed foreign nations to run roughshod over Chinese domestic affairs and sovereignty.

The 21st century has witnessed U.S. and Chinese ships coming to near-conflict over differing national interests in the South China Sea. While the USN has dominated Asian waters in general for the past half-century, China is now challenging that dominance. The USN in 2016 numbers less than half the ships it deployed in 1986, at the height of the Cold War. The Chinese People's Liberation Army Navy (PLAN) is increasing in numbers and in technological sophistication—both vital factors in making it a 21st century navy. The PLAN is the strongest navy in Asia and will be global by 2020, second only to the USN in capability, but outnumbering all other navies in East Asian waters.

The latter fact results from important differences in the U.S. and Chinese naval areas of operation. The USN continues to be tasked with global presence; the PLAN focuses for the most part on the Western Pacific Ocean, defined by the Philippine Sea and the "three seas." These are the Yellow, East China and South China Seas, all of which Beijing considers areas vital to national security because of their geographical proximity and importance to the nation's growing economy.

Chinese People's Liberation Army Navy (PLAN) officers marching, Shanghai. (GUY BROWN/ALAMY)

Maritime Asia, specifically the great oceanic sweep from the Kamchatka Peninsula and the straits leading from the Pacific to the Indian Ocean, is to an extent defined by the first and second island chains. The chains encompass not just the three seas, but also a significant area of the Philippine Sea, reaching out approximately 1,800 nautical miles (nm) from China. These two geographic lines originated in a post-World War II study by the U.S. Joint Chiefs of Staff, but are more commonly attributed to the writings of a former senior Chinese admiral, Liu Huaqing. Admiral Liu used these island chains as goals for Chinese naval modernization and capabilities, set to be achieved in the early- and mid-21st century.

The three seas certainly are of interest to the U.S., but probably not to the degree they are to China. Washington's concerns here include freedom of navigation—a global U.S. priority—as well as treaty relationships. The U.S. holds defense treaties with the Republic of South Korea, Japan and the Philippines, all of which border on the three seas. Washington further maintains a treaty relationship with Thailand—though it is currently weakened by that country's rule by a military junta. It has special defense relationships with Taiwan, under the 1979 Taiwan Relations Act, and with Singapore, and it is enlarging its defense relationships with Singapore, Vietnam, Indonesia and Malaysia.

Conflict between China and the U.S. over events in the three seas is certainly not inevitable, but maintaining peaceful relations between the two countries will continue to require carefully crafted diplomacy. The Yellow Sea is the location of relatively minor maritime boundary disputes between China and North and South Korea. The East China Sea is the setting for much more serious maritime boundary and land-feature sovereignty quarrels between China and Japan. But the South China Sea is currently the most dangerous area of contention in East Asia between regional players, and between the U.S. and China. ■

Before you read, download the companion **Glossary** that includes definitions and a guide to acronyms and abbreviations used in the article. Go to **www.great decisions.org** and select a topic in the Resources section on the right-hand side of the page.

UN Convention on the Law of the Sea

The United Nations Convention on the Law of the Sea (UNCLOS) is an international treaty that seeks to establish a globally acceptable body of maritime laws and definitions, including the categorization and description of land features. It was concluded in 1982 following a decade of negotiations. It became effective in 1994. The treaty has been signed and ratified by 167 states and the European Union. Some 14 additional UN member states have signed, but not ratified, the Convention. The U.S. is notable as a non-signatory.

Understanding the dispute over the hundreds of land features in the South China Sea first requires an understanding of how UNCLOS defines land features, including islands, rocks and low-tide elevations. Each of these entitles the host nation to certain rights. The South China Sea is marked by hundreds of land features, ranging from populated bits of land, to reefs that are fully submerged even at low tide. Most significant are the groups called the Paracel Islands, the Spratly Islands, the Macclesfield Bank and the Natuna Islands. Each of the claimants to these land features has given them a different name.

The South China Sea is approximately 1,400 nm from north to south, and 700 nm east to west, bordering the Southeast Asian mainland. It includes an area of approximately 1,423,000 square miles. It is bounded on the northeast by the Taiwan Strait (which connects it to the East China Sea); on the east by Taiwan and the Philippines; on the southeast and south by Borneo, the southern limit of the Gulf of Thailand and the east coast of the Malay Peninsula; and on the west and north by the Asian mainland. The Indonesian archipelago forms the southern boundary of the South China Sea; the northern boundary stretches westward from the northern tip of Taiwan to the coast of China's Fujian Province.

Wang Min (front left), China's deputy permanent representative to the United Nations, addresses the meeting of state parties to the UN Convention on the Law of the Sea (UN-CLOS) at the UN headquarters in New York, June 13, 2014. Wang Min forcefully refuted accusations made by Vietnam and the Philippines against China over the South China Sea situation. (NIU XIAOLEI/XINHUA/ALAMY)

These data are important to the application of international law, especially UNCLOS, as well as when considering military operations in the South China Sea. The treaty implies that there are two requirements for a land feature to be classified as an island. First, the land must be above water at all times, including during maximum high tide. Second, it must be capable of sustaining human life and/or economic life. If the land feature meets the first but not the second requirement, it is legally a rock, not an island. If it is not always above the ocean's surface, then it is classified as a low-tide elevation, neither an island nor a rock.

UNCLOS grants an island several zones of entitlement. First is the territorial sea, measured from the host nation's coastal baseline out to a distance of 12 nm. The second UNCLOS zone is contiguous waters, measured to an additional distance of 12 nm (24 nm from the host nation's coastal baseline). Third is an exclusive economic zone (EEZ), measured from the coastal base-

line to a maximum distance of 200 nm. Finally, the continental shelf is a feature defined by the ocean bottom topography and which a country may claim to a maximum distance of 350 nm from its coastal baseline. While an island is entitled to all of these zones, a rock is entitled only to 12 nm of territorial waters. A low-tide elevation is entitled to no UNCLOS zone at all, but may claim a surrounding 500 meter-wide security zone, which is a safety zone from which unauthorized ships are banned.

UNCLOS recognizes that geography may not accommodate all such zones. For instance, if two coastal nations are less than 700 nm apart, then both cannot effectively claim 350 nm continental shelves; if they are less than 400 nm apart, they both cannot effectively claim 200 nm EEZs. The UNCLOS recommends ways of resolving such disputes. Given the dimensions of the South China Sea, the claimants to various land features and associated maritime zones will almost always have to come to an agreement on where con-

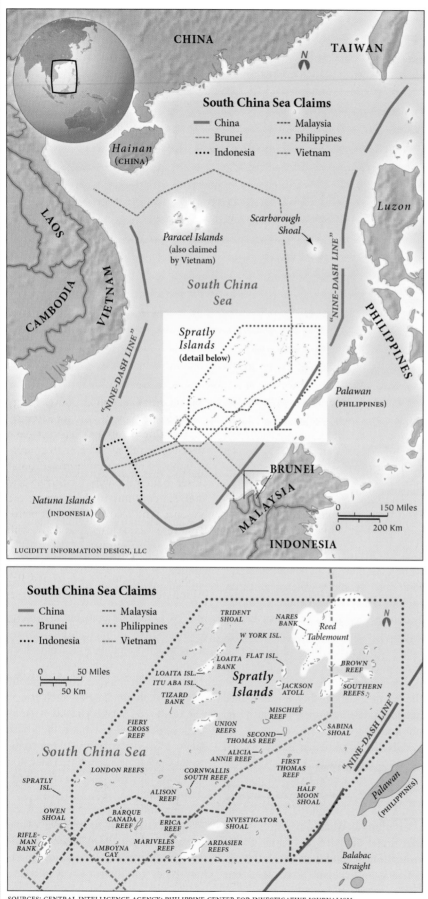

South China Sea Claims

— China   --- Malaysia
--- Brunei   •••• Philippines
•••• Indonesia   --- Vietnam

CHINA

TAIWAN

Hainan
(CHINA)

LAOS

CAMBODIA

VIETNAM

Paracel Islands
(also claimed
by Vietnam)

*Scarborough
Shoal*

Luzon

"NINE-DASH LINE"

PHILIPPINES

*South China
Sea*

*Spratly
Islands*
(detail below)

Palawan
(PHILIPPINES)

"NINE-DASH LINE"

BRUNEI

MALAYSIA

Natuna Islands
(INDONESIA)

0   150 Miles
0   200 Km

INDONESIA

LUCIDITY INFORMATION DESIGN, LLC

South China Sea Claims

— China   --- Malaysia
--- Brunei   •••• Philippines
•••• Indonesia   --- Vietnam

0   50 Miles
0   50 Km

South China Sea

TRIDENT
SHOAL

NARES
BANK

Reed
Tablemount

W YORK ISL.

LOAITA   FLAT ISL.
BANK

LOAITA ISL.

*Spratly
Islands*

BROWN
REEF

ITU ABA ISL.

JACKSON
ATOLL

SOUTHERN
REEFS

TIZARD
BANK

MISCHIEF
REEF

FIERY
CROSS
REEF

UNION
REEFS

SABINA
SHOAL

SECOND
THOMAS REEF

ALICIA
ANNIE REEF

NINE-DASH LINE

SPRATLY
ISL.

LONDON REEFS

CORNWALLIS
SOUTH REEF

FIRST
THOMAS
REEF

Palawan
(PHILIPPINES)

ALISON
REEF

HALF
MOON
SHOAL

OWEN
SHOAL

BARQUE
CANADA
REEF

ERICA
REEF

INVESTIGATOR
SHOAL

RIFLE-
MAN
BANK

MARIVELES
REEF

ARDASIER
REEFS

AMBOYNA
CAY

*Balabac
Straight*

SOURCES: CENTRAL INTELLIGENCE AGENCY; PHILIPPINE CENTER FOR INVESTIGATIVE JOURNALISM

tiguous EEZs and claimed continental shelves divide. In fact, only a relatively small area in the central part of the South China Sea is not claimed by one of the disputant countries.

Two other UNCLOS-related issues deserve discussion. First is the use of the coastal baseline as the starting point for measuring the various zones of 12, 24, 200 and 350 nm. That point is drawn on the low-water line along the host nation's coast. The baseline must follow the contours of the coast, with some exceptions for a relatively narrow break in the coastline. To draw an "excessive straight baseline" is to draw one around a group of islands, for instance, or across a wide expanse of water. Many nations, including China, are accused of drawing such excessive baselines.

The second issue of interest is that of citing "historic rights." A fundamental premise of UNCLOS is that maritime rights are based on the land, and that any professed historic rights do not annul another country's EEZ. Here, too, China is not the only party to exaggerate the applicability of historic rights as justification for various activities and prerogatives. China is of particular interest, however, since Beijing emphasizes such rights in areas of the South China Sea that are disputed by other claimants—some of whom, like Vietnam, also cite historic rights.

In this manner, both Beijing and Hanoi reference extensive historical documents and "facts" for their respective claims in the South China Sea. China's claims approach the mystical, as Beijing alleges unsubstantiated "historic rights" and pre-Common Era (BCE) "evidence." Maritime legal expert, Captain Raul Pedrozo, USN (Retired), opines that "Vietnam clearly has a superior claim to the South China Sea Islands," basing his opinion on Hanoi's "symbolic acts of sovereignty in the early 19th century, followed by peaceful, effective, and continuous administration of the islands" by Vietnamese and French colonial governments. However, the "first demonstration of Chinese sovereignty over the [islands] did not occur until 1909." This view in favor of Vietnam is at least partially negated by China's use of military force to occupy the Paracels, Mischief Reef, Scarborough Shoal and some of the Spratlys between 1974 and 1995.

Beijing seems intent on changing the definitions and privileges of land features, set out in UNCLOS. China believes that other claimants have taken advantage of past Chinese inaction by strengthening their assertions, including through land reclamation and facilities construction. Therefore, Beijing believes it must take strong action to bolster its own sovereignty claims and presence. ■

Territorial claims in the South China Sea

1. Brunei has implied a claim to Louisa Reef, which lies within its EEZ.

2. China claims all land features "and associated waters" within the current nine-dash line, including features that never appear above the sea's surface.

3. Indonesia's claimed EEZ overlaps China's (and Taiwan's) nine-dash line.

4. Malaysia claims several Spratly islands based on its continental shelf.

5. The Philippines claims several Spratlys based on various UNCLOS principles.

6. Taiwan's claims are almost entirely the same as China's.

7. Vietnam claims all the Paracel and Spratly Islands.

Current tensions in the South China Sea

Disputes in the South China Sea concern the sovereignty of the Paracel Islands, the Spratly Islands, Macclesfield Bank, the Pratas Islands and the delimitation of maritime boundaries in the adjacent seas. As of 2016, Vietnam has occupied 27 of the Spratly land features; Malaysia, nine; the Philippines eight; China, seven; and Taiwan, one.

China bases its claims on a line originally drawn as 11 dashes on a Chinese map published by a government-sponsored committee of scholars in 1922. In 2016, that line comprised ten dashes, although it is commonly referred to as the "nine-dash line," and has, at various points, consisted of nine, ten and eleven dashes. The u-shaped marker includes most of the South China Sea. No Chinese government, neither that of the Republic of China nor the People's Republic of China, has ever delineated the coordinates of the dash line, or clearly stated what it defines. China claims all land features "and associated waters" within the current line, including features that never appear above the sea's surface.

Since China seized all of the Paracel Islands (located in the north of the sea) after a brief naval battle with Republic of (South) Vietnam forces in 1974, the most unresolved, contentious claims are those concerning the Spratlys, further to the south. China maintained occupation of several of these islands after a similar battle with Vietnamese naval units in 1988.

The Spratlys includes more than 400 land features—inhabited land, rocks, sand cays and low-tide elevations. Among them, only 33 rise above the sea, while only seven of those have an area exceeding 0.3 square miles. The waters are rich in fish; they may also contain significant oil and other energy resources, although no commercially recoverable oil or gas has yet been discovered in the sea's central area, as opposed to the rich "proven" areas closer to littoral waters. Geologists and analysts continue to disagree on the presence (and recoverability) of petroleum reserves near these islands, with widely varying estimates.

Chinese surveys indicate that about 25 billion cubic meters of gas and 105 billion barrels of oil exist in the con-

A crew standing on a fishing vessel setting sail for the Spratly Islands, an archipelago disputed between China and other countries including Vietnam and the Philippines, from Danzhou, south China's Hainan Province, in May 2013. (STR/AFP/GETTY IMAGES)

tinental shelf around the Spratly Islands, but U.S. surveys are not nearly so optimistic. In fact, unsuccessful oil prospecting in the South China Sea dates back at least to Japanese efforts in the mid-1930s. Despite this uncertainty, energy reserves remain an issue of contention between China and the other regional claimants. Although important, these reserves probably are not as essential to the contesting nations as are sea lines of communication, security and national pride.

The current heightened tensions in the South China Sea may be dated to 2008–09, when China's coast guard and maritime militia—civilian fishing boats in the service of the government—harassed U.S. oceanographic survey vessels. These U.S. ships are crewed by civilians and conduct surveys that map the sea's characteristics. The data collection has both seabed prospecting and anti-submarine warfare implications. China conducts similar operations in waters it contests with Japan in the East China Sea, but repeatedly and vehemently objects to similar U.S. surveys in the South China Sea.

The disputes intensified further in 2012, when a Sino-Philippine standoff occurred over Scarborough Shoal, a series of rocks approximately 100 nm from the Philippines' Luzon Coast. Beijing used coast guard vessels to seize Scarborough, in contravention of a diplomatic agreement it had made with Manila.

China's strained relations with Vietnam then increased significantly in May 2014 when Beijing began drilling operations with an oil rig operated by the state-owned China National Offshore Oil Corporation. This deep-sea drilling platform was placed 120 nm from the Vietnamese coast, inside its EEZ, but 17 nm from China's claimed Triton Island in the Paracels, which are also claimed by Vietnam. Hanoi vehemently protested China's drilling activities. Multiple collisions and water cannon exchanges then ensued between Vietnamese and Chinese fishing boats and coast guard vessels before Beijing announced the end of approximately two months of drilling operations. Hanoi and Beijing then announced recourse to diplomacy to address their different claims, but resolution has not been achieved.

The most frequent clashes over land features and maritime boundaries have occurred between China and Vietnam, and between China and the Philippines. During 2016, however, China engaged in a new contest with Indonesia over possibly conflicting EEZs. Beijing has not disputed Jakarta's sovereignty over the Natuna Islands, which lie in the midst of especially rich energy and fishing waters north of Sumatra. The Natunas are located outside China's claimed nine-dash line, but their EEZs do overlap the area encompassed by that line. In 2015 and 2016, Chinese fishing boats repeatedly poached within Indonesia's EEZ. Such actions are intensified by the fact that these waters also contain energy fields vital to Indonesia's economy. In several instances, Jakarta had its coast guard boats seize the offending fishermen, often burning their boats. The occasional presence of Chinese coast guard vessels, which prevent their Indonesian counterparts from arresting the Chinese fishermen, heightens China's violations.

On June 19, 2016, Chinese Ministry of Foreign Affairs spokesperson Hua Chunying described the most recent incident with Indonesia as occurring "in waters that are Chinese fishermen's traditional fishing grounds." Beijing's actions against Indonesia increase tensions and raise the risks of armed confrontations with Jakarta by exaggerating the theory of historic or traditional fishing rights. Claiming historic right in this case seems directly counter to the UNCLOS basic premise that maritime rights are based on the land. Interestingly, Beijing seemed to disagree with this concept in its 2015 *Defense White Paper*. More recently, however, its July 2016 *White Paper on the South China Sea* indicated agreement that the land dominates the sea.

Prospects for diplomatic resolution

One area of at least partial successful negotiation has occurred over the Gulf of Tonkin (called the Beibu Gulf by China). A northern arm of the South China Sea, the gulf is a semi-enclosed bay bounded by mainland China and Vietnam, as well as by China's Hainan Island. It contains rich resources, including petroleum and fish stocks. Beijing and Hanoi signed the Beibu Gulf Demarcation Agreement and the Beibu Gulf Fishery Cooperation Agreement in 2000, and they came into effect in 2004.

The two countries have agreed on the width of the gulf's territorial sea

A Chinese vessel (right) using water cannons on a Vietnamese vessel near the Paracel Islands May 5, 2014. (VIETNAM COAST GUARD/EPA/REDUX)

within which each will exercise their respective jurisdictions, but have yet to fully delimit their maritime boundary. China has proposed establishing a rectangular "neutral zone" in the gulf's center, which would remain free from exploitation until the two countries could reach an agreement on the delimitation. Vietnam has never formally accepted this proposal, but, like China, has halted exploration for oil in the proposed joint development zone. Despite this partial agreement, and although Beijing and Hanoi reached agreement on settling their land boundary in 1993, their maritime boundary dispute in the South China Sea remains unresolved, and has been marked by several violent clashes. Still, Beijing and Hanoi seem determined to prevent significant armed conflict, and the Gulf of Tonkin agreements do set a precedent for cooperation in the South China Sea.

Diplomatic efforts to resolve the disputes among all the claimants have been marked by the 2002 Declaration on the Conduct of Parties in the South China Sea, between China and the Association of Southeast Asian Nations (ASEAN) member states. This agreement called for further negotiations that would lead to the implementation of a Code of Conduct, envisioned as facilitating peaceful resolution of all territorial claims. Since then, little progress has been made toward establishing a Code. While none of the claimants has shown any sign of flexibility, Beijing's insistence that negotiations must be preceded by acknowledgement of Chinese sovereignty has vitiated possible diplomatic resolution. Beijing has been loath to follow up on the Declaration and has massively outspent all disputants in building military facilities and ships to further establish and enforce its claims, especially in the Spratlys.

With the exception of the Philippines, the other claimants have been leery of directly confronting China. Vietnam has actively challenged China at sea, but at the state level, the two nations' communist parties consistently move to defuse relations following any clashes. Malaysia has been extremely reluctant to take a direct stand against

Nearly completed construction within the Fiery Cross Reef, located in the western part of the Spratly Islands group in the South China Sea. (DIGITALGLOBE/GETTY IMAGES)

Beijing. Brunei has remained silent about a possible dispute with China over Louisa Reef, while Taiwan simply agrees largely with China's claims. Indonesia is the relatively new, potentially very significant challenger to China's nine-dash line and overall maritime claims in the South China Sea.

Hence, there is little or no chance of the ten member states of ASEAN, or even the five members that dispute the South China Sea features with China, adopting a united position in opposition to Beijing. In fact, it is likely that only continued U.S. interest in the status of peace and freedom of navigation prevents the other claimants from entering into negotiations that would result in de facto if not de jure Chinese political and military domination of the sea, both within and outside the nine-dash line.

Military aspects of the South China Sea disputes

The South China Sea's most important military use would be by China as a "bastion" for its seaborne nuclear deterrent. Beijing has constructed an impressive base for its Jin-class nuclear-powered ballistic missile submarines on Hainan Island, at the northern end of the

sea. If these submarines were armed with ICBMs of sufficient range to cover the continental United States, they could restrict their operations to the South China Sea, thereby very significantly increasing its strategic importance, especially to China and to the United States.

The Spratly Islands possess strategic military significance because of their central position in the South China Sea amid vital sea lines of communication. These are the main transit routes from Southwest Asia and the Indian Ocean, and Northeast Asia and the Pacific Ocean. The military installations China has built there—and will continue building, according to the PLAN commander, Admiral Wu Shengli—may eventually be in a position to monitor and perhaps dominate most of the South China Sea.

The Chinese navy is progressing steadily toward a goal of regular global presence by 2050. The PLAN of 1996 was unable even to effectively monitor waters within 200 nm of the Chinese coast; that of 2016, just 20 years later, is a 21st century navy, regularly deploying half a world away. China's naval strength has grown at a moderate pace, but has been consistent and impressive. It now ranks second only to that of the U.S. Furthermore, China's overall maritime power, including its merchant fleet and shore-based infrastructure, is among the world's strongest.

Global ambitions demand a leadership eye on the international arena, and in Asia that means maritime. For this reason, China continues to modernize and expand its navy as its economic and political maritime interests increase. Further, Beijing's newly organized State Oceanographic Administration has taken a lead in building and deploying what is now the world's largest coast guard force. A large, growing, state-equipped maritime militia augments these new ships and helicopters. The new Chinese coast guard and expanding maritime militia

A member of the Chinese Navy stands watch as the guided missile destroyer USS Stethem arrives at the Shanghai International Passenger Quay for a scheduled port visit in Shanghai, China, in a sign that contacts between the U.S. and Chinese militaries continue despite tensions over the South China Sea, 2015. (PAUL TRAYNOR/AP)

are, in turn, backed up, and to a degree operationally controlled, by the PLAN during confrontations with the civilian and naval forces of other nations, from Brunei to the U.S.

Threats to China's perceived international interests are mostly nontraditional, but the navy's planners, like their foreign counterparts, look for the most likely opponents at sea. That selection is easy for Beijing: Japan is the historic enemy, very much a maritime nation and therefore a primary concern to planners and strategists. The PLAN is particularly concerned about 2016 reports that

Japan's navy will conduct joint patrols with the USN in the South China Sea. An increased Japanese naval presence would seriously complicate the operational picture confronting China. Beijing understands, however, that the U.S. is the only maritime power capable of frustrating China's national security interests.

U.S. interest in the South China Sea

Washington's South China Sea policy is based on the historic issue of ensuring U.S. commercial access to maritime commons around the world. This is not limited by the UNCLOS maritime zones of entitlement, but applies to all areas outside sovereign territorial waters. Guaranteeing such access was the mission of the first U.S. warship deployed to East Asia in 1832—a frigate sent to punish Sumatran pirates who had captured an American merchant ship. Ensuring access remains a primary U.S. naval mission, especially in the face of Iranian threats to close the Strait of Hormuz and Chinese talk about controlling the seas within the first and second island chains.

U.S. freedom of navigation cruises are conducted as a Department of State global program. The intent is to demonstrate U.S. disagreement with specific maritime claims. China's reaction to such demonstrations in the South China

Sea has been vocal and threatening. It includes a recent statement by Admiral Sun Jianguo—possibly the next commander of the Chinese navy—opposing "so-called military freedom of navigation" cruises, and threatening the U.S. that these "could even play out in a disastrous way."

This highlights a key difference between China and the United States: The former believes that freedom of navigation under UNCLOS and international law applies only to civilian merchant vessels, while the U.S. believes that freedom of navigation applies universally. Both civilian and military Chinese officials, as well as Chinese analysts and academics, doggedly protest that China has never and will never pose a threat to freedom of navigation. They refer, however, to Beijing's different standard, expressed in one of the declarations it made when ratifying UNCLOS. In this declaration, China stated: "In accordance with the provisions of the United Nations Convention on the Law of the Sea, the People's Republic of China shall enjoy sovereign rights and jurisdiction over an exclusive economic zone of 200 nautical miles and the continental shelf."

The United States certainly does not wish to cause an incident that might escalate to armed conflict, but does want China to understand that the U.S. is determined to ensure freedom of navigation for both naval and civilian vessels throughout the South China Sea. Chinese analysts, for their part, often cite the U.S. rebalance to Asia as evidence of containment. The rebalance was announced by President Obama in 2011 and has included actions across the political, economic and military spectra. These include increasing political, economic and security relations with Asian nations, from South Korea to Iran, as well as a more active U.S. role in regional organizations such as ASEAN. Particularly irritating to Chinese officials and analysts, both civilian and military, is the increase in U.S. military presence in the Pacific.

The belief that the U.S. is trying to contain China flies in the face of history since 1972, when President Richard

Nixon visited China and agreed with Premier Zhou Enlai to resolve many of the differences underlying antagonism in the relationship. This process matured in 1979, when the U.S. shifted diplomatic recognition of "China" from Taipei to Beijing. Since then, the U.S. has provided much of the open market that has facilitated China's economic growth into the world's second largest economy. Washington also campaigned for China's inclusion in the World Trade Organization. U.S. support for China's role on the international stage has been emphasized for decades.

China's foreign policy in the South China Sea

For China, domestic national security concerns take precedence, and the country's new and growing navy plays only a very marginal role therein. Foreign policy under President Xi Jinping is consistent with this state of affairs: It is a secondary concern, often driven by nationalism, popular pressure and the "China Dream." The latter is Xi's formulation—stated goals for the economic and security well-being of the Chinese people, to be achieved in 2021 and 2049, respectively.

The genesis of Xi's China Dream results in part from his effort to consolidate his personal and his party faction's power. More important, however, is the Dream's origin in China's history, looking back to the onset of massive foreign intervention in the 1830s, which culminated in the 1949 founding of the PRC. The year 1949 began only a phase in the great Chinese revolution—an often violent one that perhaps peaked in the Tiananmen Square massacre of June 3–4, 1989. China's then-leader, Deng Xiaoping, unleashed the army against students and workers in Tiananmen. But this was quickly followed by a continued international opening of China's economy and, to an extent, its society.

Xi Jinping appears to be striving to maintain this openness—so vital to China's ongoing economic growth and to the people's satisfaction with Communist Party rule. Simultaneously, he is fostering nationalism, again to bolster Party rule, and to heighten China's role in regional and international relations. Xi is a product of China's history. He is also seizing upon that history to enhance personal and national power. The South China Sea disputes thus directly result from, influence and may determine the fate of Xi's policies.

Beijing is, in large part, working within the established rules and procedures of the international community as it strives to attain its foreign policy objectives. Simply put, China "wants a seat at the table." It wants to be treated in accordance with the world power status it historically possessed and is now regaining. A significant problem confronting Beijing is reconciling the goals of a successful peripheral strategy—which includes central economic and "soft power" instruments—while also seeking to defend sovereignty interests. Prominent Chinese security studies analyst Michael Swaine has characterized this latter goal as pursued with "a fervent level of self-righteousness." Phillip Saunders, director of the Center for the Study of Chinese Military Affairs, has accurately described this two-sided foreign policy as having "a schizophrenic quality," which certainly complicates accurate analysis and foreign response to Chinese policies. China's attitude also contributes to its emerging maritime strategy, laid out in its 2015 *Defense White Paper*. Both soft and hard power policies are forwarded without any seeming sense of conflict between the two. Soft power is formalized in the concept of Asians solving Asian problems, while hard power is evident in China's drive for a navy capable of far-seas as well as regional operations.

Wu Shicun, head of China's National Institute for South China Sea Studies, echoes the Party line on China's interest in the South China Sea. Wu is well connected to the Hainan provincial government and to the national government: He receives financial support from the Ministry of Foreign Affairs. He describes the sea as:

a natural line of defense for Chinese national security, an important strategic waterway, and a strategic must-have for it to become a maritime power. For the U.S., controlling the South China Sea and maintaining its presence there is indispensable for its dominance in the Asia-Pacific based on its bilateral alliances formulated in the post-war era. In this sense, China-U.S. competition and rivalry in the South China Sea is structural, strategic, and irreconcilable.

Wu also claims historic rights in the Scarborough Shoal and adjacent waters.

Meanwhile, Chinese analysts deny that any of their country's actions or positions in the South China Sea violate international law, or that China claims sovereignty over the whole Sea, threatens navigation and overflight rights, intends to change the status quo, is building artificial islands, is accelerating the militarization of the sea, is damaging the environment, or is acting assertively. These protestations are problematical at best. Chinese officials and analysts continue to defend the validity of the dash line, without specifying its precise meaning or location. Chinese officials particularly and repeatedly emphasize China's support for freedom of navigation, but believe this applies only to merchant ships. However, the U.S., the great majority of the UNCLOS signatories and international law apply freedom of navigation to military vessels.

This again raises the role of military power in the South China Sea. Beijing has not hesitated to employ nominally non-naval craft, coast guard and maritime militia vessels, to enforce its territorial and maritime claims. China's employment of these "white hull" forces in the three seas has become the norm in its campaign to enforce its claims in Asian waters. The majority of these vessels do not display weapons above deck, but use water cannons and ramming to attack other nations' fishermen and coast guard.

The International Tribunal for the Law of the Sea (ITLOS)

The UN created the International Tribunal for the Law of the Sea (ITLOS) to resolve disputes that arise under UNCLOS. In 2013, the Republic of the Philippines appealed to ITLOS in part because of frustration at its inability to effectively negotiate with China over disputed claims in the South China Sea. The Sino-Philippine disputes revolve around land features in the Spratly Islands, particularly the Scarborough Shoal. China has insisted from the onset of the case that it would neither participate in nor adhere to any of the court's proceedings and rulings.

Importantly, ITLOS did not consider questions of sovereignty over the South China Sea land features, but focused instead on China's maritime claims. The Philippine requests were limited and germane to the sovereignty conflicts in the South China Sea. Manila was focused on China's claims to land features that lie on the Philippine-claimed continental shelf, not to broader issues of maritime law and sovereignty issues. The Philippines asked the tribunal to rule on several submissions across three groups of issues. Particularly significant was Manila's argument that China's nine-dash line claim is contrary to UNCLOS. The Philippines also requested the tribunal to determine the statuses of land features occupied by China, arguing that most are rocks or low-tide elevations rather than islands. The Philippines further asked that the tribunal cite China for violating UNCLOS environmental rules, referring to Chinese fishing activities and island construction that destroy coral.

China had argued repeatedly that ITLOS did not have jurisdiction over the South China Sea disputes, and also complained about betrayal by the Philippines, which had previously agreed to settle their disputes through negotiation, to the exclusion of any other means. Finally, China issued a declaration when it ratified UNCLOS in 2006, refusing to "accept any of the [settlement] procedures provided," thus in effect reserving resolution of maritime boundary and land feature sovereignty disputes to Beijing to negotiate directly.

ITLOS first stated in October 2015 that it would not rule on China's artificial island construction, since this was "military in nature" and hence not within its authority under UNCLOS. Exercising its civilian jurisdiction in July 2016, it ruled almost entirely in Manila's favor. This was an unexpectedly overwhelming win for the Philippines, especially the ITLOS statement that none of the land features in the South China Sea qualify as "islands."

The ruling was issued in a 501-page document and contained the following primary "holdings":

1. UNCLOS "comprehensively" governs the parties' respective rights to maritime areas in the South China Sea. Therefore, to the extent that China's nine-dash line is a claim of "historic rights" to the waters of the South China Sea, it is invalid. ITLOS did not describe the dash line as illegal, just irrelevant. "Historic rights" do not supersede another nation's EEZ.

2. None of the features in the Spratly Islands generates an EEZ, nor can the Spratly Islands generate an EEZ collectively as a unit.

3. China violated the Philippines' sovereign rights in its EEZ. It did so by interfering with Philippine fishing and hydrocarbon exploration, constructing artificial islands and failing to prevent Chinese fishermen from fishing in the Philippines' EEZ. China also interfered with Philippine fishermen's traditional fishing rights near Scarborough Shoal. China's construction of artificial islands at seven features in the Spratly Islands, as well as illegal fishing and harvesting by Chinese nationals, violate UNCLOS obligations to protect the marine environment. Finally, Chinese law enforcement vessels unlawfully created a serious risk of collision by physically obstructing Philippine vessels at Scarborough Shoal in 2012.

4. China has aggravated and extended the disputes through its dredging, artificial island building and construction activities.

China's reaction to the ruling has been loud and repetitive. Its refusal to acknowledge the validity of the ITLOS decision reflects its traditional refusal to settle maritime sovereignty disputes, although it has settled many continental disputes. In response to the ruling, China issued a white paper reaffirming its "territorial sovereignty and maritime rights and interests in the South China Sea." Beijing insists that it holds sovereignty over all the South China Sea "islands," citing various Chinese laws, "historic rights" and UNCLOS.

China's ambassador to the U.S. accused the Philippines of attempting to "use legal instruments for political pur-

(Left) Protesters outside of the Chinese Consulate hours before ITLOS announced its ruling on the South China Sea, July 12, 2016. (BULLIT MARQUEZ/AP) *(Right) Pro-Beijing protesters shout slogans against U.S.support for the ITLOS ruling outside the U.S. Consulate in Hong Kong, July. 14, 2016.* (KIN CHEUNG/AP)

poses," with U.S. "military coercion as a backdrop." He further accused the U.S. of having a "Cold War mentality" and attempting to subvert diplomacy with "a fleet of aircraft carriers." Military officers and civilian officials and analysts in China continue to blame Washington for instigating Manila (and the other South China Sea claimants) to challenge Beijing.

Finally, China's foreign minister described the ruling as "a political farce" and "an attempt to undermine China's territorial sovereignty and maritime rights and interests in the South China Sea." He reiterated that the decision "shall not be affected by the award of the Arbitral Tribunal." In short, China's reaction to the ITLOS decision was "no acceptance, no participation, no recognition, and no implementation."

The ITLOS ruling placed China very much on the defensive and illustrated the weakness of the nation's international behavior. The tribunal did note, however, "We should not assume that these disputes are the product of *bad faith* on the part of the PRC; rather, they are the result of basic disagreements about respective rights and obligations and the applicability of UNCLOS." This statement did nothing to salve Chinese resentment.

The case's greatest legal significance, however, may lie in providing the first precedent defining specific criteria for what constitutes an "island" as opposed to a "rock." In fact, ITLOS ruled that none of the land features in the South China Sea are legally "islands." They cannot, therefore, generate any geographic zone beyond a 12 nm territorial sea. This ruling affects all the land feature claimants in the South China Sea, not just China.

Furthermore, although not specifically addressed in the ITLOS ruling, the description of what constitutes an "island" strongly implies that many other land features around the world are not legally so categorized. This includes Japan's claim to Okinotorishima, as well as claims by the U.S. to such features as the Howland, Johnston and Midway "islands," for instance. ∎

Looking forward

The sovereignty of the many land features in question was deliberately not addressed in the ITLOS ruling, and the tribunal has no power to enforce its nominally binding decisions. Despite low key urging by Washington and several other capitals that Beijing follow the rulings, China refuses to do so. Instead, Beijing issues belligerent denials of any wrongdoing or willingness to adhere to the UNCLOS interpretations supported by the great majority of the treaty's signatories.

Underlying China's actions in the South China Sea and its reaction to the ITLOS ruling is the belief that the U.S. poses the primary threat to its national security interests, especially in view of the 1979 Taiwan Relations Act and the 1996 Taiwan Strait crisis, both of which attest to the U.S. commitment that reunification of Taiwan with the mainland must be peaceful. China's containment accusations continue to gain credence among Chinese analysts, who often focus on U.S. alliances with South Korea, Japan, the Philippines, Australia and Thailand, deriding them as "relics of the Cold War."

China is also wary of the strengthening of U.S. relations with Vietnam, Singapore and India. These are seen by Beijing as facets of the U.S. rebalance to Asia. Hence, they are often and perhaps disingenuously interpreted as U.S. efforts to prevent China from assuming its deserved role as a leading Asian and global power. As noted above, increased U.S. military relations with these and other Asian nations are particularly troubling to Beijing.

China's future actions could be escalatory. Beijing might declare an Air Defense Identification Zone over the South China Sea. Most dangerous would be turning Scarborough Shoal into an artificial island and military base, as it has with three Spratly land features. This shoal lies little more than 100 nm off the Luzon coast. Its role as a Chinese military installation

would directly challenge the U.S.' ability to fulfill its responsibilities under the U.S.-Philippine Mutual Defense Treaty. Chinese withdrawal from UNCLOS has been discussed by analysts in Beijing, but is not likely since the country has too much at stake in the treaty's provisions about deep seabed mining concessions and its own maritime claims in the three seas.

In short, Beijing apparently believes that any U.S. disagreement with a Chinese position is an attack on China's interests. That also means, of course, that relations with the U.S. are at the top of China's foreign policy concerns and may temper future actions in the South China Sea. The U.S. could strengthen its position vis-à-vis the South China Sea by signing and ratifying UNCLOS. Every president since Ronald Reagan has stated that the U.S. will accept the treaty as international law; secretaries of defense, secretaries of the navy and chiefs of naval operations since then have all urged the Senate to ratify the treaty, to no avail.

Other U.S. future actions are more certain: ongoing insistence on the peaceful resolution of sovereignty disputes; adherence to alliances in Asia, including that with the Philippines; and freedom of navigation operations. The U.S. will continue to insist on free access for both commercial and military vessels throughout the maritime commons, as codified in UNCLOS.

Government officials in the U.S., China and the Philippines have all called for "turning a new page" following the ITLOS ruling, and for peacefully resolving the disputes in the South China Sea. This will require the disputants to negotiate joint ventures and other arrangements without dealing with sovereignty issues, since neither China nor the other claimants have demonstrated flexibility on that issue. The ITLOS decision certainly will not resolve the disputes in the South China Sea, nor will it ease the considerable tensions there. ∎

discussion questions

1. Why hasn't the U.S. ratified UNCLOS? What would be the costs and benefits of doing so, as they pertain to U.S. interests in the South China Sea?

2. Given that UNCLOS has no enforcement mechanism, is the 2016 ITLOS ruling on China's claims in the South China Sea likely to have any significant affect on the situation on the ground? If so, how?

3. Beijing cites the U.S. "rebalance to Asia" as evidence of containment. To what extent is that perception justified, or is it totally unjustified?

4. What influence do Chinese domestic political concerns have on Beijing's calculations in the South China Sea?

5. Should China's historical experience during the "100 Years of Humiliation" figure more prominently in U.S. and international policy considerations in the South China Sea?

6. China rejects multilateral negotiations in South China Sea disputes, claiming that direct negotiations between the relevant parties is the better approach. Many criticize this position as a way for China to maintain the upper hand in disputes with less powerful countries. Are disputes in the South China Sea better solved bilaterally or multilaterally?

Don't forget: Ballots start on page 115!

suggested readings

Coker, Christopher, **The Improbable War: China, the United States and the Logic of Great Power Conflict**. Oxford: Oxford University Press, 2015. 256 pp. Coker maintains that the rise of China will seriously disrupt the U.S.-led international order, and, if mishandled, could lead to war.

French, Howard W., "China's Dangerous Game." **The Atlantic**, November 2014. Available free online: <http://www.theatlantic.com/magazine/archive/2014/11/chinas-dangerous-game/380789/>. This article attempts to answer the central question: Does China's aggressive assertion of its maritime claims indicate that Beijing is increasingly powerful, or that it is facing a legitimacy crisis?

Hayton, Bill, **The South China Sea: The Struggle for Power in Asia**. New Haven, CT: Yale University Press, 2014. 320 pp. Journalist Bill Hayton presents a history of territorial disputes in the South China Sea, suggesting avenues for resolution. He contends that the U.S. maintains a vast technological advantage over the PLAN, bolstered by regional alliances.

Jenner, C.J. and Thuy, Tran Truong, eds., **The South China Sea: A Crucible of Regional Cooperation or Conflict-making Sovereignty Claims?** Cambridge: Cambridge University Press, 2016.

382 pp. This book provides a detailed empirical study of conflict in the South China Sea, examining the issue from the subnational to the international level.

Kaplan, Robert D., **Asia's Cauldron: The South China Sea and the End of a Stable Pacific**. New York: Random House, 2014. 256 pp. Kaplan analyzes the conflict in the South China Sea, reviewing U.S. and Chinese interests, and offering an explanation of Chinese political and cultural motivations there.

Poling, Gregory B., "The South China Sea in Focus: Clarifying the Limits of Maritime Dispute." **Center for Strategic & International Studies**, July 2013. 48 pp. Available free online: <https://csis-prod.s3.amazonaws.com/s3fs-public/legacy_files/files/publication/130717_Poling_SouthChinaSea_Web.pdf>. This report uses analysis of maritime law, satellite imagery, public source data and geographic information systems to better define the areas under dispute in the South China Sea.

Rosario, Albert F., "Statement Before the Permanent Court of Arbitration." **The Hague**, July 8, 2015. Available free online: <http://www.chicagopcg.com/sfa%20speech.pdf>. In his speech on the maritime dispute case between the Philippines and China at the UN Arbitral Tribunal, the Philippine Department of Foreign Affairs Secretary Albert F. Rosario articulates the implications of the case for his country, the region and the world.

To access web links to these readings, as well as links to additional, shorter readings and suggested web sites,

GO TO www.greatdecisions.org

and click on the topic under Resources, on the right-hand side of the page

Saudi Arabia in transition
by Lawrence G. Potter

King of Saudi Arabia Salman bin Abdulaziz Al Saud (center), Deputy Crown Prince Mohammed bin Salman Al Saud (right) and Crown Prince, First Deputy Prime Minister and the Minister of Interior Muhammad bin Nayef (left) pose for a photograph before the announcement of the economic reform plan known as "Vision 2030" in Riyadh, Saudi Arabia on April 25, 2016. (BANDAR ALGALOUD/ANADOLU AGENCY/GETTY IMAGES)

As 2017 began, the incoming administration of Donald J. Trump was faced with a difficult situation in the Middle East, with active conflicts in Iraq and Afghanistan, the nuclear agreement with Iran under renewed attack, the peace process between Israelis and Palestinians still stalled, and strained relations with Egypt and Turkey. Proxy wars between Iran and Saudi Arabia continued in Yemen and Syria, drawing in the U.S. A military offensive against Mosul and Raqqa, with American participation, is now contesting ISIS' control of parts of Iraq and Syria, but this will be a prolonged struggle.

The Arab Spring, the region-wide upheaval demanding reform and democracy that swept the Middle East starting in early 2011, led to the downfall of rulers in Tunisia, Libya, Egypt and Yemen, yet did not lead to the reforms ardently wished for. Gulf rulers were alarmed by

demands for political reform, and responded by blaming Iran, seeking to buy off political opposition and stepping up internal repression.

The situation in Saudi Arabia has now been transformed by the accession to power of King Salman bin Abdulaziz Al Saud, 81, in January 2015 following the death of his half-brother, King Abdullah, who had ruled the country since 2005. The new leadership includes the crown prince, Muhammad bin Nayef, 57, also the interior minister, who

LAWRENCE G. POTTER *is director of research and publications for Gulf/2000, a major research and documentation project on the Persian Gulf states based at Columbia University, where he also teaches. He is a longtime contributor to* GREAT DECISIONS *and published "The Persian Gulf: Tradition and Transformation" in FPA's* Headline Series *Nos. 333–334 (Fall 2011).*

Mohammed bin Salman Al Saud (left), deputy crown prince and defense minister of Saudi Arabia, and U.S. President Barack Obama meet at the White House in Washington, D.C, on June 17, 2016. (ANADOLU AGENCY/GETTY IMAGES)

has a background in counter-terrorism. The king's son, Mohammed bin Salman, 31, is deputy crown prince and the person many regard as the real decision-maker. Ambitious and brash (he did not hesitate to upbraid President Obama over U.S. policy), he is spearheading major changes in domestic policy. The new team has also embarked on a much more aggressive foreign policy to oppose Iranian inroads in the region, intervening in the conflict in Syria and initiating a disastrous war in Yemen.

The change in government coincided with a precipitous drop in the price of oil—the state's main resource—which started in mid-2014, after a decade of high prices. Prices fell from a peak of $145 per barrel in 2008 to below $30 in 2016, ending the year in the $50 range. This has led to an economic crisis and a massive budget deficit of $98 billion in 2015, and a projected $87 billion in 2016. In response, the government has introduced

Before you read, download the companion **Glossary** that includes definitions and a guide to acronyms and abbreviations used in the article. Go to **www.great decisions.org** and select a topic in the Resources section on the right-hand side of the page.

a plan for major reforms and reductions in expenditure, dubbed "Saudi Vision 2030." These reforms amount to a rewriting of the "ruling bargain" long in effect between the government and its citizens during the age of plenty: As long as the government took care of people's needs, including employment, housing, education and health care, and did not tax them, they would delegate decisions of how to rule to the Al Saud. Such major policy changes have unsettled Saudis, and, if implemented, there is no guarantee they will work.

The U.S. hope of reducing its footprint in the Middle East, especially the Persian Gulf, has had to be repeatedly deferred. The wars in Afghanistan and Iraq that President Obama inherited from his predecessor, George W. Bush, were supposed to be over by now, but American troops are still fighting in both. Official ties with Saudi Arabia, the U.S.' most important Arab ally, are badly strained, and support for the Saudis has plummeted in public opinion. On September 28, Congress overrode the president's veto of a bill (the Justice Against Sponsors of Terrorism Act or JASTA) that would allow families of victims of the September 11 attacks to sue the Saudi government for any role in the event. Although

the official investigation of the 9/11 attacks concluded that there was "no evidence" that they were funded by the Saudi government or senior officials, questions have persisted as to whether lower-level officials or other Saudis were complicit and information was being suppressed. The Saudis have threatened to retaliate by selling off their assets in the U.S.

The war in Yemen, which has so far claimed an estimated 10,000 casualties, has put the U.S. in an untenable position. The Obama administration has reluctantly supported the air war that began there in 2015 in hopes of reinstalling President Abdu Mansour Hadi, who was removed from power by Iranian-aligned Houthi rebels. U.S. assistance has included aircraft, munitions, training and in-flight refueling. This support is partly payback for Saudi acquiescence in the Iranian nuclear deal. In the opinion of the *New York Times*, "If the Saudis refuse to halt the carnage and resume negotiations on a political settlement, Mr. Obama should end military support. Otherwise, America could be implicated in war crimes and be dragged even deeper into the conflict."

Saudi Arabia is also facing criticism for the export of Wahhabism, its austere version of Islam that is widely believed to have contributed to the spread of jihadist violence. The paradox is that although the country is accused of funding and exporting terrorists, it has been fighting a homegrown terrorist movement since al-Qaeda first targeted the Al Saud, and is now experiencing attacks by ISIS.

In the face of perceived U.S. unreliability, coupled with financial crisis at home, Saudi Arabia has undertaken dramatic policy changes. According to Prince Turki Al Faisal, former ambassador to the U.S. and former head of intelligence, "America has changed, we have changed and definitely we need to realign and readjust our understandings of each other." Americans have started to wonder: Should they regard Saudi Arabia as a friend or foe? Clearly, some readjustment of relations is in store.

Religion and state in Saudi Arabia

Tribes were the key to forming modern states in the Arabian Peninsula, although the dynasties ruling there are mostly of urban origin. Particularly significant was a religious reform movement known as the Wahhabis, which arose in the central region of Najd in the 18th century. It was founded by Muhammad ibn Abd al-Wahhab (d.1792), a preacher who formed a partnership in 1744 with a local chieftain, Muhammad ibn Saud (d. 1765), and went on to conquer much of the peninsula.

This led to the formation of three Saudi states, the first lasting from 1744 to 1818 (destroyed by the governor of Egypt, acting on Ottoman behalf); the second from 1824 to 1891 (put to an end by the Rashidis, a tribal dynasty); and the third state, founded by Abdulaziz Ibn Saud in 1902, which persists today. Although Ibn Saud incorporated much of Arabia into what became the new state of Saudi Arabia in 1932, he was prevented by the British from swallowing up the small shaikhdoms they protected along the Gulf coast, or expanding into Iraqi and Jordanian territory. The discovery of oil in 1938 by American prospectors ensured the state's survival. Since Ibn Saud died in 1953, only his sons have ruled the country, including the present King Salman.

Wahhabi Islam

The Wahhabi version of Islam is austere. Like other Islamic schools, it emphasizes monotheism and the obligation to pay *zakat,* or taxes to be remitted to the leader of the community. Its theology, however, rejects any form of intercession with God, such as visiting the shrines of saints. Wahhabism seeks a return to a purified faith and opposes all it regards as *bid'a* (reprehensible innovation), such as Sufism and Shi'ism. It enjoins believers to carry out jihad ("holy war") against those who do not follow these principles. This led in the

early 19th century to attacks on Shi'a holy places in present-day Iraq, as well as in Medina.

While religion was the main animating force of the movement, economic reward was also a key to its success. Historian Hala Fattah notes that the Wahhabi tendency to label Muslim opponents as unbelievers (*kafir,* plural *kuffar*), and thereby excommunicate them by the act of *takfir,* led to an early struggle over pilgrimage and communication routes in the Arabian Peninsula, as well as to attempts to collect protection money and impose a trade monopoly. Before oil, the annual Hajj pilgrimage was a significant source of income. Today, Saudi control of the Hajj is very important for political and economic reasons.

The use of the derogatory term "Wahhabi" is, however, problematic, and it was originally introduced by the opponents of Muhammad ibn Abd al-Wahhab. By naming a movement after a man (like the analogous "Muhammadism"), it seeks to emphasize that its doctrines were created by a man and that its followers belong to a heretical cult, not mainstream Sunni Islam. The current use of the term to refer to (and delegitimize) movements outside of Saudi Arabia is also misleading. Most Saudis regard themselves as Sunni Muslims who adhere to Salafism; that is, they follow the example of the Prophet Muhammad and his Companions, who constitute the worthy ancestors of today's true Muslims (*al-salaf*). Salafists are mainly concerned with problems of the Islamic world and questions of individual piety, not international relations or even politics. The Western media usually refer to the radical and militant branch of Salafists as "Jihadi" or "Salafi Jihadi."

"Salafism morphed into a religious movement with a number of political manifestations, only one of which was the blend of social conservatism

and political quietism represented by the official Saudi variant," according to F. Gregory Gause III, professor at the Bush School of Government at Texas A&M University. While acknowledging that the Saudis have set up institutions and networks to spread a puritanical, intolerant form of Islam abroad, he points out that they long ago lost control of the global Salafi movement, if they ever had it, and it is unrealistic to think that they control it. "This means that leaning on the Saudis to become 'less Wahhabi' is unlikely to have much effect on jihadist movements like Al Qaeda and Islamic State [ISIS]."

The role of the ulama

Like other religions and religious tendencies, over more than 250 years the doctrine and practice of "Wahhabism" has undergone an evolution. In the beginning, it was a partnership between a religious and a secular figure, in which the descendants of Muhammad bin Saud provided "secular" leadership of the state, and the descendants of Muhammad ibn Abd al-Wahhab (the Al Shaikh family) provided religious leadership. As Ibn Saud consolidated his power in the early 20th century, this balance had to change. In 1929, the Ikhwan (Brethren), his fervent tribal warriors, wanted to attack the British Mandate of Iraq against his wishes. A major battle took place (Battle of Sibila), in which the forces of the king vanquished these religious zealots.

From then on, the balance between religion and state changed. The role of the Wahhabi *ulama* (Muslim religious scholars with recognized authority in matters of sacred law and theology), originally partners with the secular Al Saud, was increasingly circumscribed. While the state pays deference to the ulama, since the defeat of the Ikhwan it has always been

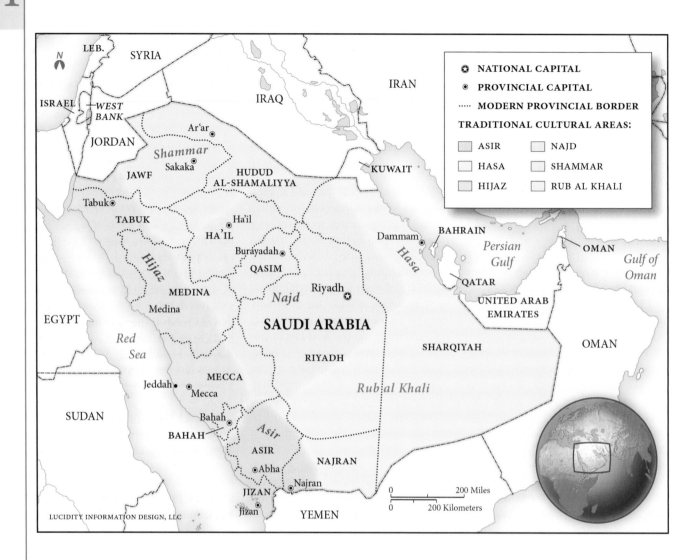

in charge, and most ulama have been part of the government bureaucracy. While some marriages have occurred between the Al Shaikh family and the Al Saud family since the 1940s, these are not important when it comes to the political affairs of the country. In 1971, King Faisal created a Council of Senior Ulama, which, by means of its *fatwas* (religious edicts), provides religious sanction for state policies.

The support of the Wahhabi ulama remains a key source of legitimacy for the rule of the Al Saud. "In Saudi Arabia, stability depends to a large degree on cooperation between the ruling family and the *ulama*," according to Czech scholar Ondrej Beranek. "During the second half of the twentieth century...the expression of traditional Abd al-Wahhab's doctrine changed from the revivalist Salafi movement to apologetic institutionalized religion, which has supported two very controversial, yet very frequent political habits in the history of Islam: hereditary political power and absolute submission to the ruling authority."

National identity

Since the current state was founded in 1902, it has tried to foster a sense of national identity where none existed before. As Saudi historian Madawi Al-Rasheed explains, "Saudi historical narratives create a memory of a population riven by warfare, instability, and rivalry as a prelude to the paramount role of the Wahhabi call...more importantly, the narrative asserts the leading role of the Najdi population." Ignoring the unique identity and historical roles played by regions such as Hijaz, Asir and al-Ahsa, Saudi texts speak of the country's "unification" rather than "conquest."

The result is a skewed portrayal of pre-oil Arabia and the Gulf, with a loss of the diversity and ambiguity that characterized it. Thus the heritage of the sedentary Najdi population is emphasized to the exclusion of other elements. However, rather than a state based on Bedouin and "tribal values," in reality Saudi Arabia was very much the exclusive project of those living in settled communities who were often in conflict with Bedouins, cautions Saudi scholar Abdulaziz Al-Fahad.

Today, all the Gulf Cooperation Council (GCC) states are trying to create a historical memory and sense of loyalty to the ruling dynasties. This is promoted partly by state-sponsored histories, which omit or downplay the role of groups such as the Shi'a, who have responded by writing their own histories to correct the record. Regional identities nevertheless live on, especially in the Hijaz, the "cradle of Islam" which contains the cities of Mecca and Medina and the outward-looking seaport of Jiddah. According to anthropologist Mai Yamani, the Hijazis regard themselves as superior to the less-sophisticated Najdis, who run the country, while the Najdis regard Hijazis as being tainted by impure lineage and too liberal and westernized. The strict Wahhabi interpretation of Islam and the privileging of the conservative Najdi lifestyle and values has little appeal in the Hijaz or Shi'a parts of the country, and its attraction to the modern middle class is questionable.

In the past, there were a variety of identities that took priority over state identity in Saudi Arabia, including tribe, religion, ethnic group, city and province.

Now, according to Professor Al-Rasheed, "the old, mild nationalism that immediately followed the establishment of Gulf nation-states is developing into an assertive, hypernationalist trend centered on militarization—specifically in the UAE [United Arab Emirates] and Saudi Arabia, where both countries project themselves as being at war with an Iranian proxy whose tentacles reach their own backyard in Yemen."

The Islamic opposition in Saudi Arabia

The resurgence of religion in personal and political life that has marked the Middle East since the 1970s also affected the Arabian Peninsula. Ostensibly, Saudi Arabia was the most "Islamic" of states, being the birthplace of Islam and strictly ruled according to the Sharia, or Islamic law. However, in the Muslim world, political action has often been taken in the name of religion by governments and opposition groups alike. The Muslim Brotherhood, a Sunni Islamist movement active for decades in Egypt, was welcomed in the Gulf in the 1950s and 1960s and played a big role in the educational system. In 1979, Saudi security forces fought a bloody battle to oust Islamic militants who had taken over Islam's holiest site, the Grand

Mosque in Mecca, in a protest over the rule of the Al Saud. After that time, the state lavished attention on the Wahhabi ulama and gave them greater control over public space and behavior, including television and radio programming, as well as the educational system.

The Gulf War, in which a U.S. military coalition evicted Iraqi forces from Kuwait (1990–91) changed everything and led to the rise of a potent Islamist opposition. "The post-war resurgence of Islamism was a reaffirmation of identity, a protest movement against the monarchy and its Western allies, and for some, a means to achieve social influence and, perhaps, a takeover of power," according to political scientist R. Hrair Dekmejian. A new generation of clerics known as the "Sahwa" (Awakening), influenced by the Muslim Brotherhood, led resistance to state policies. They accused the ruling Al Saud of squandering resources, being puppets of the West, and not being sufficiently "Islamic" in their rule. A bitter split developed between the "official" religious establishment, supported by the state, and the outlawed opposition. Thus the fatwa, or ruling, allowing non-Muslim forces to enter Saudi Arabia in 1990, issued by the senior religious

scholar, Shaikh 'Abd al-'Aziz bin Baz, was criticized as a sellout on the part of some Wahhabi ulama.

The Islamic opposition took an ominous turn when new groups inspired by militant ideologies of jihad in Afghanistan began to carry out violent attacks and to challenge the Sahwists for influence. Osama bin Laden, a Saudi of Yemeni origin, formed a transnational Islamist network, al-Qaeda, in 1988, which carried out a number of terrorist attacks, including the 9/11 attacks on the U.S. (Many were shocked that 15 of the 19 airplane hijackers were identified as Saudi.) Support for the Afghan *mujahideen* in the 1980s eventually led to blowback for the Al Saud, as radicalized Arab fighters returned home and created an offshoot, al-Qaeda in the Arabian Peninsula (AQAP). AQAP carried out a number of violent attacks against the state between 2003 and 2006. By 2008, the AQAP campaign had failed because of a government crackdown, lack of popular support and a split among jihadists, some of whom gave priority to struggle in war zones such as Iraq and Afghanistan.

A new branch of AQAP has been active in Yemen since 2009. While AQAP remains a threat in Saudi Arabia, today

Saudi Governor of Medina Faisal bin Salman bin Abdulaziz (second right) and security officers look at blood stains on the ground after a suicide attack near the security headquarters outside one of Islam's holiest sites, the Prophet's Mosque in Medina on July 4, 2016. (STR/AFP/GETTY IMAGESS)

Saudi society: the urgency of reform

Saudi security men bombard a building near the site where police exchanged fire with suspected al-Qaeda militants in the city of Dammam, September 6, 2005. (STR/AFP/GETTY IMAGES)

Riyadh faces a more potent challenge from ISIS, which it also regards as a "deviant sect." ISIS has mainly targeted Shi'a mosques and the security services, but an attack last July on the Prophet's Mosque in Medina shocked Saudis. Their declaration of a caliphate in 2014 was a direct challenge to Saudi pretensions to be the leader of the Islamic world.

How dangerous is the Islamic opposition in Saudi Arabia? At present, it constitutes a security threat, but not a threat to regime stability. The Al Saud can count on the support of the Wahhabi ulama, revel in their custody of the holy cities in the Hijaz, and still have vast financial resources at their disposal. The legitimacy of the royal family to rule is well-established and religiously justified, and the unrest in nearby states such as Iraq, Syria and Yemen has made Saudis think twice about replacing their government. The ulama stood by the Al Saud during the Arab Spring protests.

A more recent concern is how winding down the wars in Iraq and Syria will affect Saudi Arabia. These conflicts have served as a destination of Saudi jihadists, who have gone there to fight against the Shi'a and the Americans. The Saudi government fears that these forces will receive training and experience, only to later return home and foment instability.

The succession

King Salman is likely to be the last of the sons of Ibn Saud to rule, and the transition to a new generation of leaders has begun. The crown prince, Muhammad bin Nayef, favored by the U.S., is next in line to the throne. Should King Salman die early, it is possible that Muhammad bin Nayef, as king, could dismiss Mohammed bin Salman and install a new deputy crown prince. It is unclear how this would affect the policies, such as the war in Yemen, that are identified with his rival.

Political decisions in Saudi Arabia are traditionally taken by consensus among a small family elite, with input from the Sunni ulama. There is also an appointed 150-member Shura Council that provides limited advice. Although given wide powers by his father, Mohammed bin Salman's youth and inexperience are concerns in a society that venerates and defers to its elders. However, the crown prince does reflect the young society he rules over—in Saudi Arabia, 70% of the population is under 30—and he will presumably have different priorities than his predecessors. He is not believed to be overly wedded to tradition. "The next generation of Gulf leaders will likely embrace an alternative model: good governance. Specifically, they will concentrate on delivering public services effectively, improving their management of public administration, and pursuing economic reforms that ensure the long-term prosperity of the GCC," according to RAND analysts Becca Wasser and Jeffrey Martini.

The new generation

Saudi Arabia is experiencing a "youth bulge" and needs to create about 226,000 jobs a year, although in 2015 only 49,000 were added. As in other GCC states, there is a widespread preference on the part of nationals to work in the public sector, since this assures them of higher wages, shorter working hours and longer holidays, plus the probability that they cannot be fired. However, it has led to a "culture of entitlement" and criticism that the new generation is not prepared to work hard.

Thanks to new information technology such as smart phones and satellite TV, governments no longer have a monopoly on information and the younger generation are much more aware of what is happening in their own country, the region and the world than in the past. Saudi youth are known to be heavily addicted to social media. The rulers, for their part, are making skillful use of such media to introduce the Vision 2030 plan, with a reported 190,000 Twitter users participating in a discussion about it. Mohammed bin Salman has cultivated younger clerics, who have millions of followers on social media. Government officials must now worry about accountability, and have to monitor their social media accounts to make sure they respond to any criticism.

The role of women

The role of women in Saudi Arabia is severely circumscribed compared to that in neighboring Islamic states. This is partly due to the religious necessity to separate the sexes. Modest dress is, of course, essential for both men and women. Without the permission of a male guardian, women can't leave their homes, get a passport, marry, travel or receive higher education. Last September, around 15,000 Saudis signed an online petition to the government to end the male guardianship system now in place. The younger generation still finds ways to have fun, such as meeting in malls and flirting on social media. While women make up an estimated 60% of university students, there are few jobs for them when they graduate, a situation that increasingly poses a financial hardship. So far they cannot drive, but this may change be-

Female genetics researchers at King Faisal Specialist Hospital and Research Center on April 14, 2016, in Riyadh. (DAVID DEGNER/GETTY IMAGES)

fore long. Nevertheless, more women are now entering professions such as law. In 2013, King Abdullah appointed 30 women to the Shura Council, and in 2015, women were allowed to vote and run in municipal elections for the first time. Mohammed bin Salman has indicated that he wants women to be a more productive part of the economy, and he may be sympathetic to the loosening of social codes. He already has reined in the morality police who patrolled streets and malls, which was one of the most-criticized mechanisms of social control imposed by the Wahhabi ulama.

Human rights

When President Obama met with King Salman in Riyadh in April 2016, the sharpest exchanges came as he criticized the Saudi record on human rights, noting harsh sentences and beheadings, while the king defended the justice system. The Saudis are not interested in American advice about their domestic affairs. The U.S. has typically softpedaled criticism of Saudi Arabia, notably during the Arab Spring. According to the Human Rights Watch report for 2015, "The United States largely did not criticize Saudi human rights violations beyond congressionally-mandated annual reports."

The situation has not improved under King Salman. The Human Rights Watch

report charged that Saudi authorities continued arbitrary arrests, trials and convictions of peaceful dissidents. They discriminated against religious minorities and sent people to prison for criticizing the authorities. Freedom of expression and freedom of worship do not exist. The rate of executions, including beheadings, rose dramatically in 2015. In one notorious example, in 2014 blogger Raif Badawi was sentenced to ten years in prison and 1,000 lashes (50 have been administered so far) for setting up a liberal website and "insulting Islam" online. This even prompted an objection from the State Department. Nevertheless, last October, Saudi Arabia was re-elected to the UN's Human Rights Council.

In a recent report, Hala Aldosari, a visiting scholar at the Arab Gulf States Institute in Washington and the director of an online project on women's rights in Saudi Arabia, points out that human rights activists in Saudi Arabia are a diverse group containing many women, liberals and Shi'a. In the aftermath of the Arab Spring, social networks in Saudi Arabia and abroad have been drawing attention to human rights abuses. She believes that the newly announced reforms can give activists an opportunity to press their case. However, she notes that "the king and his circle retain absolute authority to override otherwise binding laws, international treaty commitments, or other apparently official decisions."

The economy: end of an era

In the GCC states, the "ruling bargain" that evolved after the discovery of oil and development of a rentier economy (one that depends on revenue from oil rents) is now badly in need of reformulation. This is especially true in Saudi, whose population (31.7 million, about 33% of whom are estimated to be foreign) is higher and per capita income ($54,730) lower than other petro-states. As long as oil revenue was high, the government could take care of people's needs, such as employment, housing and health care, and expected obedience in return. The drastic reduction in income has now led to reduced salaries (even for princes) and subsidies, and the beginning of taxation. Presumably in return people will now expect more accountability and participation in affairs of state. But opening up society could in turn shake the legitimacy of monarchs who don't want to share power. Ruling families thus face a conundrum about how much to liberalize.

How bad is the situation? Deputy Crown Prince Mohammed bin Salman warned in April 2016, "We have developed an oil addiction in the kingdom of Saudi Arabia, among everyone. That is dangerous, and that is what has hampered the development of many different sectors in recent years." At the end of 2014, Saudi Arabia had a comfortable $740 billion in foreign currency reserves, but in light of its huge deficit took out about $115 billion in 2015, and clearly cannot sustain withdrawals at that clip. The International Monetary Fund, in a report released in late October, cited a breakeven oil price for Saudi Arabia of $80 a barrel—much more than it is earning now or is expected to earn in the near future. The Arabian Peninsula states all ultimately face a post-oil future. This is already arriving in Bahrain, Oman and Yemen, although it could be delayed by decades in Saudi, the UAE and Kuwait. Adjusting to the new reality will be painful after decades of excess, but there seems to be no alternative to implementing long-overdue structural reforms.

"Saudi Vision 2030," announced in the spring of 2016, is a major set of reforms that aim to reduce government subsidies,

The Saudi Shi'a

In Saudi Arabia, the official Wahhabi school ignores other strains of Islam such as Sufism found in the Hijaz, the Shi'a in the Eastern Province, and smaller minorities such as the Ismaili Muslims and Christian foreign workers. But the most angst has been caused by the Shi'a, who have periodically dared to express open opposition to the Riyadh government.

Eastern Arabia, with strong historical links to Bahrain, has been predominantly Shi'a for hundreds of years. Both areas were conquered by Najdis and retain a myth of a "golden age" when Shi'a ruled. In other Gulf states, such as Kuwait, Qatar and Oman, the Shi'a are more recent arrivals and tend to support Sunni governments.

Relations between the Wahhabis and the Shi'a have varied since the area was conquered by Ibn Saud in 1913. At first, the Shi'a did not resist the Saudi takeover, hoping that the new rulers would establish peace in the region. The Al Saud practiced what Laurence Louër of the Center for International Studies and Research at Sciences Po, Paris, has characterized as "pragmatic sectarianism" in order to build the new state, for example allowing the Shi'a to have their own religious judges. However, following the politicization of Islam during the Iranian revolution (1978–79), and especially the takeover of the Mecca mosque by Sunni militants in November 1979, the Shi'a issue in Saudi Arabia became politically charged and the group was regarded as a threat. This led to what Louër describes as "a widespread state-sponsored policy of sectarian discrimination."

Saudi Shi'a have not lobbied for an independent state, but have been subject to discrimination in employment and religious expression, and are now feared to be a fifth column for Iran. Wahhabi ulama who have been sent to Eastern Arabia preach that Shi'a are apostates. A major grievance is that although Shi'a live in a major oil-producing area, little money has been returned to develop their region.

The rise of identity politics in the Gulf, and the politicization of religious movements, has led to anti-state activism. From 1979 until 1993, relations between the Saudi government and the Shi'a were confrontational. The first steps to reconcile were taken by King Fahd in 1993, and things improved under his brother, King Abdullah (r. 2005–15). Since the Arab Spring and the uprising in Bahrain, however, conflict has reignited. The execution in January 2016 of a Shi'a religious leader, Shaikh Nimr al-Nimr, who criticized the monarchy, led to outrage among Shi'a throughout the Gulf, especially in Iran, where it inspired attacks on Saudi diplomatic posts and the breaking of diplomatic relations. According to Dr. Toby Matthiesen, a senior research fellow at St Antony's College, Oxford, "As long as the state legitimises itself through a religious nationalism based on the Wahhabiyya the situation of Shia Muslims in Saudi Arabia will remain precarious."

Saudi Shi'a children take part in a street procession commemorating Ashura in the Shi'a-dominated Gulf coast city of Qatif on October 11, 2016. Ashura mourns the death of Imam Hussein, a grandson of the Prophet Muhammad, who was killed by armies of the Yazid near Karbala in 680 AD. (STR/AFP/GETTY IMAGES)

cut dependency on oil and empower the private sector. The plan would help the country live on less oil revenue, as well as provide jobs for many of the younger generation who are now unemployed. Some two thirds of employed Saudis work for the state, and in September, the government announced drastic cuts in salaries and perks. One of the most dramatic proposals is to sell 5% of the shares of Saudi Aramco, the state oil company, although investors would not have control over output, production or contracts. The huge amount of money raised will be key to carrying out the broad vision of change ahead. "Read in one way, the documents are an ambitious blueprint to change the Saudi way of life. Read in another, they are a scathing indictment of how poorly the kingdom has been run by Prince bin Salman's elders," according to Mark Mazzetti and Ben Hubbard, writing in the *New York Times*.

Can this plan work? "Broadly, the direction is right, but there are a lot of question marks about implementation and the size of what they are promising," according to Steffen Hertog of the London School of Economics. One serious problem is the education system, which promotes a religious education and does not prepare students with skills needed in a modern economy. According to an analysis by Theodore Karasik and Joseph Cozza of Gulf State Analytics, a Washington, D.C.-based geopolitical risk consultancy, "The NTP [National Transformation Plan] and Vision 2030 could make Saudi society more vibrant and sustainable. Or they could undermine the kingdom's relative stability and create devastating consequences for the greater Middle East region, as well as global energy and financial markets."

Saudi foreign policy: a new activism

Traditionally the Saudis took a cautious approach to regional developments and preferred to exert their influence behind the scenes, as they are now doing in Syria. The new, more muscular foreign policy is inspired by the regional turmoil and a fear that Riyadh can no longer rely on the U.S. for protection. Since the overthrow of Saddam, Iraq has no longer been a counterweight to Iran, and for the first time, that country's government has been run by Shi'a. Iranian-supported Shi'a militias now play a significant role in Iraqi politics. GCC States fear increased Iranian influence in the Middle East, and new demands for political and social recognition on the part of their Shi'a minorities. For the first time, Saudi Arabia and the UAE have publicly constructed a military coalition to wage war on their periphery in Yemen. Saudis regard the Yemen conflict as a war of necessity, and so far it has had popular support. They are being subjected to missile attacks, and fear an unstable, failed state on their border that is a haven for terrorists or non-state actors that are proxies for Iran.

The rise of sectarian politics

One of the most harmful effects of the Iraq War in 2003 was the rise in sectarian discourse and a new conception of Shi'ism not merely as a different school of Islam, but an actual security threat to Sunni-led states. In December 2004, King Abdullah of Jordan warned that if the new Iraqi government fell under Iranian influence, a "crescent" of Shi'a movements would result, threatening Sunni governments. Former Egyptian President Mubarak, reflecting usually unstated anxieties, said in April 2005 that "[Shi'a] are mostly always loyal to Iran and not the countries where they live." This fear is especially salient in

Saudi and Bahrain, which have substantial populations that they fear Iran may be manipulating. The increased influence of Iran in Iraq and Syria has put Saudi Arabia on the defensive, and in the fall of 2016 Riyadh was wary of the role Iranian-backed militias were playing in the battle for Mosul.

Many analysts conclude, however, that fears of a rising "Shi'a crescent" are misplaced. For one thing, the Shi'a community is not unified but divided, with many clerics competing for leadership. The most prominent clergyman outside Iran at present is Ayatollah Ali al-Sistani in Iraq, whose teachings many Arab Shi'a in the Gulf follow,

and he strives to avoid political involvment except in dire circumstances.

In the Gulf states, Iranian influence is much more limited than in Iraq or Lebanon, according to Laurence Louër. She found that Shi'a movements in the Arab Gulf states were offshoots of Iraqi (not Iranian) movements, and there was a division between pro- and anti-Iranian Shi'a. Shi'a in the Gulf have generally sought to demonstrate loyalty to their own states rather than to Iran. The change of government in Iraq in 2003 did lead to an improvement of the lot of Gulf Shi'a, but this progress was reversed after the Arab Spring.

Israel and Saudi Arabia: a thaw in relations?

One recent regional trend is the strengthening of Israeli ties with the GCC states, stimulated by common hostility to Iran, aversion to radical Islamist groups and apprehension over the Obama administration's policies toward the Middle East. Although the Palestinian issue has always prevented formal bilateral ties between Israel and the GCC, there has recently been an upsurge in informal contacts based on mutual interests. The public visit of a delegation of Saudi academic and business figures to Israel in July 2016 may have been a trial balloon to test public opinion, while discreet off the record talks and business deals are known to have been taking place in recent years. Shared interest in fields such as desalination, renewable energy and military technology, and an appreciation for innovation, are behind such talks.

Despite an absence of formal ties, Israel has maintained discreet relations with its Gulf neighbors. It opened trade offices in Oman and Qatar in 1996, although both were subsequently closed. Israeli tourists are acknowledged to be visiting Dubai, where Mossad as-

sassinated a top Hamas operative in 2010. Saudi Arabia's Crown Prince (later King) Abdullah's peace initiative, unveiled in Beirut in 2002, would have normalized relations between Israel and Arab states.

The current rapprochement has grown out of a new political realignment in the Gulf and the region since the Arab Spring. During the talks over the Iran nuclear issue, Israeli intelligence officials communicated with their Arab counterparts in Gulf states, and both were unhappy that an agreement was reached. Israel is not believed to have objected to the transfer of two small islands in the Red Sea from Egypt to Saudi Arabia in 2016. Trade between Israel and the GCC states does exist, but it is conducted through third parties.

It is likely that for the foreseeable future, a new generation in both Israel and the Arab states will take advantage of the changing regional realignment to make pragmatic decisions on cooperation, although any normalization has to await settlement of the Palestinian issue.

4

War of words

For some time, both Saudi Arabia and Iran have engaged in heated rhetoric couched in sectarian terms. The death of almost 500 Iranian pilgrims in a stampede at the annual Hajj in September 2015, and the execution of prominent Saudi Shi'a cleric Nimr al-Nimr in January 2016, was followed by an attack by demonstrators on Saudi diplomatic missions in Iran in January 2016 and the breaking of relations by Riyadh. Saudi Foreign Minister Adel al-Jubeir said at the time, "The history of Iran is full of negative and hostile interference in Arab countries, always accompanied with subversion." This is a feeling shared by all the GCC states to some extent. Abdullah Al-Shayji, a political science professor at Kuwait University, wrote regarding the nuclear agreement: "The deal will embolden Iran, rehabilitate it, enrich it with cash and make it act with hubris and confidence to advance its hegemonic project to dominate the region and undermine our security, sovereignty and stability through its proxies in Iraq, Syria, Lebanon and Yemen, and its interventions in GCC states."

In September, the Iranian foreign minister, Mohammad Javad Zarif, wrote an op-ed in the *New York Times* entitled "Let Us Rid the World of Wahhabism," in which he blamed the ideology for instigating terrorism throughout the Middle East. The Iranian Supreme Leader, Ayatollah Ali Khamenei, said that "Saudi rulers' refusal to offer a simple verbal apology [for the Hajj incident] was indicative of their ultimate impudence and shamelessness." He went on, "the stampede demonstrated that this government is not qualified to manage the Two Holy Mosques."

How serious is this war of words? Although Saudi Arabia is very concerned about the Iranian threat, the Iranians do not seem too worried about Saudi but keep their focus on relations with major states such as the U.S., Russia, China and Europe. Sectarian rhetoric plays a role in poisoning public opinion and is a factor behind the "proxy wars" around the region. In an interview with *The Economist* in January 2016, Deputy Crown Prince Mohammed bin Salman said that "a war between Saudi Arabia and Iran is the beginning of a major catastrophe in the region...for sure we will not allow any such thing." In a similar vein, a former top Iranian diplomat, Seyed Mohammad Kazem Sajjadpour, acknowledged the reality: "Security interests of nations and governments in this region are intertwined and security of one country cannot be ensured by fomenting insecurity in another country. On the contrary, when the entire region is made secure, security of all countries will be guaranteed."

Sponsors of global jihadism?

The greatest concern of the U.S., and the hardest one for Saudis to refute, is that the state's vigorous export of Wahhabi ideology has served as the rationale for jihadist groups such as al-Qaeda and ISIS. A classified memo sent by then-Secretary of State Hillary Clinton in December 2009, revealed

King Faisal of Saudi Arabia (Faisal ibn Abdulaziz Al Saud) at a luncheon being held at the Dorchester Hotel, London, May 12, 1967. (PIERRE MANEVY/EXPRESS/HULTON ARCHIVE/GETTY IMAGES)

by WikiLeaks, concluded that "donors in Saudi Arabia constitute the most significant source of funding to Sunni terrorist groups worldwide." (It should be noted that such "donors" are private citizens who do not have the approval of the Saudi government.) An important goal of al-Qaeda and ISIS, after all, is to overthrow the ruling Al Saud family.

Since the time of King Faisal (r. 1964–75), Riyadh has vigorously promoted Islam abroad, always in the Wahhabi version. It has supported a plethora of Islamic organizations, dispatching imams and spending freely to build 1,359 mosques, 210 Islamic centers, 202 colleges and 2,000 schools in countries that do not have an Islamic majority. The Saudis have helped finance mosques in the West, including 16 in the U.S. Saudi religious textbooks have been widely distributed, although their contents have been found to insult other religions, promote jihad and offer a harsh, exclusionary view of other Islamic sects and other religions. ISIS adopted official Saudi textbooks for use in its schools until it published its own in 2015.

Although considerable evidence exists, the Saudis have rejected accusations that their religion has radicalized foreign Muslims and negatively impacted the more moderate, tolerant Islam that exists in many countries, such as Indonesia. The previous king, Abdullah, maintained that "Saudi Arabia stands in the face of those trying to hijack Islam and present it to the world as a religion of extremism, hatred, and terrorism." The Saudi government claims to be cracking down on religious extremism: It fired some 3,500 imams between 2004 and 2012 for refusing to renounce radical views, according to the Ministry of Islamic affairs. While there is no denying the effect of Wahhabi ideology on jihadi groups, there are many other sources of terrorism, notably repressive ruling structures in states that do not provide any hope of change for their people. Internet recruiting is now very effective yet beyond the control of states.

U.S.-Saudi relations: time of testing

The religion, lifestyle and values of Saudi society may be different from those of most Americans. However, the bargain reached in the post-World War II years that Saudi would supply oil to the world, especially U.S. allies, and the U.S. in return would guarantee its security, has continued to hold. Saudi Arabia has long been one of the closest U.S. allies in the Middle East. During the Cold War, it was a reliable friend that opposed any Soviet inroads. From the time the British voluntarily withdrew from the Gulf in 1971 until the Iranian revolution in 1979, Saudi Arabia and Iran constituted the "Twin Pillars" that protected American interests. In the 1980s, Saudis worked closely with the U.S. in Afghanistan, providing money and fighters to the mujahideen resistance, which eventually expelled the Soviet invaders. The Saudis also funded anti-communist movements and organizations throughout the world. The one big issue on which the countries differed was Israel and the Palestinians, and during the 1973 war between Israel and Arab states, Saudis acted with others to embargo oil to the U.S. in protest.

Today, the relationship has deteriorated in an alarming fashion. This is partly because of popular and media criticism that foreign policy elites can no longer control. Saudis felt betrayed during the Arab Spring when the U.S. did not prevent the overthrow of President Mubarak of Egypt, a close ally. Similarly, when Syria crossed Obama's redline by using chemical weapons in 2013, and the U.S. did not respond, Saudis questioned U.S. credibility. Worst of all, it seemed to Saudis that the U.S. under President Obama preferred Iran to the Sunni states who historically were the closest U.S. allies in the region.

When Obama was asked if he regarded the Saudis as friends, he replied, "It's complicated." His last official visit to the country in April 2016 revealed

President Barack Obama and King Salman walk to President Obama's motorcade after meeting at Erga Palace in Riyadh, Saudi Arabia, April 20, 2016. The president began a six day trip to strategize with his counterparts in Saudi Arabia, England and Germany on a broad range of issues with efforts to rein in the Islamic State group being the common denominator in all three stops. (CAROLYN KASTER/AP PHOTO)

deep differences, despite critical cooperation over security and counterterrorism. King Salman did publicly endorse the nuclear deal with Iran, to U.S relief. And a broader rapprochement between Iran and the U.S. has not developed as many in the region feared. Obama pressed the king to be willing to "share" the neighborhood with Iran — an appeal he did not appreciate. He has criticized the kingdom's harsh human rights record, as well as dissatisfaction with the war in Yemen. Obama also reiterated his view that Saudi Arabia and the GCC states in the future needed to rely less on the U.S. for their security.

The top U.S. priority in the region is neutralizing militant jihadist groups like al-Qaeda and ISIS. However, the Saudi priority is to counter Iranian and Shi'a influence, which U.S. actions seem to have increased. Since March 2015, a Saudi-led coalition has carried out airstrikes in Yemen in hopes of put-

ting down an insurrection by the Iranian-backed Houthis. (The amount of actual Iranian support for them is often exaggerated.) In response to a series of airstrikes on October 8 that "wrongly targeted" a funeral in the capital, Sanaa, more than 140 people were killed, leading to an international outcry. The National Security Council spokesman, Ned Price, said the U.S. would conduct an immediate review of its support for the Saudi-led coalition. (The administration could, as in the case of Bahrain's desire to buy additional F-16s, put the government on notice that it will not approve the sale unless there is progress on human rights issues.) The war in Yemen is an urgent policy concern, as the U.S. considers whether to scale back military assistance. If it does not, Congress could act to force it to do so.

There have been calls in Congress for the U.S. to take some action to curb the export of Wahhabism, regarded by

Children sit amidst the rubble of a house hit by Saudi-led coalition air strikes two days earlier on the outskirts of the Yemeni capital Sanaa on November 14, 2016. (MOHAMMED HUWAIS/AFP/GETTY IMAGES)

many as the root cause of terrorism. For example, Chris Murphy, a Democratic senator from Connecticut, charged in a January 2016 speech that "though ISIS has perverted Islam...the seeds of this perversion are rooted in a much more mainstream version of the faith that derives, in substantial part, from the teachings of Wahhabism." Professor Gause writes in *Foreign Affairs* that much of this is true: "Wahhabism is indeed intolerant, puritanical, and xenophobic... furthermore, ISIS and al Qaeda do share many elements of the Wahhabi worldview, especially regarding the role of Islam in public life." However, he points out that the Islam that Saudi Arabia was exporting until the time of the conflict in Afghanistan (1979–89) was not politicized, and by the 1990s the Saudis no longer controlled the global Salafi-Wahhabi movement. "What all of this means," Gause observes, "is that no amount of U.S. pressure on Saudi Arabia will alter the trajectory of Salafi jihadism, for that ideological movement is now independent of Saudi control."

Some point out that Saudi Arabia, especially at this time, is too important to lose as an ally. It is one of the few functioning states in the Middle East, and continues to supply the world with 13% of its oil—badly needed by U.S. allies—and as of October 2016 was the second largest supplier to the U.S. itself.

Washington depends on close cooperation with Saudis on counterterrorism, and they have provided warnings of imminent attacks—for example, a tip in 2010 foiled an attack on two American cargo planes. Saudi Arabia has also been a reliable customer for arms for decades, with some $110 billion sold under the Obama administration. Tens of thousands of Saudis have been educated in the U.S., and thousands of Americans have lived and worked there to build the modern state.

David B. Ottaway, longtime *Washington Post* reporter, believes that the effort to vilify Saudi Arabia is badly misplaced. He comments, "At a time when the United States is struggling mightily to find Middle East partners to implement its counterterrorism agenda, Saudi Arabia remains indispensable and still a willing one." Last October, a senior official in charge of blocking terrorist financing had praise for Saudi efforts to cut off funds for groups like al-Qaeda.

A struggle over U.S. legislation that would embarrass the Saudis and open the possibility of suing the government for supporting the 9/11 terrorists played out during 2016. The Justice Against Sponsors of Terrorism act (JASTA) was passed by overwhelming majorities in Congress, only to be vetoed by President Obama in September. With an eye on upcoming elections, and feel-

ing a duty to support the 9/11 families, Congress voted to override the veto on September 28. This bill was opposed by the administration on the basis that it would overturn longstanding principles of international law that protect sovereign states from lawsuits. It opens the door to lawsuits against individual Americans in foreign courts and puts U.S. assets at risk of seizure by overseas litigants.

Saudis had threatened that should the legislation pass, they would be forced to withdraw hundreds of billions of dollars in assets from U.S. jurisdiction, to protect themselves. So far, they have not done so. Some congressmen had second thoughts after the vote, and the administration hoped to make some adjustments in the lame-duck Congress. Even though they had hired an army of lobbyists to defeat the legislation, the vote clearly demonstrated that Saudi Arabia's clout with Washington is not what it used to be.

The next administration

What are the implications of a Trump presidency for U.S. policy in the Persian Gulf? Since the election, there has been much speculation about this, although little to go on given President-elect Trump's lack of specifics during the campaign. A lot will depend on who Trump chooses as advisors. Obviously his comments on banning Muslims from entering the U.S. and use of the term "radical Islamic terrorism" has upset some regional allies. The president-elect made clear his hostility to the Iranian nuclear deal, which he may seek to abrogate or more likely renegotiate. Trump clearly sides with the Sunni monarchs in their struggle against Iran, which could lead to improved ties with Saudi Arabia. However, he has also said (like Obama) that the Gulf monarchies were "free riders" that were dependent upon the U.S. for their security and have to "pay their way" in return for our defending them. It is likely that periodic U.S. complaints about human rights abuses and advocacy for democracy promotion in the region will be toned down. Saudi officials do not necessarily favor democratization, which they associate with the disastrous civil war in Iraq and the failed Arab Spring.

Trump seems to have a neo-isolationist bent and is disinclined to support sending U.S. ground forces to the region, which could affect the outcome in Iraq, Syria and other places. It is possible that by the time he takes office, successful offensives against Mosul and Raqqa, the main urban centers of ISIS, could have eliminated the threat of a territorial "caliphate." A major unknown is whether the U.S. could work with Russia against ISIS and acquiesce in leaving Bashar al-Assad in power in Damascus, at least in the short term. This would upset Gulf monarchs who see this as a win for Iranian policy.

★ ★ ★

These are difficult times in the Middle East, with the lack of effective regional leadership, the rise of sectarian politics, and drought, migration and economic crisis made worse by the plunge in oil prices. All these factors have helped produce radical Islamic groups and fueled wars in the region. The implosion of states such as Iraq and Syria that emerged after the collapse of the Ottoman Empire has led to a questioning of the borders imposed by colonial powers. The younger generation that drove the Arab Spring has been bitterly disappointed that its aims of democracy and better governance have not been met. A blame game is taking place among governments that are acting defensively and refuse to take responsibility for their actions.

Outside powers, such as the U.S., do not have solutions or even expertise, and have been worn down by never-ending conflicts in the Middle East. They would rather focus their attention elsewhere. But, inevitably, the Persian Gulf region is still important, above all as a major source of oil and gas and a market for U.S. goods. The countries of the Gulf Cooperation Council, especially Saudi Arabia, are critical allies in fighting the terrorist threat, and they can play a role in resisting extreme jihadi Islam.

A picture taken on January 17, 2016 in the Saudi capital Riyadh shows a portrait of Saudi King Salman bin Abdulaziz (center), Crown Prince Mohammed bin Nayef (left) and Deputy Crown Prince Mohammed bin Salman. (FAYEZ NURELDINE/AFP/GETTY IMAGES)

How much should it matter if many are repressive societies? How important should human rights be in forming U.S. policy toward the region? In the past, the answer was, not very. Should the U.S. push them to democratize? So far this has not worked well: Nation-building as it has played out in Afghanistan or Iraq has been a disaster. Should the U.S. press harder for women's rights, and if it does, will it get anywhere? Is it good policy to assuage Saudi anger by supporting their war in Yemen, as the U.S. and Britain have done?

Americans and U.S. policymakers are torn. The Saudis did not seem to appreciate that the Iran nuclear deal would protect them first and foremost, but were obsessed that the U.S. now seemed to favor a larger regional role for Iran at their expense. Conspiracy theories are the lifeblood of the region, after all. According to Robert S. Ford, former U.S. ambassador to Syria and Algeria, "Americans like to have someone to blame—a person, a political party or country. But it's a lot more complicated than that. I'd be careful about blaming the Saudis." Making foreign policy in a democracy is always a lot harder than in a country where one person, such as the Shah of Iran, or a small elite like the Al Saud, make all the decisions. Despite many predictions of its inevitable downfall, the House of Saud is still standing after 250 years.

The issue of terrorism troubles Americans greatly, and on this Saudi sends mixed signals: Wahhabism is clearly a source of radical Islamic ideology, but on the other hand, the Al Saud themselves are targets for not being Islamic enough. So far they have been helpful to the U.S. in exposing terrorists and warning of imminent attacks. Perhaps more of a distinction should be made between state policy and private support for jihadis. This is also a question of leverage, and the U.S. does not seem to have much at the moment.

For all its faults, Saudi Arabia is still one of the most stable countries in the Middle East. Of course, if the Vision 2030 plan fails, oil prices stay low and the government hesitates to impose a new social contract, the danger is there that things could go wrong quickly. The possibility of another change in Saudi leadership in the near future is unsettling. The U.S., it seems, is as divided over how to interpret Saudi actions as the Saudis are about U.S. fidelity. The reputation of Saudi these days in Washington is at a nadir, and defenders are hard to find. They may be "free riders" but they buy billions of dollars worth of weapons from the U.S. There is an important legacy of decades of friendship and security cooperation between the two countries, but it is clear that the relationship must continue to evolve. It is now up to the Trump administration to devise policies for a new era in the Middle East. ■

discussion questions

1. In formulating U.S. policy toward Saudi Arabia, how much emphasis should be placed on human rights? Should the U.S. continue to soft-pedal criticism out of strategic concerns?

2. Is "Wahhabism" the main problem in international terrorism?

3. The U.S. has talked about reducing its footprint in the Gulf and pivoting to Asia. Is this a realistic goal any time soon?

4. What has been the fallout of the Iraq War in the region? Why has sectarianism become worse afterward?

5. The U.S., Iran and Saudi Arabia all view the war in Yemen differently. How would you characterize the positions of the various sides, and how do you think the U.S. should proceed?

6. Should Saudi Arabia be willing to "share the neighborhood" with Iran, as President Obama suggested?

Don't forget: Ballots start on page 115!

suggested readings

Al-Rasheed, Madawi, **A History of Saudi Arabia (2nd ed.)**. New York: Cambridge University Press, 2010. 342 pp. This overview by a prominent expatriate Saudi historian discusses the challenges facing the state in the 21st century.

Gause, F. Gregory, III, "The Future of U.S.–Saudi Relations: The Kingdom and the Power," **Foreign Affairs**, vol. 95 no. 4, 2016, pp. 114–26. This article by a leading scholar provides a recent update on the U.S.-Saudi relationship.

– – –, **The International Relations of the Persian Gulf**. New York: Cambridge University Press, 2010. 270 pp. This one-volume treatment covers the wars that have reshaped the region since 1980.

Haykel, Bernard, Hegghammer, Thomas and Lacroix, Stéphane, eds., **Saudi Arabia in Transition: Insights on Social, Political, Economic and Religious Change**. Cambridge: Cambridge University Press, 2015. 360 pp. In this book, prominent Saudi and foreign scholars present the conclusions of their research on the Kingdom's society, culture, economy and politics.

Long, David E., and Maisel, Sebastian, **The Kingdom of Saudi Arabia (2nd ed.)**. Gainesville: University Press of Florida, 2010. 176 pp. Long and Maisel present a general survey of Saudi Arabia, based on extensive firsthand experience.

Matthiesen, Toby, **The Other Saudis: Shiism, Dissent and Sectarianism**. Cambridge: Cambridge University Press, 2015. 292 pp. This book examines the role of Saudi Arabia's marginalized Shi'a minority, who are geographically focused in the Kingdom's oil-rich Eastern Province.

Munif, Abdelrahman, **Cities of Salt** (trans. Peter Theroux). New York: Vintage Books, 1989. 640 pp. Banned in Saudi Arabia, this novel chronicles the profound changes caused there by the discovery of oil.

Potter, Lawrence G., "The Persian Gulf: Tradition and Transformation." **Headline Series**, Nos. 333–34. New York: Foreign Policy Association, 2011. 136 pp. This publication provides an overview of the recent historical evolution of the Persian Gulf.

To access web links to these readings, as well as links to additional, shorter readings and suggested web sites,
GO TO www.greatdecisions.org
and click on the topic under Resources, on the right-hand side of the page

U.S. foreign policy and petroleum

by Jonathan Chanis

The overground drives for reciprocating piston pumps (also known as pump jacks, horse heads or nodding donkeys) at the Lost Hills oil field in California. (DAVID MCNEW/GETTY IMAGES)

During the last 45 years, the United States has experienced alternating periods of energy security and insecurity. There were the oil shocks of 1973–74 and 1979–81; the quiescent phase of the mid-1980s through the very early 2000s; the more difficult years of 2004–12; and now the current period of lower energy prices and more secure supplies. During all of these phases and even earlier, U.S. foreign policy was shaped either directly or indirectly by energy and petroleum security concerns. While energy security and foreign policy success are not mutually exclusive, each influences and often constrains the other.

The relationship between petroleum and foreign policy is difficult to analyze with precision. Especially today, after the vast increase in domestic U.S. petroleum production, i.e., the "energy revolution," some look at the geopolitics of oil and ask if this revolution improved U.S. foreign policy.

Many find the benefits hard to see. While U.S. energy security has clearly improved, its contribution to the success of U.S. foreign policy has been uncertain at best. There are several reasons why.

JONATHAN CHANIS *has worked in investment management, emerging markets finance, and commodities trading for over 25 years. Currently he manages New Tide Asset Management, a company focused on global and resource consulting. He previously worked at Tribeca Global Management and at Caxton Associates where he traded energy and emerging market equities, and commodities and currencies. Mr. Chanis holds a Ph.D. in political science from the Graduate School, CUNY, and a B.A. in economics from Brooklyn College. Over the last seven years, he has taught graduate and undergraduate courses on, among other subjects, energy security, international politics, and political economy.*

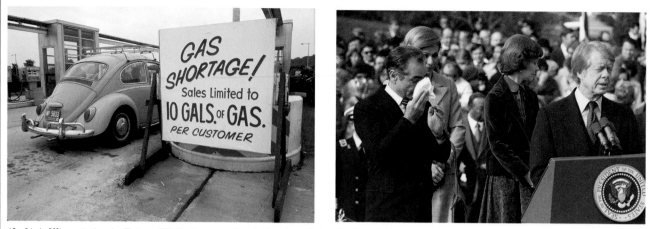

(Left) A filling station in Eaton, CT, limits gas sales during the oil shock of 1973–74. (OWEN FRANKEN/CORBIS/GETTY IMAGES) (Right) The Shah of Iran wipes tear gas from his eyes as President Jimmy Carter speaks in Washington, D.C., November 15, 1977. Empress Farah Pahlavi of Iran and Mrs. Carter turn away during ceremonies on the South Lawn. The tear gas came from a demonstration outside the White House. (AP PHOTO)

First, proving causality between anything as complicated as U.S. foreign policy and a single variable is difficult, and often impossible. In contrast to the physical world, the causes of an action or policy by a person or country can be obscure. And while it may be intellectually or emotionally satisfying to offer mono-causal explanations, complex phenomena such as U.S. foreign policy often have multiple causes. For example, why did the United States invade Iraq in 2003? Was it for the oil? Perhaps the George W. Bush administration did not think it could continue to contain Iraq. Or maybe the administration learned the wrong lessons from the successful use of force in the Balkans and thought it could reshape the Middle East with a single military act. Analysts and historians will argue about this for years and the best that might be expected are differing interpretations based on ideology and changing social values.

Second, even if improved U.S. petroleum security circumstances provide new opportunities for more

successful policies, these new circumstances have to be recognized by policymakers. There is a reason that the events of 1973–74 were called an "oil shock." The shortages and price rise not only disrupted the economy, but caught most policymakers completely by surprise. Similarly today, policymakers and pundits may fail to appreciate the threats and opportunities that are created by changing social forces and petroleum supply-demand dynamics.

Third, while the improvement in U.S. energy security has reduced America's energy vulnerability, it has not eliminated it. As discussed below, the energy security gains over the last ten years have been substantial, but the "energy revolution" has not liberated the United States from dependence on foreign suppliers, nor has it disconnected the domestic market from global price trends.

In spite of the limitations on our understating of the relationship between foreign policy and petroleum, a number of interesting and useful observations can be made. Moreover, when examining this relationship, several policies and actions tend to repeat themselves. Awareness of these repetitive patterns may improve discussions of U.S. foreign policy; it may even lead to improved policy.

In order to analyze these patterns, this narrative will proceed by defining

energy security and the U.S. oil revolution; examining the role of prices and the investment cycle; reviewing the history of petroleum's impact on U.S. foreign policy; and concluding with several policy questions.

Energy security defined

It is easy to forget that coal, natural gas and petroleum are vital to the daily lives of people in the developed world. If a product is not made from stone or wood, it is almost always made from or with coal, natural gas and/or petroleum. And virtually everything is transported by burning refined petroleum products, natural gas or coal. The key component of fossil fuels, the hydrocarbon molecule, is the basis of modern life. While the evidence is increasingly clear that fossil fuels have contributed to global warming, the debate continues over when society will achieve the transition away from hydrocarbons. But whether that transition is 30 years away or 100, countries still must obtain and often increase an affordable and uninterrupted supply of these fuels over the next one to two decades. To do otherwise risks severe economic hardship for most, and continued energy deprivation and poverty for many. As has been seen from occasions like Superstorm Sandy or Hurricane Katrina, inadequate fuel supplies can have disastrous consequences.

A comprehensive understanding of energy security includes threats not just from the malicious actions of states or non-state actors, but also from unintentional, man-made accidents, and from natural disasters. Consequently, energy security covers the ability to manage supply disruptions and recover quickly through the establishment and maintenance of resilient infrastructure. Secure energy is readily available, affordable and not subject to interruption. In its broadest sense, a discussion of energy security includes all primary sources of energy—from coal, natural gas, nuclear and petroleum, to alternatives like biomass, geothermal, solar, hydroelectric and wind.

For the United States, petroleum has an oversized role in energy security discussions because the other sources of energy are largely abundant domestically and thus less vulnerable to disruption by foreign states. Unlike in the power generation sector, there are virtually no short or near-term substitutes for petroleum in the transportation sector. Electric cars probably will dominate the global vehicle fleet in 30 or 40 years. Right now, according to the International Energy Agency (IEA), they constitute less than 0.1% of all vehicles. It will be a long time before everyone drives an electric car. In the interim, the world is almost entirely dependent on gasoline, diesel fuel and jet fuel for transportation.

Petroleum also looms large in energy security because it remains absolutely necessary for the maintenance of national defense and the conduct of modern war. According the to the U.S. Defense Science Board, the amount of petroleum consumed in World War I (WWI) was less than one gallon per U.S. soldier per day. This figure rose to slightly less than two in World War II (WWII), ten in Vietnam, and almost 30 in the Second Gulf War. The contrast between the increasing energy efficiency of civilian transportation and manufacturing with ever increasing military consumption is stark. It is for this reason that the U.S. Department of Defense has become one of the most significant supporters of alternative energy research.

In thinking about energy security, an important distinction can be made between "sensitivity" and "vulnerability." As political scientist Joseph Nye has written, sensitivity is how quickly change in one part of a system brings change in another part of that system. Vulnerability is about how "costly" it is to change the structure of sensitivity. It is about the ability to cope with, or adjust to the consequences of a change in the system. In order to be vulnerable, a country must be sensitive. But not all sensitivity leads to vulnerability.

For petroleum, not every change to the global system of production and consumption affects energy security. For example, a production outage in any single producer country may or may not affect global consumers. Whether the outage is costly depends on factors such as local or global inventory levels, global spare production capacity or existing logistical linkages.

An easy way to observe U.S. sensitivity is by measuring how much of total petroleum consumption comes from foreign suppliers (i.e., net imports divided by consumption). Peaks in this net import dependency have tended to be accompanied by peaks in concern about U.S. energy security. Simply, if a country imports a large amount of foreign petroleum, it may be damaged if this petroleum is cut off. Conversely, if it imports no foreign petroleum, its foreign supply cannot be cut off. If there is no sensitivity (e.g., imports), there is no (or less) vulnerability. The graph below, left, illustrates how U.S. sensitivity to a foreign petroleum cutoff has declined markedly in the last several years. However, other factors, such price (i.e., affordability), also have to be considered in order to gain a complete picture of U.S. vulnerability.

The U.S. oil revolution

The substantial decline in U.S. import dependence was due exclusively to an increase in U.S. domestic petroleum (and natural gas) production. When assessing U.S. production and security, it is usually better to examine "liquids" production, rather than just crude oil production, because refined products are made from more than just crude oil. Liquids production includes crude oil, condensate, tight and heavy oils, natural gas plant liquids, biofuels, and refinery processing gains. Between 2008 and 2015, U.S. "liquids" production increased 90% from 7.8 million barrels per day (mmbd), to 14.8 mmbd.

The United States has been the world's leader in liquids production since 2013 and it is unlikely to give

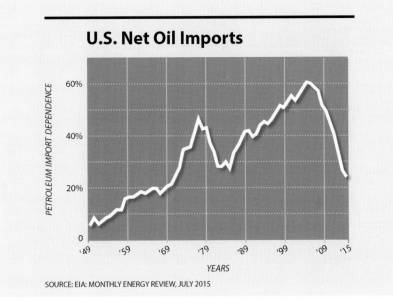

U.S. Net Oil Imports

PETROLEUM IMPORT DEPENDENCE

60%

40%

20%

0

'49 '59 '69 '79 '89 '99 '09 '15

YEARS

SOURCE: EIA: MONTHLY ENERGY REVIEW, JULY 2015

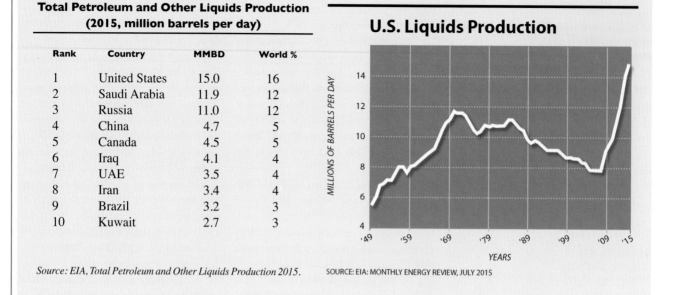

Total Petroleum and Other Liquids Production (2015, million barrels per day)

Rank	Country	MMBD	World %
1	United States	15.0	16
2	Saudi Arabia	11.9	12
3	Russia	11.0	12
4	China	4.7	5
5	Canada	4.5	5
6	Iraq	4.1	4
7	UAE	3.5	4
8	Iran	3.4	4
9	Brazil	3.2	3
10	Kuwait	2.7	3

Source: EIA, Total Petroleum and Other Liquids Production 2015.

U.S. Liquids Production

SOURCE: EIA: MONTHLY ENERGY REVIEW, JULY 2015

up this position unless there is a major change to domestic U.S. energy policy. As is indicated by the table above, the United States is an energy superpower. And this advantage is further solidified by its high production of energy though natural gas (where it is first), coal (where it is second to China), hydro (where it is fourth behind China, Brazil and Canada) and nuclear (where it is first).

While the common picture of the oil industry is of men in dirty coveralls huddled on a drilling platform, the reality is that oil production is a high-tech industry. Advances in petrology (the study of rocks), fluid dynamics, engineering and computing pioneered during the last 20 years have allowed the industry to extract oil (and natural gas) from reservoirs that were previously thought to be uneconomic. The basis of this revolution is found in three technological developments: hydraulic fracturing, horizontal drilling and advanced 3D seismic imaging (*See adjacent box*).

Notwithstanding concerns over global warming and "fugitive" methane emissions, ground water pollution and earthquakes, the domestic U.S. industry is now heavily dependent on hydraulic fracturing. According to the EIA, more than half of all U.S. crude oil production, and approximately two thirds of natural gas production come from fracked wells. If the United States stopped hydraulic fracturing, its domestic oil and gas production would decline sharply over a very short period of time. Not only would this completely reverse the U.S. import dependency ratio and increase U.S. sensitivity and vulnerability, but it would substantially raise domestic gasoline and electricity prices. ■

Hydraulic fracturing, horizontal drilling and advanced 3D seismic imaging

Hydraulic fracturing increases the permeability of a hydrocarbon reservoir by pumping large amounts of water with specialty chemicals at high pressure into the reservoir. This fractures the rock and increases the flow characteristics of the reservoir.

Horizontal drilling is a process in which the drilling starts vertically at the surface and then extends to a subsurface location where it veers off on an arc and continues at a near-horizontal tangent. This ultimately allows the production pipe to access more of the reserves, since reservoirs usually are much larger horizontally than they are vertically.

Advanced 3D seismic imaging uses geophones and other devices to create high-definition pictures of subsurface geology. By sending and recording sound waves as they bounce off underground rock structures, the petroleum or natural gas (if they exist) are better revealed. Increasingly sophisticated computer software also is used for data analysis.

Prices, the investment cycle and petroleum security

In many ways, the current oil revolution is not a revolution but a renaissance. Historically, the current period repeats a pattern of surging U.S. domestic production and dramatically falling prices. What is clear from this pattern of abundance and scarcity is that abundance phases tend to be much longer than scarcity phases. The real historical problem of the oil and gas industry is not shortages and high prices, but surpluses and low prices. This is why the industry has been so prone to collusion (i.e., the Rockefeller Trust during the 1880s, "Seven Sisters" dominance from the 1920s through the 1960s and OPEC since the 1970s).

Discoveries in 1899, 1901, 1921 and 1926 all created vast surpluses of oil. Shortly after each of these discoveries, prices collapsed. A more contemporary example is the 1980s surge in production from the North Slope of Alaska and the deep waters of the U.S. Gulf of Mexico. This additional production (together with increased North Sea production) suppressed prices for almost a decade and a half.

When prices rise, people are incentivized both to look for petroleum in more remote locations and to improve the technology to extract these resources. Consequently, the "frontier" of oil production continually moves into locations that were previously inaccessible or unprofitable to exploit. In earlier days, the oil frontier was primarily geographic and geologic: Companies had to go to the far corners of the earth to find petroleum. Today, however, we largely know where most of the petroleum is located. The oil frontier is primarily about land access, technology, management skills and capital. The role of capital, or funding for oil exploration and devel-

The largest oil refinery in the U.S. at that time in Richmond, California, 1912. It was in the possession of the first world-wide oil company, the Standard Oil Company of John D. Rockefeller. The refinery is still in operation today and it is owned by the Chevron Corporation, a Standard Oil successor company.(SZ PHOTO/BRIDGEMAN IMAGES)

opment, is particularly critical because it vastly complicates the management of energy security.

After the 1980s production surge, companies drastically reduced their capital expenditures for exploration and development. By 2000, the industry globally was spending less than $250 billion a year. As a result, when demand in China and other locations rose dramatically in the mid-2000s, the production capacity to meet this demand did not exist and prices rose sharply. Eventually, with demand and prices higher, the industry responded with a significant increase in capital expenditures. The only problem is that most of this spending took years to produce more oil. In any event, by 2014 the industry was spending more than $680 billion per year on exploration and development. This investment surge

was the primary cause of the current oil surplus and lower prices. But now, as a result of this current over-supply, the industry has drastically reduced investment spending and it is expected to spend approximately less than $440 billion in 2016.

The oil industry is unique in both the scale of its investments and the time necessary to realize a return. Virtually no other industry has to invest as much money or wait as long to earn a return. As a result, the petroleum investment cycle is extremely volatile and it swings from massive overfunding, to extreme under-investment. (While the advent of shale and tight oil has marginally changed this, the bulk of future production gains still has to come from multibillion dollar projects stretching out for a decade or more.) The problem with this in-

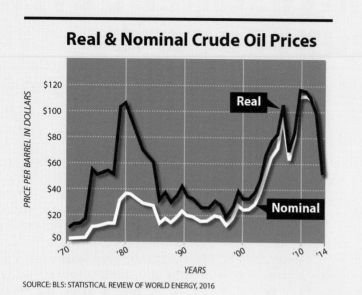

Real & Nominal Crude Oil Prices

PRICE PER BARREL IN DOLLARS

Real

Nominal

YEARS

SOURCE: BLS: STATISTICAL REVIEW OF WORLD ENERGY, 2016

Gasoline & Other Energy Expenditures

PERSONAL CONSUMPTION

- Change the pattern of spending.
- Lower the profitability of most industries, especially manufacturing.
- Transfer income from consumers to producers.
- Make sizable parts of the capital stock obsolete.
- Increase the wealth of oil exporting countries and decrease the wealth of oil importing countries

The negative impact of higher petroleum prices on non-petroleum producing economies depends on a number of variables, especially the energy intensity of the economy (i.e., energy consumption per unit of gross domestic product [GDP]). Obviously, the more petroleum used to produce a unit of GDP, the greater the disruption from higher prices. In general, however, the degree of disruption is dependent on the magnitude of the price increase, the speed with which it arrives and its persistence.

The political problem of higher energy prices in the United States is straightforward. Besides the more complicated economic problems mentioned above, the basic issue is that most Americans do not like to pay, and often many cannot pay, high prices for gasoline. This is particularly true at lower income levels where people have to pay a much higher percentage of their income for gasoline.

An easy way to understand this is to look at the price of gasoline as a percentage of what Americans earn, and then correlate it with news stories indicating dissatisfaction with high gasoline prices. Clearly, there is a percentage of personal expenditures for gasoline beyond which people become very dissatisfied and complain politically. The accompanying chart is based on *pretax income and it excludes electric and gas service charges.* Based on the experiences of 1970–85, 2006–08, and 2011–14, one can say that in the United States, when expenditures on gasoline approach 3% of pretax income, people start to question why prices are rising and they resentfully adjust their budgets to reallocate more

vestment cycle is that at the ends of each phase there are either massive shortages or enormous surpluses of oil. This leads to large misallocations of capital when petroleum is oversupplied (because many investments have zero or negative return), and heightened political vulnerability and economic dislocation when petroleum is under-supplied.

The consequences of high petroleum prices

The deleterious impact of extremely high oil prices on the non-petroleum producing economies is well known. Extremely high prices:

- Lower real wages.
- Lower overall consumer spending.
- Cause either inflation or a decline in living standards (or both).

The impact of petroleum on U.S. foreign policy

money for fuel. When prices approach 4%, people complain about price gouging, denounce "exorbitant" oil industry profits, and ask for government investigations and other actions to lower prices. At close to 5%, violence by motorists and truckers to try to force prices lower is not unknown, and Congress summons oil industry leaders to Washington to testify under oath (and peril of perjury) and then threatens them with anti-industry legislative action. The ubiquity and visibility of gasoline prices tends to make it a proxy for how people feel about their own economic situation. Paying "too much" for gasoline disturbs consumers, and there even tends to be an inverse correlation between gasoline prices and presidential approval ratings. Clearly, a politician vying for popularity wants to keep gasoline prices closer to that 3% pretax figure.

In the earlier description of the U.S. petroleum investment cycles, the period between the 1930s and the 1980s was omitted. This was because the investment response to the oil shortage scare at the end of the Second World War was to expand exploration and development in the Middle East, not the United States. By the end of the WWII, the "easy" U.S. oil was discovered and largely depleted. The accessible and inexpensive oil was now predominantly in the Persian Gulf. This transfer of the geographic center of the industry to the Middle East confirmed that the world was, once again, *not* running out of petroleum. But this transfer also compounded the traditional investment cycle challenge with a new geographic challenge. Not only was the oil "in the wrong place," but these local governments were determined to gain control over their resources and break the integrated system of private company investment planning. So, how did the U.S. government transition to a petroleum world not dominated by the United States? And how, specifically, has petroleum interacted to shape or constrain U.S. foreign policy before, during and since this transition? ∎

As stated by the political scientist Karl Deutsch, a policy is an "explicit set of preferences and plans drawn up in order to make the outcomes of a series of future decisions more nearly predictable and consistent." Consequently, foreign policy consists of those preferences and plans that guide the actions and relations of a state with other states. When the United States has had the ability to pursue its petroleum preferences, it has revealed a number of consistent patterns. One of the most enduring preferences is the use of petroleum to supply fuel to allies and deny it to adversaries. Many other U.S. preferences, such as heightened concern for the political (i.e., pro- or anti-American) orientation of particular petroleum producing states, the

A tanker ship leaves San Francisco Bay, 2006. (PAUL COLLIS/ALAMY)

provision of security guarantees to selected states and, to a lesser extent, the U.S. naval role in supporting the international movement of petroleum, can be understood as derivative from this dominant preference.

Another way to understand this is by distinguishing between petroleum as an "end" of policy, and petroleum as an "instrument" of policy. If the goal of policy is to ensure adequate petroleum for the military and domestic society, it is an end. If policy is concerned with using petroleum to further other foreign policy objectives, it is an instrument. Insofar as petroleum is just another instrument of power, it is no different than economic, diplomatic or military instruments. Manipulating the supply of energy to enemies or allies in periods when the country is not at war is neither moral nor immoral. If one takes a strong position on the need for the United States to protect the physical and economic wellbeing of its population by acting internationally, then potentially using petroleum as an instrument of policy, or as a "weapon" is logical.

For most of the period since petroleum has been internationally relevant (roughly 1900 to today), it has usually been an instrument of U.S. foreign policy. When not forced by domestic petroleum insecurity to do otherwise, the U.S has pursued its preference to supply petroleum to allies and potentially or actually threaten adversaries with energy denial. Based on studies by historians and analysts such as David Painter and Daniel Yergin, the phases of U.S. petroleum and foreign policy can be divided into the six periods below. To a small extent, several dates are arbitrary, but for the purposes of this analysis, the existing divisions illustrate the necessary points.

Phase 1: production dominance and political advantage, 1900–45

From 1900 until 1945, the United States was not only able to meet its own petroleum demand from domestic production, it also was able to export petroleum to the rest of the world. Consequently, petroleum was an instrument of U.S. policy. During WWI, the United States supplied over 80% of the fuel consumed by its European Allies. During WWII, the United States was the primary supplier of fuel to Britain and other allies. Additionally, the 1941 U.S. decision to embargo gasoline sales to Japan clearly illustrated the use of petroleum as an instrument of policy. Although Japanese consumption of gasoline and other petroleum products constituted less than 10% of its total energy consumption, it was heavily dependent on U.S.-sourced gasoline for civilian and military transportation uses. By embargoing the sale of gasoline, the United States thought it could force Japan to withdrawn from recently conquered French Indochi-na and other areas. However, Japan refused to comply with America's terms, and instead it decided to attack U.S. forces at Pearl Harbor, Hawaii, and invade the Dutch East Indies oil fields. The U.S. entry into WWII followed less than five months after the U.S. gasoline embargo.

Other U.S. preferences, such as heightened concern for the political orientation of particular petroleum-producing states and intervention into local producer state affairs also became evident during this period. This was particularly important by the mid-1930s, when the U.S. ability to maintain high global exports began declining as its own oil fields depleted. In order to source petroleum to sell abroad, especially to Europe, U.S. companies began producing and exporting petroleum from Mexico, and then Venezuela. This third country sourcing encouraged the United States to promote more actively pro-U.S. governments and pro-U.S. corporate regimes, especially in Venezuela. An illustration of deep U.S. involvement in the local affairs of a producer country in support of international oil company (IOC) interests occurred in 1943, when the U.S. government helped the IOCs resolve a number of disputes with the Venezuelan government over profit-sharing and the nature and duration of their concessions. U.S. government intervention in Venezuela allowed the IOCs to secure and expand their oil production in that country. This was important not just in fueling U.S. and allied war efforts between 1943 and 1945, but also in allowing the U.S. IOCs to dominate the global supply of fuel during the next phase.

Phase 2: supply and demand transformed and policy blindness, 1946–73

During the Cold War, the manipulation of oil supplies became integral to U.S. foreign policy. Neither Western Europe nor Japan had significant supplies of locally produced petroleum, and the United States facilitated fuel acquisition by these countries. While on the one level this was virtuous, on the other it clearly created an asymmetric dependence on the United States that was ripe for exploitation. A few examples of this dependence or its consequences include:

- Under the U.S. Marshall Plan, approximately 10% of aid was used to pay for petroleum purchased from American companies.
- In 1949, the Truman administration made the first of several security guarantees to Saudi Arabia. Also in 1949, unbeknownst to Saudi Arabia and the other local governments, the United States and Britain developed detailed plans and capabilities to destroy the Saudi and other Middle East oil fields in the event of a Soviet attempt to seize them.
- In 1953, the United States worked with Britain to overthrow the legitimately elected government of Iran in order to reverse that country's nationalization of the Anglo-Iran Oil Company.
- In 1956, after Britain, France and Israel seized the Suez Canal from Egypt, President Dwight Eisenhower threatened them with

Men studying an oil flow chart showing the course of oil through a refinery to supply fuel for American combat units fighting in World War II, 1944. (GRANGER, NYC)

(among other things) restricted oil access if they did not withdraw. The 1956, use of petroleum is especially interesting because it did not follow the traditional pattern of supporting the IOCs and foreign control. Eisenhower thought that by backing Gamal Abdel Nasser, Egypt would become more supportive of U.S. interests. Instead, President Nasser went on to lead the anti-Western, pan-Arab nationalist movement, to more strongly align Egypt with the Soviet Union and to undermine U.S. regional interests, especially in Iraq. Years later, Eisenhower was said to have told his former vice president, Richard Nixon, that Suez "was his major foreign policy mistake."

- From 1968–71, as the British withdrew from east of the Suez, the United States increased its military presence in the region in order to support its existing security guarantees and to assume the freedom of navigation role formerly undertaken by Britain.

As the United States was increasing its regional commitments and using petroleum for policy advantage, it also was losing its position as the globally dominant petroleum producer. Few diplomats or analysts perceive this change, and U.S. policymakers rushed headlong into the disaster of 1973. From 1945 until 1970, U.S. oil production almost doubled from approximately 5 mmbd to more than 9 mmbd. But this was insufficient to meet the rapid growth of U.S. or global demand. From 1965 through 1974, global petroleum consumption increased 45% from 30.7 mmbd to 55.6 mmbd. This coincided with the peaking of U.S. crude oil production in November 1970 at 10 mmbd.

Internationally, changes were also becoming obvious. In 1951 (as noted), the popularly elected Iranian government nationalized the Anglo-Iran Oil Company. In 1956, in response to the Suez seizure, Saudi Arabia and several other Arab oil pro-

In a simple ceremony in the White House Rose Garden, President Truman and members of his cabinet bid farewell to Ambassador W. Averell Harriman, just before he left for Iran to seek a peace in the British-Iranian oil dispute. Left to right are: Secretary of State Dean Acheson, Harriman, President Truman, and Defense Secretary George C. Marshall. (BETTMANN/GETTY IMAGES)

ducers first used the "oil weapon" by organizing (an unsuccessful) oil boycott of Britain and France. In 1960, in order to improve the commercial terms of their relationships with the IOCs, Venezuela, Iran, Saudi Arabia, Kuwait and Iraq formed the Organization of Petroleum Exporting Countries (OPEC). The founding OPEC states were dissatisfied with the price they were receiving for their oil and their lack of control over production decisions. In particular, the IOCs maintained a pricing formula that allocated most of the production profits to themselves and not to the producer countries. OPEC's founding was the beginning of the producer countries successful efforts to take control of their resources.

In 1967, Saudi Arabia and several other Arab oil producer states again tried to use the "oil weapon" by organizing (an unsuccessful) boycott of several Western countries over support for Israel in the Six Day War. Several Arab oil producers hoped that by restricting sales to the United States, Great Britain and West Germany, and by keeping the Suez Canal

closed even after the war, they could force a less favorable settlement on Israel. However, Iran, the United States and Venezuela all increased production and compensated for the lost Arab production. Additionally, after the experience of the 1956 Suez disruption, the industry began building and using "supertankers" (or Very Large Crude Carriers, VLCCs). This allowed them to reroute the new supplies efficiently without transiting the Suez Canal. One of the more interesting possible effects of the 1967 experience was that it may have lulled U.S. policymakers into believing they could successfully manipulate oil as an instrument of foreign policy. This belief was to be seriously undermined during the next phase.

Phase 3: the crisis years, 1974–81

During this phase, the United States was confronted with an economic and political crisis. In 1949, the U.S. import dependency was under 5.5%, but by 1973 it was nearly 35%. In the wake of the October 1973

Mideast War, the Arab members of OPEC embargoed shipments of crude oil to the United States and several other countries, and reduced production. Although the reduction was only 7–8% of global supply, this modest cutback (not the embargo) was sufficient to raise prices from approximately $3 per barrel to over $12 in March 1974. (While the embargo was symbolically very important for both the Arab producers and the targeted consumer countries, its primary impact was to create a logistical headache for the IOCs. It was not the major cause of the price rise.) After the 1979 Iranian Revolution and the ensuing production decline in that country, prices rose from approxi-

A demonstrator in front of a burning car during a riot in response to the gas shortage in Levittown, Pa., on June 25, 1979. Hundreds of police later dispersed a crowd of thousands and at least 16 persons including six police officers were injured. (SUZANNE PLUNKET/TRENTON TIMES/AP PHOTO)

mately $12, to over $40. Securing an adequate and affordable supply of petroleum became a dominant end of U.S. foreign policy. The United States no longer had the luxury of using petroleum as an instrument. U.S. efforts to secure adequate petroleum supplies during this period were complicated by a wave of expropriation and nationalization of IOC assets in most all producing countries.

While U.S. vulnerability was not as extreme as in Europe, or especially Japan—where import dependence was much higher—it was still profoundly disruptive. The direct domestic economic consequences of the price rises included a decline in real wages and consumer spending; high inflation; less profitable or uncompetitive manufacturing industries; and income and wealth transfers from U.S. consumers to oil producers.

This was a particularly difficult time for Americans not simply because they were spending more than 5% of their pretax income on fuel, but also because there were periods when fuel was unavailable at any price. Americans were not assaulting each other by the hundreds of thousands at the gas pumps, but extreme violence was not unknown. One of the more spectacular episodes of civil disorder occurred in June 1979 in Levittown, PA, when more than 2,000 rioters clashed with police over three days.

The oil shocks also fractured U.S. alliance relationships by exposing the inability of the United States to guarantee petroleum supplies to allies. As noted previously, one of the points of manipulating petroleum as an instrument of foreign policy is to make other states beholden to the supplier for the security of their energy supplies. If the United States were unable to provide this energy security, then the West Europeans and Japanese would have to secure their own supply and a U.S. advantage in the relationship would disappear. Further disturbing these allied relationships was the fact that by 1976, the Soviet Union had emerged as the largest global producer of petroleum. The U.S.' ability to use petroleum as an instrument of foreign policy was declining, while Soviet ability to use it as an instrument was increasing.

While the United States briefly considered invading Saudi Arabia and seizing the oil fields in 1974 and 1975, this was ultimately abandoned for an approach that included a number of positive inducements. The U.S. increased diplomatic contacts (including between Israel and its Arab enemies), weapons sales, security training and military basing. And although invasion was not publicly spoken of by U.S. officials, surely the threat could never be completely forgotten by those in the region.

Underlying U.S. policy at this time was an effort to create offsetting dependencies. In order to balance the newfound U.S. petroleum vulnerability, Washington sought to make regional states beholden in other areas—their physical security, especially. A very public affirmation of the U.S. security guarantee occurred after the fall of the Shah of Iran, when President Jimmy Carter affirmed the U.S. willingness to use force to protect the Middle East oil fields in 1980. In retrospect, the promulgation of the Carter Doctrine was the watershed moment in U.S. involvement in the Middle East. By declaring the Middle East vital to U.S. interests, the intellectual justifications and military-industrial incentives for what later would become decades of intervention and war were created.

Phase 4: managing the supply surplus, 1982–2003

Phase 4 saw the United States again treating petroleum as an instrument of policy. Part of the evolving U.S.-Saudi understanding was that Saudi Arabia would attempt to use its influence to keep oil prices moderate, or just high enough to meet their fiscal objectives, but not so high as to damage the economic interests of the United States. While not the only basis for the U.S.-Saudi relationship, the "oil for security" element clearly was paramount. What made the bargain immensely easier was that the investment boom of the late 1970s resulted in massive petroleum production overcapacity. There was too much production capacity not just in the aforementioned Alaskan, Gulf of Mexico and North Sea fields, but also in most all producing countries from Saudi Arabia and Kuwait, to Russia and Venezuela. During this phase, prices tended to gyrate between $10 and $25 per barrel, and U.S. consumers reaped the benefits by not paying more than 2.5–3% of pretax income for gasoline. Remarkably, during this phase the United States even complained to Saudi Arabia on at least two occasions that petroleum prices were too low.

During this period, the United States confirmed its security guarantee to various Middle East countries when it intervened in the 1984–88 Iran-Iraq Tanker Wars, and when it liberated Kuwait from Iraqi occupation in 1991. In 1987, the U.S. Navy began escorting Kuwaiti and Saudi oil tankers out of the Persian Gulf in an effort to protect them from Iranian attack. The liberation of Kuwait stopped Iraq from gaining control over Kuwaiti production and reserves, and it (temporarily) removed the threat to Saudi Arabian production and reserves. Both instances, as well as the stationing of U.S. forces in Saudi Arabia after the First Gulf War, demonstrated the U.S. commitment to guarantee the global supply

of oil and protect its allies. It also reaffirmed the role of petroleum as a valuable instrument of U.S. policy. But the United States was now extraordinarily intertwined in the politics of the region and its commitment to the survival of various regimes such as Saudi Arabia was very high. The events of 9/11 caused many to question the basis for U.S.-Saudi cooperation, but it did not cause a decline in the flow of oil out of the region, or fundamentally disturb the existing U.S. security guarantees.

Paradoxically, the very low oil prices of the late 1980s and 1990s probably were a factor in the U.S. decision to invade Iraq in 2003. Had global oil supplies been tighter, the perceived risk of the invasion triggering a disruptive oil price increase would have been higher. In any event, the Second Gulf War was at least coincident with the start of a multiyear trend toward higher oil prices. While the price rise arguably had more to do with the global petroleum investment cycle, the loss on average of over half a million barrels per day of Iraqi production from 2003 through 2007 (as compared to 1998 through 2002) clearly pressured prices higher.

Phase 5: revenge of the investment cycle and constrained policy options, 2004–12

Phase 5 is particularly interesting because it (again) caught many analysts and policy makers by surprise. Beginning in 2003, oil prices began to increase, and except for a brief interruption due to the 2008 financial crises, they did not peak (on an annual basis) until 2012. As prices began to climb, the United States was presented with an array of problems that looked eerily similar to those it faced in the 1970s. By 2005, U.S. import dependency was an astonishing 60%, and the higher prices were beginning to disrupt the domestic economy and cause political discontent. People started complaining about oil company price gouging; the media and some

policy institutes denounced "exorbitant" oil industry profits; government investigations, both at the state and federal level were organized. As a Gallup Poll in 2005 stated: "Americans' negative views of the oil and gas companies—and their desire to see the government do something about them—are certainly related to the fact that gas prices continue to be seen as the top economic problem facing the country today."

Internationally, higher prices and the revenue they generated for states like Iran, Russia and Venezuela also were undermining a number of U.S. foreign policy goals. While it is difficult to connect petroleum to any single foreign policy act, it can be said that the substantially increased revenue generated by higher prices made it easier for those states to pursue policies at odds with U.S. goals (e.g., Iran's nuclear weapons program, Russia's increased defense spending and Venezuela's support for anti-U.S. Latin American states). And even with countries where the United States did not have adversarial relationships such Brazil and Nigeria, higher prices were contributing to a number of negative changes, such as an increase in corruption. As prices climbed, the United States began to be more concerned with petroleum as an end of policy.

This period, like the one that preceded it, may be dubbed "the revenge of the investment cycle." As noted earlier, investment in petroleum exploration and development was drastically reduced in the 1990s. As a result, when prices started rising in 2004, there was little ability to increase oil production. Economically, the supply curve went "vertical": Higher prices could not increase supply in any meaningful timeframe, and the only way to clear the market was to force consumers to stop buying by making petroleum prohibitively expensive.

The most significant petroleum and foreign policy changes during this period have to be China's increasing petroleum consumption and its reliance on foreign suppliers. Although China

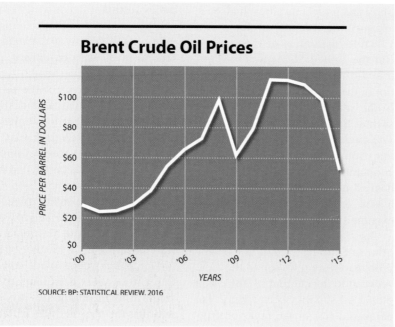

Brent Crude Oil Prices

SOURCE: BP: STATISTICAL REVIEW. 2016

became a net importer of petroleum liquids in 1993, its purchases were not large until 2003, when they reached 2 mmbd. China's increase in consumption was a major source of the upward pressure on petroleum prices.

The rising purchases of petroleum by China had at least two additional consequences. First, they encouraged the Chinese to "go out" and seek their own sources of supply without the intermediation of U.S. or European IOCs. China did this both by investing directly in production that was accessible to foreigners (e.g., Canada, Sudan), or by signing direct purchase agreements with national oil companies. This complicated U.S. foreign policy since Chinese companies, personnel and political interests were now active in places that had previously been of little or no concern to the country (e.g., Angola, Sudan and Venezuela). Secondly, China became vulnerable to U.S. naval disruption of its waterborne supplies. While it may sound implausible to some that the United States would ever attempt to stop this petroleum flow, the very existence of this capability forces China to prepare for its possibility. The Chinese even named this the "Malacca Dilemma" after the straits that oil tankers transit in order to reach China after

leaving the Persian Gulf or Africa. China's new and growing dependence on petroleum brought in by sea increased the strategic value of the U.S. Navy by creating greater opportunities for the United States potentially to disrupt these supplies.

Phase 6: supply surpluses, new opportunities or new dangers? 2013–present

In 2008, U.S. liquids production was 7.8 mmbd. By 2015, it was an astounding 14.8 mmbd. The petroleum investment cycle and the petroleum revolution transformed the U.S. supply situation. The United States now consumes approximately 19 mmbd of petroleum and imports 5 mmbd for an import dependence ratio of 26%. This vast dependency reduction has dramatically changed the range of policy options open to the United States. Most importantly, there has been a perceptible reduction in the level of U.S. engagement in the Middle East. The failure to intervene decisively in Libya, Syria and Yemen, and the continued reduction in U.S. involvement in Iraq are arguably caused—at least partially—by lessened concern over the global supply of petroleum.

Another way increased policy freedom was evident was with the last round of Iranian energy sanctions and the current Russian energy sanctions. These policies were predicated upon the vast global petroleum surplus created primarily by the change in U.S. production. This excess supply reduced the risk of sharply higher global prices due to an actual reduction in Iranian supply and the potential reduction in Russian supply.

The significant petroleum price decline that began in mid-2014 is expected to reduce U.S. production in 2016 by approximately 600,000 barrels per day from its 2015 average. Without higher prices, continued improvements in technology and management, or changes to U.S. regulatory policies, U.S. production is unlikely to increase much in 2017 and beyond. Some, including the IEA, have begun to think that a continuation of low prices will once again place OPEC, and particularly the Persian Gulf, back at the center of global petroleum. The potential negative foreign policy ramifications of declining U.S. production and increasing OPEC/Persian Gulf dominance are clear: higher U.S. import dependency, greater vulnerability to foreign disruptions and increased incentive for the United States to intervene abroad to maintain the stability of global petroleum supplies. ∎

Saudi Arabia's oil minister, Ali Al Naimi, (center) arrives for the OPEC meeting, in the Qatari capital Doha, on April 17, 2016.
(KARIM JAAFAR/AFP/GETTY IMAGES)

Looking forward

Since the beginning of the 20th century, the United States has not hesitated to use petroleum as a coercive instrument of foreign policy. At various times this has contributed to wider foreign policy success, at other times this has created circumstances that undermine foreign policy objectives and create dreadful problems. The connection between U.S. international petroleum policy and the last 36 years of nearly endless intervention and war in the Middle East is difficult to deny. Many, such as historian Andrew Bacevich, have argued that without oil, the motivation to intervene militarily would be greatly diminished. While the United States has other interests in the Middle East besides oil, it is oil that makes the region vital to the United States and the global economy.

The United States is now at an important crossroad in its domestic energy policy and this policy's relationship to its foreign and military policies. The "oil revolution" has created conditions whereby the United States can continue to increase significantly its domestic petroleum production and further reduce its vulnerability to foreign disruptions. Increased U.S. production adds to the global supply and pressures prices lower. But the key to greater domestic petroleum production is not just modestly higher global prices (over which the United States has little control), but U.S. domestic energy policy and regulation (over which the United States has total control).

While the exact contours of President-elect Donald J. Trump's energy and foreign policies are not yet known, he has said that he wants to make "American energy dominance a strategic economic and foreign policy goal." Among other things, he wants to remove various federal regulations on the industry and open up more federal lands for energy exploration and development. How any of this will be achieved is yet to be seen, but several issues and questions are clear:

- There is a definite connection between U.S. domestic petroleum

A U.S. Navy sailor protects oil tankers in the Houston Ship Channel, Texas. (SARAH LEEN/ NATIONAL GEOGRAPHIC CREATIVE)

production, foreign import dependence and U.S. intervention abroad. If one increases domestic petroleum (and natural gas) production, it reduces the pressure—or some might say, the need—to intervene abroad. Should this oil-intervention trade-off figure more prominently in the public discussion?

- The environmental consequences of greater domestic petroleum (and natural gas) production are substantial. While the petroleum and natural gas industries, like all extractive industries, are dirty and dangerous, we cannot do without them, at least for several more decades. How can smart regulations, especially at the state level, be designed and implemented to balance the needs of producers—and the consumers they represent— and other interest groups, such as some environmentalists, landowners, and Native Americans?

- Changes to domestic petroleum policy along the lines President-elect Trump have indicated would substantially and quickly increase U.S. domestic petroleum production. Many, such as environmental policy expert Ted Nordhaus, have examined alternative energy proposals that are supposed to transform the U.S. energy system in short order, and have found them utopian and counterproduc-

tive. Alternative energy solutions that take 15, 20 or 30 years, would not affect the *immediate incentive* for foreign intervention. What timeframe for considering domestic energy policy alternatives and their foreign policy consequences is appropriate?

- The military cost of protecting the international trade in petroleum (and natural gas) is substantial. Should the new administration stop protecting the flow of energy from the Middle East to Europe and insist that the Europeans do this themselves?

Conceivably, the United States could do little to increase domestic petroleum production and instead simply withdraw from the Middle East, but might not this just exacerbate U.S. and global problems? Might the United States end up with destructively higher energy prices, and an intensification of the localized wars and humanitarian disasters that accompany them? Politics is about choosing the least bad solution to a problem. Ideal solutions that perfectly reconcile domestic U.S. petroleum production and the U.S.-managed global petroleum supply system do not exist. How the U.S. policy balances domestic petroleum production and foreign engagement to promote global energy access is, indeed, a great decision. ∎

discussion questions

1. In what ways has the U.S. "energy revolution" improved or not improved U.S. foreign policy?

2. Should the United States continue using petroleum as an instrument of leverage, supplying energy security to allies and denying it to adversaries? What are some current examples of this practice?

3. To what degree should the U.S. government and public care about the economic interests of domestic petroleum producers? Should it aggressively promote U.S. domestic petroleum production in order to minimize U.S. import vulnerability and decrease the incentive to intervene abroad?

4. How far should the U.S. government go in supporting its international oil companies? In an era of increasing state capitalism, are U.S. companies disadvantaged without strong government support?

5. Should U.S. taxpayers continue to fund the U.S. Navy's role in protecting the international shipment of petroleum? Is it possible to separate petroleum from non-petroleum transport?

6. Are the security guarantees provided to Saudi Arabia and other Persian Gulf states really necessary? What would happen if the U.S. renounced this commitment? Would the Chinese or Europeans have to intervene to replace the U.S.? If regional war(s) broke out, would U.S. interests be secure?

Don't forget: Ballots start on page 115!

suggested readings

Bryce, Robert, **Power Hungry: The Myths of "Green" Energy and the Real Fuels of the Future**. New York: PublicAffairs, 2010. 416 pp. Bryce emphasizes a critical role for fossil fuels now and in the years to come, challenging narratives that promise a "clean energy future."

Emerson, Sarah A. and Winner, Andrew C., "The Myth of Petroleum Independence and Foreign Policy Isolation." **The Washington Quarterly**, vol. 37 no. 1, 2014. pp. 21–34. Available free online: <https://www.ciaonet.org/attachments/24671/uploads>. This article argues that linking energy independence with the promise of reduced military commitment in the Persian Gulf is a political myth.

Hofmeister, John, **Why We Hate the Oil Companies: Straight Talk from an Energy Insider**. New York: St. Martin's Press, 2010. 256 pp. Hofmeister, previously the president of Shell Oil, provides an insider account of the relationship between energy companies and politicians, and offers his own paradigm for clean and affordable energy solutions.

Humphreys, Macartan, Sachs, Jeffrey D. and Stiglitz, Joseph E., eds., **Escaping the Resource Curse**. New York: Columbia University Press, 2007. 432 pp. In this book, leading economists, lawyers and political scientists present policy options for remodeling how the world's natural resources are managed.

Ladislaw, Sarah O., Leed, Maren and Walton, Molly A., "New Energy, New Geopolitics: Balancing Stability and Leverage." Center for Strategic and International Studies, April 2014. 64 pp. Available free online: <https://csis-prod.s3.amazonaws.com/s3fs-public/legacy_files/files/publication/140514_Ladislaw_NewEnergyNew-Geopolitics_REVISED.pdf/>. This report presents potential geostrategic implications of the "shale revolution." Intended to inform policymakers, it provides a framework for assessing the risks and rewards of shale gas and tight oil resources.

Roberts, Paul, **The End of Oil: On the Edge of a Perilous New World**. New York: Mariner Books, 2005. 416 pp. This book investigates a future where oil is scarce, analyzing the economics and politics of oil and of alternative energy sources.

Yergin, Daniel, **The Prize: The Epic Quest for Oil, Money & Power**. New York: Free Press, 2008. 928 pp. This Pulitzer Prize-winning history of oil recounts the global contest for power and wealth that surrounds the resource.

To access web links to these readings, as well as links to additional, shorter readings and suggested web sites,

GO TO www.greatdecisions.org

and click on the topic under Resources, on the right-hand side of the page

Latin America's political pendulum
by Michael Shifter and Bruno Binetti

People line up outside a supermarket in Caracas, Venezuela, to buy price regulated toilet paper made available for sale by the government, in January 2016. (FERNANDO LLANO/AP PHOTO)

In the early 2000s, many Latin American countries witnessed the emergence of leaders and parties of the political left, in its many variants. This group combined a commitment to expansive social policies to redress long-standing inequalities and a more active government with adherence to electoral democracy. Much of the media dubbed this the "pink tide" of Latin America, to distinguish it from the communist-inspired movements of the Cold War era.

These new forces rose to power as a product of citizens' dissatisfaction with previous governments. At the turn of the century, Latin Americans were demanding change and a renewed emphasis on social policy—such as anti-poverty measures and more access to public services—after years of neglect by traditional political parties. Leftist political movements were also reinforced by increasing anti-Americanism in the region, fueled by what was widely perceived as an imperialistic and aggressive U.S. foreign policy after September 11, 2001.

Although the pink tide label is useful to frame this period,

it should be employed carefully, as it can obscure the many differences among governments of the new left. Each country experienced its own particular version of this tendency, based on distinct national realities. In Brazil, President Luiz Inácio Lula da Silva (known as "Lula"), a pragmatic union leader, expanded social protection but maintained pro-market economic policies. By contrast, in Venezuela, Hugo Chávez, a highly ideological army officer, largely stifled the private sector with a relentless push toward nationalization, especially in the oil industry.

The period of left-leaning rule coincided with unprecedented levels of economic growth and political stability,

MICHAEL SHIFTER *is president of the Inter-American Dialogue and an adjunct professor of Latin American Studies at Georgetown University's School of Foreign Service.*

BRUNO BINETTI *is research associate at the Inter-American Dialogue. He holds a Master's degree from the Elliott School in International Affairs of George Washington University. .*

particularly in South America. The economic expansion was largely the result of a staggering rise in exports of raw materials, mainly to China. Economic growth, in turn, helped lift millions out of poverty and reduce unacceptably high levels of income inequality. On the other hand, Mexico and Central America did not perform as well: Their manufacturing sectors suffered from Asian competition and the effects of the Great Recession in the U.S.

Today, as analysts point to the bust of the commodity boom and the unmistakable signs of economic stagnation, the pink tide is receding. Incumbents who had enjoyed broad popular support for nearly a decade are being defeated at the polls because their capacity to deliver social and economic progress has substantially diminished.

After achieving a higher standard of living, Latin American citizens have increased demands and expectations, and are protesting—at the ballot box and in the streets—against corruption and mismanagement. New governments are promising transparency, more effective institutions and market-oriented economic reforms. In the next months and years, these new leaders will be severely tested as to whether they can deliver on those promises. ∎

The political pendulum

Gen. Augusto Pinochet, center, presides over a meeting with his military staff in Santiago, Chile, on September 20, 1973, days after seizing power from President Salvador Allende. (AP PHOTO)

Historically, Latin American politics have been cyclical and marked by the alternation between leftist and right-wing forces. Many analysts have long referred to the "political pendulum" of Latin America. Left-leaning movements tended to focus on addressing the region's high levels of poverty and inequality through redistributive government policies. More rightist parties, usually with the support of the military, generally favored an alignment with the Western world, in the context of the

Cold War, and more market-friendly economic management.

This debate now takes place peacefully and within a democratic framework in most countries, but that has not always been the case. In fact, from the 1930s to the 1980s, sharp ideological differences frequently led to violent clashes and coups across the region. Especially during the Cold War, divisions between leftist and rightist groups became so acute that they led to civil wars in some Central American nations. Throughout this period of geopolitical competition, moreover, the United States actively intervened to promote friendly governments in Latin America, either through invasion (as in the Dominican Republic in 1965 or the failed Bay of Pigs invasion of Cuba in

1962) or by tacitly supporting military coups (as in Chile in 1973).

During the 1980s, a number of countries in Latin America experienced transitions back to democracy after decades of brutal military dictatorships and armed conflict. Economically, however, this was a turbulent period for the region, and most countries were unable to repay mounting foreign debts. In 1982, Mexico was forced to declare default, and many others followed. The combination, in most countries, of financial crisis with deteriorated social conditions is why the 1980s are commonly referred to as the "lost decade" in Latin America.

The crisis in Latin America coincided with an ideological shift in the developed world, particularly within some U.S. universities (most notably, the University of Chicago) and international financial institutions such as the World Bank and the International Monetary Fund (IMF). The new economic approach—known as "neoliberalism"—argued that Latin America's crisis was mainly due to an oversized and poorly managed public sector, and a lack of incentives for private initiative.

In response, neoliberal economists recommended a series of structural reforms: privatization of state-owned companies, elimination of barriers to trade and foreign investment, reduction of public spending and tax breaks for the business sector. The financial crisis of the 1980s provided an opportunity to apply these policies in Latin America. Incapable of repaying their debt with their own budgets, governments turned

Before you read, download the companion Glossary that includes definitions and a guide to acronyms and abbreviations used in the article. Go to **www.greatdecisions.org** and select a topic in the Resources section on the right-hand side of the page.

to the IMF and the World Bank for financial assistance. These institutions granted countries much-needed funds, but only after they had implemented profound structural reforms with a markedly neoliberal orientation.

Some Latin American politicians rapidly adopted this new economic creed. As a reaction to the crisis, in the late 1980s citizens began to elect a new series of leaders who applied these pro-market policies, which were known as the "Washington Consensus" and inspired by Ronald Reagan in the U.S. and Margaret Thatcher in the United Kingdom.

At the same time, relations between the U.S. and these market-friendly governments became much stronger. In 1994, during the first Summit of the Americas (a triennial meeting of all heads of government in the hemisphere), there was unanimous agreement on a program based on open markets and democratic governance. Even Mexico, a historically statist country, ended decades of economic nationalism and, in 1993, signed the North America Free Trade Agreement (NAFTA) with the U.S. and Canada. The Argentinian foreign minister famously described his country's relations with the U.S. during this time as "carnal."

For nearly a decade, neoliberal presidents were successful in stabilizing their economies, promoting foreign investment and taming inflation. Argentina, a country renowned for its economic decline since the early 20th century, elected Carlos Menem president in 1989. Menem quickly reneged on the policies of his Peronist party, which were nationalistic in character, coming from the party associated with former President Juan Domingo Péron who governed in the 1940s. Instead, Menem embarked on a vast program of privatization in all sectors of the economy. Most state-owned industries were sold, including oil company YPF. Menem and his minister of the economy also pegged the value of the Argentine peso to the dollar. That decision ended high inflation, but also hurt the competitiveness of Argentine exports.

Neoliberalism likewise took hold in Peru, after Alberto Fujimori became president in 1990. When he took office, he was a political outsider with no government experience. The country's economy was in shambles, and terrorist organizations—especially the infamous Sendero Luminoso ("Shining Path")—were staging attacks and kidnappings on a frightening scale.

Fujimori rapidly cemented his power, stabilized the economy with a program of privatization and liberalization, and launched a campaign to defeat terrorist organizations, which, while effective, was accompanied by widespread human rights violations and massive corruption. While he remained popular for most of the 1990s, his rule quickly became more authoritarian: In 1992, with the support of the military, Fujimori shut down Congress, and only reopened it after drafting a new constitution that granted him enhanced powers.

In Brazil, Fernando Henrique Cardoso, a former leftist intellectual, became president in 1995, and implemented a program of stabilization and liberalization that ended hyperinflation and allowed the economy to grow again. Cardoso's embrace of Washington Consensus policies exemplified the new era of Latin American politics and economics.

The neoliberal model, however, soon found its limits. Despite economic growth, the withdrawal of the state had made the population more vulnerable to economic shocks. Further, economic liberalization and the elimina-

Peruvian President Alberto Fujimori is surrounded by members of the military during an appearance in July 1992 in Lima, Peru.
(HECTOR MATA/AFP/GETTY IMAGES)

tion of trade barriers did not bring the benefits that had been anticipated. In many countries, local industries were unable to compete with cheaper foreign goods, and unemployment rose as factories were forced to close. In addition, financial reforms had attracted speculative capital, making Latin America even more vulnerable to external shocks than in the past. As capital was free to move based on economic conditions, financial instability spread: When doubts emerged about the region's economic performance, investors rapidly left.

The last years of the 20th century saw the unraveling of the neoliberal paradigm. By the end of the 1990s, economic stagnation had returned. Many countries were heavily indebted once again, and corruption scandals further eroded the credibility of incumbents. Once praised as models of successful economic management, countries where the Washington Consensus was applied with most vigor suffered the worst.

One of the earliest and most notable examples of the economic and political impact of neoliberal reforms was in Venezuela. A bipartisan agreement between the social-Christian COPEI and the social-democratic Acción Democrática had maintained an electoral democracy for decades. But as political elites became increasingly isolated from popular demands, the costs of this model mounted.

Facing low oil prices and continuous economic crisis during the 1980s, the administration of Carlos Andrés Pérez implemented a drastic program of reducing public spending and eliminating gasoline subsidies. But such policies were short-lived. When the cost of living dramatically increased, Venezuelans took to the streets: The so-called "Caracazo" of 1989—a series of protests in the capital, Caracas, of unprecedented virulence and size—inaugurated a long period of social violence and political instability.

A few years after the Caracazo, in 1992, leftist colonel Hugo Chávez led an attempted coup by young army officers against President Pérez. Although the coup failed, Chávez became a symbol of the resistance to neoliberal policies, and his popularity soared.

Some years later in Peru, the Fujimori government, associated with

Cuban President Fidel Castro and Venezuelan President Hugo Chávez wave in Havana, Cuba, on February 02, 2006. Venezuela's president received a UN prize named for Cuban independence hero Jose Martí a day after the Bush administration likened Hugo Chavez to Hitler. (PHOTO BY JOSE GOITIA/GAMMA-RAPHO/GETTY IMAGES)

neoliberal prescriptions, collapsed, essentially for institutional and political reasons. The end came as a result of massive corruption scandals and strong evidence of electoral fraud during Fujimori's bid for a third term as president. After more than a decade in office, Fujimori fled Peru in 2000 and requested asylum in Japan, from where he faxed his resignation letter. He spent years in self-imposed exile to avoid the mounting number of cases against him in Peruvian courts. In 2005, however, he decided to fly to Chile, expecting most charges to be dropped and to make a triumphant return to Peruvian politics. Fujimori's calculations proved wrong: He was arrested in Chile and extradited to Peru in 2007, where he is still serving a 25-year prison sentence for crimes committed during his term in office.

The following year, Argentine President Fernando de la Rúa stepped down amid a profound recession and heightened social tension. A political adversary of Menem, de la Rúa nonetheless maintained his economic policy. The economy contracted by 4.4% in 2001, and collapsed by nearly 11% in 2002. Further, Argentina declared a default on its massive public debt—at the time, the largest default in world history—and was forced to free the peso from the dollar to regain competitiveness. Soon af-

ter de la Rúa's downfall, Bolivian President Gonzalo Sánchez de Lozada, also a proponent of neoliberal recipes, was forced to leave office and flee the country amid violent protests, road blockades and a profound economic crisis.

The resurgence of the left

It was hardly surprising that, having failed to produce sustained growth and stability, neoliberal economic policies became increasingly unpopular for many Latin Americans. In one country after another, citizens rejected pro-market forces and looked for alternatives. The stage was set for the beginning of a new era led by politicians from the opposite side of the political spectrum.

The first case of this new political moment was Venezuela. Once in office in 1999, Hugo Chávez used rising oil revenues to expand access to public services such as education and health, responding to the Venezuelan population's legitimate grievances and demands for greater social justice. At the same time, Chávez imposed state control over the economy and removed all obstacles in his path to power.

Inspired by the Pan-American ideology of independence hero Simón Bolívar, the new Venezuelan strongman sought to build a regional zone of influence and attract other countries

to his Bolivarian socialist ideology. A disciple of Cuban leader Fidel Castro, Chávez forged a strong alliance with the island's communist regime, which served as a permanent symbol and rallying cry for the continent's left. He started sending subsidized oil to impoverished nations in the Caribbean and Central America. As oil prices climbed from less than $10 a barrel to well over $100 during his term, Chávez was able to finance both domestic social policies and his grandiose regional project. That largesse would not last forever.

Within a few years, more left-leaning governments took power in other countries, as traditional parties collapsed, discredited by failed economic policies and increasingly acute social tensions. In 2005, Bolivia elected Evo Morales, a populist social leader who became the country's first indigenous president. He drafted a new constitution that recognized indigenous rights, nationalized Bolivia's natural gas industry and set a new drug policy that allowed the traditional uses of coca (but not the production of cocaine).

After a long period of political instability in Ecuador (there were six presidents in a decade), economist Rafael Correa became president in 2006 and aligned his government with Chávez's "socialism of the 21st century." That same year, in Nicaragua, leftist strongman Daniel Ortega returned to power, having ruled in the 1980s after winning the civil war. This time, he formed a political alliance with the business elites he once combated.

Yet not all leaders of the pink tide shared Chávez's statist and increasingly authoritarian policies. A second, more moderate version of the Latin American left also rose in the early 2000s. As in Venezuela and Bolivia, these center-left leaders argued for the need to reduce inequality by expanding public services and increasing the role of the government in the economy. Unlike Chávez, however, more pragmatic leftist governments generally respected democratic institutions, the rule of law, and the role of the private sector and foreign investment in fostering economic growth.

In other words, the moderate left accepted most of the tenets of the Washington Consensus (there was no attempt to restore government control over privatized companies, nor were there sudden changes to trade policy), but complemented them with more vigorous social programs. Examples of this tendency include Ricardo Lagos (2000–06) and Michelle Bachelet (2006–10; 2014–present) in Chile, and Luiz Inácio Lula da Silva in Brazil (2003–11).

In Chile, the governments of the center-left coalition Concertación increased social spending, but maintained most economic policies of the pro-market dictatorship of Augusto Pinochet (1973–90), including an aggressive search for markets for the country's exports, mainly copper. In Brazil, Lula quickly dissipated investors' concerns about his suspected radical ideological tendencies and implemented a pragmatic economic policy that lifted millions out of poverty, but also boosted Brazilian companies and private investment. The signature social policy of Lula's term was Bolsa Família, a conditional cash-transfer program that consolidated and expanded on previous initiatives. The program continues to provide financial aid to poor families, as long as they send their children to school and get them vaccinated.

Meanwhile, Argentina under Néstor Kirchner (2003–07) and his wife and successor Cristina Fernández de Kirchner (2007–15) shifted Peronism back to its traditional nationalistic ideology, but, within this wider regional turn, pursued a middle course. While the South American nation maintained close relations with Chávez—and distant relations with Washington—it nonetheless fashioned its own particular model between Chávez's more radical version of the left and the more pragmatic and market-friendly "Lula model." The Kirchners maintained a long dispute in New York courts with holders of Argentinian defaulted bonds, staunchly rejected any cooperation with the IMF and implemented more heavy-handed economic policies. Further, Argentina nationalized the YPF oil and gas company back from its private owners and relied on public

Supporters deploy a huge flag with the portrait of late President Nestor Kirchner, celebrating after Congress approved the bill nationalizing the oil company YPF, on May 3, 2012, in Buenos Aires, Argentina. (JUAN MABROMATA/AFP/GETTYIMAGES)

spending to foster economic growth. Benefiting from the collapse of the bipartisan party system after the crisis, the Kirchners became immensely popular, and concentrated most decision-making in the presidency.

Not every country joined the pink tide, however. In Colombia, conservative Álvaro Uribe cemented his popularity through his frontal offensive against armed groups, and was a close ally of U.S. President George W. Bush. In Mexico, meanwhile, the once-hegemonic Institutional Revolutionary Party (PRI) was replaced by the conservative National Action Party (PAN). During the administrations of Vicente Fox (2000–06) and Felipe Calderón (2006–12), the country continued pro-market reforms. After NAFTA, Mexico became increasingly intertwined with the U.S. economy, which brought economic growth, but had a limited impact in terms of reducing high levels of inequality and poverty. This dependency—roughly 80% of Mexico's exports go to the U.S.—has become a potential liability for Mexico now more than ever, given the protectionist promises of President-elect Donald Trump, who has pledged to renegotiate NAFTA. In economic policy, Peru, often a regional outlier, largely reflected continuity in the post-Fujimori period.

A more assertive foreign policy

Political changes in the region also led to changes in Latin American foreign policy, especially vis-à-vis Washington. The governments of Bolivia, Ecuador, Cuba and Nicaragua joined the Bolivarian Alliance for the Peoples of Our America (ALBA), a staunchly anti-American regional bloc led by Chávez and funded by Venezuelan oil revenues. The intention of ALBA was to create an alternative to U.S.-led regional institutions and to curtail Washington's influence in the region. However, the group remained dependent on Venezuela, and its membership was limited to a few Central and South American allies of Chávez, along with a number of small Caribbean nations.

While only ALBA countries expressed a markedly anti-American discourse (Chávez called Bush "the devil" before the United Nations General Assembly in 2006), hemispheric relations overall were marked by tension. In 2005, for instance, Lula, Kirchner and Chávez joined forces to defeat a U.S.-backed project to create a Free Trade Area of the Americas (FTAA) during the Summit of the Americas held in Mar del Plata, Argentina. Further, most governments in the region were uneasy with a unilateralist government in Washington that was focused on the war on terror and military adventures in Afghanistan and Iraq. In addition, in a number of nations, the U.S. still represented the neoliberal ideology that Latin Americans held responsible for years of economic hardship and social distress.

In a context of economic growth and diversification of their foreign relations, most countries in the region were confident in their capacity to set a new course. The rise of Brazil as an example for the developing world was a critical factor in this new sense of self-reliance. Under Lula, the country combined successful social policies and poverty reduction with high rates of economic growth—reaching 7.5% in 2010.

The international popularity of the Brazilian president was at least as high as his domestic support. His personal story inspired people all over the world: He rose from absolute poverty to become a factory worker, union leader, president of his country and an international celebrity. In 2009, during the G20 summit in London, President Barack Obama said Lula was "the most popular politician on Earth." That same year, Brazil entered the BRIC group of emerging economies together with Russia, India and China. A cover of *The Economist* in November 2009— titled "Brazil takes off" and illustrat-

ed by a rocket-propelled Christ the Redeemer—symbolized this optimism.

Latin America's renewed assertiveness led to the creation of new regional institutions. For 50 years the only multilateral body that included all countries in Latin America and the Caribbean (with the notable exception of Cuba, suspended from 1962 to 2009) was the Organization of American States (OAS), based in Washington. As the pink tide consolidated—and building on a strong tradition of regionalism—a number of governments decided it was time to create new regional institution without the U.S. or Canada.

Although most countries, especially Brazil, saw this as a way to regain autonomy, some governments, like those of Venezuela, Ecuador and Bolivia, were also irritated with the constant criticism from OAS bodies such as the Inter-American Commission on Human Rights. According to left-leaning leaders, the OAS was politicized and applied double standards, being especially tough on them while ignoring abuses by the U.S. and its closest regional allies.

In 2008, governments created the Union of South American Nations (UNASUR), a sub-regional group led by Brazil that also includes countries with centrist leaders such as Colombia and Peru. A few years later, all countries in the region founded the Community of

Latin American and Caribbean States (CELAC). These two organizations have become political forums where countries in the region can discuss common problems without Washington's presence or involvement, although their capacity to implement effective policies has been limited.

In addition, nearly all countries in the region worked to increase their political and economic links with countries other than the United States. The emergence of Asia Pacific as the new engine of the world economy and the relative decline of the U.S. and Europe after the 2008–09 financial crisis intensified these efforts. In 2011, the governments of Peru, Chile, Mexico and Colombia created the Pacific Alliance to further trade liberalization and economic integration among its members, while articulating and forging common approaches toward Asia.

Meanwhile, Brazil, Argentina, Paraguay and Uruguay remained part of Mercosur, a much-less ambitious bloc marred by the protectionist policies of its two largest members. The incorporation of Venezuela as a member in 2012–13 only worsened these problems. In 2016, the governments of Argentina and Brazil pushed for the suspension of Venezuela from the trade bloc, as the country failed to meet Mercosur human rights and immigration standards.   ∎

Commodity super cycle: From boom to bust

The changes in Latin America's foreign policy were deeply intertwined with global economic trends. As China became an increasingly important engine of global growth, demand for commodities produced by most South American countries—including soy, minerals, oil and others—increased dramatically, lifting international prices and generating a massive influx of resources.

The numbers speak for themselves: Trade between Latin American countries and China went from little over

$12 billion in 2003 to more than $289 billion ten years later. By 2013, moreover, China had become the second largest source of regional imports, and the second largest origin of its imports. China's role was even greater for commodity exporters in South America.

Chinese leaders began to visit Latin America with unprecedented frequency, promising billions of dollars in investment and infrastructure projects. According to the database developed by the Inter-American Dialogue and Boston University, since 2005 China

has provided over $125 billion in loan commitments to the region, more than the World Bank and the Inter-American Development Bank combined. Following the model of the Summit of the Americas, the first China-CELAC summit took place in the capital Brasília in 2014.

The commodity boom is a key factor in understanding the popularity and durability of leftist leaders. What sustained them in power for many years was less ideology than economic performance and the ability of governments to deliver to their constituents, who had been pressing for better social conditions. Between 2003 and 2013, economies in Latin America and the Caribbean grew by 3.6% annually on average, while GDP per capita rose by 2.4%. This favorable economic environment allowed governments from the left to apply their ideas of more state interventionism, expansion of public services and poverty reduction.

The combination of economic growth with active government policies—such as cash-transfer programs, including Bolsa Família in Brazil—had significant social consequences. According to the World Bank, the poverty rate in Latin America as a whole fell from over 40% in 2003 to just over 25% in 2012. Extreme poverty fell from nearly 25% to just over 12% in 2011. In the same year, more Latin Americans were part of the middle class than were in poverty for the first time in history. This progress did not, however, reach all countries equally. In Mexico, for instance, poverty levels decreased somewhat during the 2000s, only to return to be higher than 50% by the end of the decade.

Despite this uncommonly favorable economic context, Latin American countries failed to take advantage of the opportunity to invest in long-term economic development through innovation, private initiative and infrastructure. Ten years after the start of the commodity boom, South America still depends on commodity exports: minerals in Chile and Peru, oil in Venezuela, soybeans in Argentina, and iron and soy in Brazil. According to the United Nations Economic Commission on Latin America and the Caribbean (ECLAC), just five products, all of them commodities, represented 3/4 of the value of regional shipments to China in 2013.

Further, manufacturing regions such as Mexico and Central America suffered from increasing competition from China and other industrializing countries in Asia. They also took longer to recover from the Great Recession in the United States, their main trading partner and source of foreign investment. Although manufacturing countries grew during the 2003–13 expansion, high levels of

Iron ore bound for exportation sits in railway wagons at Tubarao Harbour in Vitoria city, Brazil. (PHOTO BY RICARDO FUNARI/BRAZIL PHOTOS/LIGHTROCKET VIA GETTY IMAGES)

poverty and inequality remained almost unchanged. In addition, drug-related violence and organized crime also hurt economic performance in these nations.

To be sure, governments did improve social standards and public services during this period. But these efforts were inadequate and poorly planned given the dimension of the challenges facing Latin America. For instance, more people are now enrolled in formal education than ever before, but international tests such as the Program for International Student Assessment (PISA) indicate that the level of learning in the region remains considerably below that of developed countries and even emerging Asian nations.

Countries further failed to make the necessary investment in infrastructure—including roads, airports, ports and electric distribution—that would spur economic diversification and growth. Throughout the commodity boom, countries invested only 2–3% of their GDP in infrastructure, while the World Bank states that at least 5% a year would be needed to gradually close Latin America's "infrastructure gap."

The end of the "commodity boom"—triggered by the slowdown of the Chinese economy that began in 2014—brought policy failures to the fore. As Chinese demand decreased, Latin American governments began to run deficits, and

underwriting expanded social programs became increasingly difficult. Despite important social progress during the early 2000s, the region remains vulnerable to external shocks because of some dubious economic policies and missed opportunities.

Economic stagnation and political turmoil

The end of the economic boom threatens recent social progress and has contributed to the weakening of the Latin American left. The UN's Economic Commission for Latin America and the Caribbean (ECLAC) projects that poverty in Latin America, which had declined for many years, ticked up slightly in 2015. In general, Latin American countries emerged from the 2008–09 global crisis relatively quickly, but since 2014, regional economic growth has been lower than the world average.

Economic problems have led to heightened political tension. In a context of economic contraction and cutting of social services, corruption became increasingly intolerable for many Latin Americans. Incumbents' popularity dropped sharply, and in country after country citizens began to demand change and greater transparency. Across the region, governments of varied ideological stripes began to crack in the face of an alliance of a mobilized civil society, a more active judiciary and the media. In an unprecedented event, for example, the president of Guatemala was forced to resign in 2015 after weeks of protests in the streets, and was immediately arrested for his alleged involvement in a massive corruption scheme in the country's customs system.

One of the most emblematic cases of this dual political and economic crisis is Brazil. Lula remained immensely popular when he left office in 2011 (some polls showed an approval rating of 80%), and got his chief of staff, Dilma Rousseff, elected as his successor. Soon, however, the limits of the commodity-based economic model became evident: The largest economy in Latin America grew by a meager 0.2% in 2014, and entered a deep recession a year later: GDP fell by nearly 4% in 2015 and is expected to contract by almost as much in 2016.

The economic crisis has been worsened by an unprecedented period of political instability. Soon after Rousseff's reelection in 2014, a multi-billion dollar corruption scandal surrounding state-owned oil company Petrobras led to growing distrust and anger against the entire political class. An activist judiciary has prosecuted corruption cases with unprecedented vigor, leading to the arrest of prominent businessmen and politicians. In this context, the coalition of leftist and rightist parties built by Lula began to unravel. With her approval rating at a dismal 10%, Rousseff was impeached by the Brazilian Congress for fiscal irregularities, and removed from office in August 2016.

Rousseff's vice president and successor Michel Temer, from the centrist Brazilian Democratic Movement Party (PMDB), supported her impeachment. Temer has promised to restore growth, tame inflation and implement pro-market reforms, but the lack of confidence in the political system puts the stability of his government at some risk. It is estimated that 60% of the members of the Brazilian Congress are under investigation for accusations of corruption and other irregularities. Lula himself has been formally charged for the first time, his political future hanging in

the balance. The consequences of this unprecedented political and economic crisis are yet to be known, but the optimism that surrounded Brazil during the boom years has largely dissipated.

Meanwhile, Venezuela is immersed in a dramatic economic, social and political crisis that is turning into a humanitarian disaster. After Chávez's death from cancer in 2013, his handpicked successor Nicolás Maduro has proven alarmingly incapable of governing the country.

The lack of sensible economic policies since Chávez came to office, combined with the drop in oil prices since 2014, have led to the implosion of the Venezuelan economy: GDP dropped significantly in 2014 and 2015, and the IMF expects a contraction of 10% in 2016. Meanwhile, inflation is expected to exceed 700% in 2016, and a staggering 1600% in 2017. The national currency, the bolívar, has an official rate of 6 to 1 dollar, but most Venezuelans can only buy foreign currency in the black market, where the rate is $1 per 1000 bolívares.

The collapse of foreign currency reserves has led the government to drastically restrict imports. In an economy that has been practically destroyed by the use of the state to reward Chavistas and punish opponents, including the private sector, basic goods have become increasingly scarce and the health system is on the verge of utter collapse. Venezuelans spend most of their day waiting in lines to obtain basic food and household products.

Maduro's only response to the crisis has been to ratchet up repression against the political opposition, who gained a clear majority of the National Assembly in December 2015. The regime has used its control over the judicial system and other institutions to block the assembly, leading to political gridlock. Governments in the region are attempting to promote dialogue between the regime and the opposition, but differences regarding the release of political prisoners and a recall referendum (which Maduro resists because he will almost certainly lose) are practically insurmountable.

Although Bolivia managed its

economy prudently during the years of the commodity boom, the era of high growth is over in the Andean nation, and there are signs of political dissatisfaction with President Morales. For the first time since he came to office in 2006, Morales faced defeat in the polls: In February 2016, voters rejected his proposal to reform the constitution to allow another reelection. His image among indigenous groups and new middle classes has suffered as a result of corruption scandals. Many of the groups and leaders that supported Morales in 2005 are now part of the opposition.

Meanwhile, in Ecuador, President Rafael Correa is not running for reelection in 2017, amid a sharp economic slowdown. He has anointed Lenín Moreno, his former vice president, as his chosen candidate. Also affected by the drop in oil prices, Ecuador has turned to China for desperately needed financial assistance, although it is doubtful if this will be sufficient to prevent deepening economic problems.

The era of pragmatism

Out of this political crisis, new leaders are emerging, albeit slowly. They promise to rekindle economic growth and strengthen democratic institutions. Most notably, in Argentina, Mauricio Macri—a former businessman and mayor of Buenos Aires—became president in 2015 after defeating the handpicked successor of President Cristina Kirchner. Macri's political challenges are many, including dealing with an opposition-controlled congress and Peronist provincial governors. But he has had significant accomplishments during his first months in office.

The new administration has moved quickly to launch economic reforms and restore badly strained relationships with the U.S. and Europe. The country entered a recession in 2016 (the economy is expected to contract by at least 1%), and the government has been criticized for suddenly lifting massive subsidies on electricity, water and natural gas, leading to higher rates. However, Macri's popularity remains high, and he has promised that economic reforms, although painful, will lead to lower inflation and higher growth in 2017. The private sector, foreign investors and governments in the U.S. and Europe share this optimism, and the IMF expects the economy to rebound by 3% in 2017. Meanwhile, Kirchnerism has been weakened by judicial investigations over massive corruption schemes during its 12 years in office.

It is tempting to label this new political period—which includes leaders like Macri, Temer and the new Peruvian president, market-oriented economist Pedro Pablo Kuczynski—in Latin America as "the return of the right." However, for a number of reasons, this characterization fails to capture the complexities of the current situation.

First, political changes taking place in the region are more related to economic conditions and the natural erosion of long-term incumbents than ideology. Latin American democracies are just like any other: They voted for left-leaning leaders in the 2000s because they promised to upend the failed neoliberal model and improve social conditions. Now, a decade later, they are electing alternatives who promise to generate growth and deliver results.

Second, this narrative does not describe the situation in many countries, where pro-market forces are still in power. In Colombia, President Álvaro Uribe was succeeded in 2010 by centrist Juan Manuel Santos, and the political divide in the country is focused on the ongoing peace process with armed guerrillas, not on economic policies. In Mexico, the PRI returned to power after 12 years with an agenda of economic modernization and partial privatization of the energy sector, a symbol of Mexican nationalism. Ironically, in times where some announce the return of the right, after the relative failure of governments from the PAN and the PRI to improve social conditions, a victory of the left in the presidential elections of 2018 cannot be ruled out.

Moreover, the return of the right narrative overlooks that while many left-leaning leaders are leaving the political scene, their social agenda is very likely to endure. Latin American governments cannot afford to ignore so-

cial demands, especially from the poor and excluded. The expansion of public health, access to education and cash-transfer programs changed the lives of millions. It would be almost impossible for market-friendly governments to eliminate these social programs, as people would defend them with their votes and in the streets.

Further, the emergence of new middle classes has positively transformed Latin America. Political systems will have to adapt to a citizenry that is more active and better informed. Although economic and social demands are still fundamental, citizens are also demanding transparency, infrastructure, public safety and better government policies. The organization of civil society groups through social media is a groundbreaking phenomenon that is here to stay.

Center-right leaders, therefore, will have to preserve the social agenda of leftist parties while implementing reforms to strengthen democratic institutions and rekindle economic growth. In many ways, the movement of the Latin American historical pendulum has become somewhat less pronounced: A centrist, pragmatic way of governing could emerge.

Nonetheless, this new political cycle will likely be more turbulent—and shorter—than the pink tide of the 2000s. Citizens' patience is limited, and so are government resources. If pro-market reformers do not get economic results soon, Latin Americans will look elsewhere for solutions.

Policy options for the U.S.

During the years of the pink tide, Latin American countries sought to diversify their international relations and reduce their dependency on the U.S. This was a product of the economic boom, but also a reaction against the foreign policy of the George W. Bush administration, which was perceived as unilateral and aggressive. The U.S. invasion of Iraq in 2003 in particular touched a nerve among Latin American governments and people, as the region has experienced numerous U.S. military interventions since the proclamation of the Monroe Doctrine in the early 19th century.

Bush's initial term in office was characterized by tensions with Latin America, symbolized in the defeat of the U.S.-backed FTAA in 2005. In his second term, the approach shifted, becoming more pragmatic and less confrontational. This tendency was continued by President Barack Obama. Overall, Obama has been successful

U.S. President Barack Obama (L) walks with Argentinian President Mauricio Macri as he pays homage to the victims of Argentina's Dirty War at the "Parque de la Memoria" (Remembrance Park) in Buenos Aires on March 24, on the 40th anniversary of the 1976 military coup. Obama paid tribute to victims of Argentina's former Washington-backed dictatorship at a memorial on the banks of the River Plate, a monument to the estimated 30,000 people who were killed or went missing under the 1976–83 military regime. (NICHOLAS KAMM/AFP/GETTY IMAGES)

in lifting important obstacles to hemispheric relations and establishing a more positive rapport with many governments in the region.

The surprising election of Donald Trump as the next U.S. president, however, creates considerable uncertainty for Washington's relations with the region. The aggressive campaign rhetoric of the now president-elect has had a significant impact in Latin America, and especially in Mexico. If Trump fulfills his promises on various issues of importance to the region, U.S.-Latin America relations could be heading to a new era of tension and mutual distrust.

One of the most salient campaign issues of the new occupant of the White House has been his opposition to immigration, especially that of Mexican origin. For instance, Trump has promised to build a wall across the southern border of the United States, which is an impractical and offensive idea (although, in truth, a third of the border with Mexico is already blocked by a wall or fence). He has, furthermore, pledged to make Mexico pay for that wall, which the Mexican government has emphatically rejected.

Moreover, Trump has accused immigrants of Mexican origin of being criminals, and has pledged to deport the more than 11 million undocumented immigrants living in the U.S.—most of them of Mexican origin. Obama was incapable of approving a comprehensive immigration reform during his term, largely because of the opposition of Republicans in Congress and judicial blockage of his executive orders aimed at protecting at least a portion of those immigrants. Trump's campaign rhetoric, if put in practice, could result in human rights violations and cause lasting damage for the U.S. image in the world, and particularly in Latin America.

A second area of potential tension between the Trump administration and Latin America is trade. Paradoxically, the U.S. seems to be entering a protectionist phase while most of Latin America is looking for new trade and investment opportunities after years of maintaining fairly closed economies. President-elect Trump has promised to renegotiate or withdraw from NAFTA, a trade agreement that represents around 25% of all U.S. foreign trade, and countless jobs in the US, Mexico and Canada. During the more than two decades of NAFTA, North-American value chains have developed, and suddenly reinstating trade restrictions could have dramatic consequences for the entire region.

On a broader scale, Trump's decision to pull the plug on the Trans-Pacific Partnership and a potential increase of trade barriers in the U.S. could leave a void in Latin America, one that could be filled by other emerging powers. Immediately after Trump's electoral victory, for instance, Chinese president Xi Jinping promised more trade and economic cooperation to Latin American countries. A relative withdrawal of Washington from world trade could turn into a historical setback for U.S. interests in the hemisphere—just as Latin America's political climate has become increasingly propitious for enhanced U.S. engagement.

Trump's electoral victory has increased uncertainty regarding other issues of hemispheric cooperation. It remains to be seen, for example, if the new president will continue Obama's anti-drug efforts in Latin America. Obama sharply criticized the "war on drugs" approach, pledging to reduce the law enforcement component of U.S. anti-narcotics cooperation and increasing funding for economic and social development, especially in Central America. Although Obama marked a change in tone, U.S. anti-drug initiatives in Latin America lack effective coordination and some agencies remain locked in a "war on drugs" mentality based almost exclusively on law enforcement. Whether Washington returns to more traditional policies against drug trafficking or continues a transition to a more balanced approach remains to be seen.

While Trump has displayed very liberal views about drugs in the past, it is unclear if he will implement a hardline policy that could alienate partners in the region and return to purely prohibitionist policies that have been widely questioned and have proven ineffective. Another question is what Trump will do regarding Cuba, one of Obama's most significant accomplishments in the Americas. Obama's decision to normalize diplomatic relations with the island, after decades of a failed policy of isolation and punishment, removed a longstanding obstacle to productive hemispheric relations. Although Trump was the only Republican candidate who supported Obama's rapprochement during the primaries, he reversed his stance during the general election. Polls indicate that a majority of Americans, and even most Cuban-Americans, support the normalization with the island, and so do many American corporations and businesses. It is unlikely that Trump would be willing to incur the political cost of reinstating all the economic and diplomatic restrictions Obama has lifted. However, a lifting of the U.S. trade embargo and further engagement with Cuba are probably off the table under a Trump administration.

A third challenge will be the situation in Colombia. In 2000, under President Bill Clinton, the U.S. launched Plan Colombia, a bipartisan cooperation package that helped the South American nation strengthen state capacity and push back against armed guerrillas and other criminal groups heavily involved in drug trafficking. Under Obama, the U.S. strongly backed the Colombian government in its efforts to reach a peace agreement with the FARC, the country's largest armed group. Colombian voters, however, rejected the deal in a referendum in October 2016. The new U.S. president will have to support efforts to revive the peace process, while continuing collaboration in combating drug trafficking, all while respecting Colombian sovereignty and desires.

A final issue that will be critical for the next administration is the situation in Venezuela. For some time now, the South American nation—which holds the largest oil reserves in the world—has been suffering from a dramatic economic collapse and a relentless political standstill. Despite its massive unpopularity, and the violation of its own constitution, the Venezuelan government has used its absolute control over the country's courts to block the opposition-led Parliament, and has rejected pressures to release political prisoners and open a political dialogue. In the context of a dramatic humanitarian crisis, the U.S. will likely continue efforts to articulate a regional coalition to mount diplomatic pressure on Caracas and contribute to finding a peaceful solution. All in all, Trump's frequent changes of opinion and his lack of political experience and policy knowledge mean that, for now, uncertainty is the name of the game for Latin American countries that want to engage with the U.S.

The next U.S. president will inherit hemispheric relations that seem to be heading in a more positive direction, although Trump's rhetoric during the campaign has already affected the U.S. image in the region. If Trump wants to engage the region constructively, there is already much work to be done. However, relations with Latin America will hardly be a priority for the new occupant of the White House. The region's problems—inequality, growth, governance, rule of law, drug trafficking—are significant but not urgent, compared to other global crises. Still, political changes in Latin America could offer the new president with an opportunity to renew and deepen hemispheric cooperation.

More broadly, the biggest challenge for the next U.S. president will be to provide a reinvigorated framework for relations with Latin America. Economic development and integration will remain crucial, but the old, heavily free trade-focused agenda of the past is not suitable for the 21st century. People in Latin America and in the U.S. are increasingly wary of the effects of globalization and trade, and their demands will need to be taken into consideration.

The challenge is to develop new partnerships and approaches toward Latin America that take into account the region's progress during the early 2000s, as well as its rapidly evolving political landscape. President Obama's trip to Argentina in March 2016, only months after the inauguration of the

People wait for President-elect Pedro Pablo Kuczynski before the swearing-in ceremony at the National Congress in Lima on July 28, 2016. (LUKA GONZALES/AFP/GETTY IMAGES)

centrist Mauricio Macri as president, was a step in this direction. Further, a more nuanced policy toward the region implies avoiding one-size-fits-all programs, and building regional coalitions to address common problems. The U.S. can do more to engage Latin America as a partner in tackling global issues from food security to climate change.

In that sense, the emergence of centrist, market-friendly governments in the region could offer an opportunity for better relations with the U.S. and more work on common challenges. If Obama's main contribution was to remove obstacles and facilitate open dialogue, his successor could build on this legacy to set a more constructive relationship, valuing concrete steps toward more cooperation on a variety of issues like energy, infrastructure, education and innovation.

In doing so, the next U.S. administration should bear in mind the lessons from the 2000s. Latin American countries are historically averse to foreign interventionism and very protective of their sovereignty, especially vis-à-vis the United States. Therefore, policies that seek the promotion of democracy, transparency and human rights should only be pursued in close concert with countries in the region. The U.S. has a role to play in defending democratic governance in Latin America, but its capacity to unilaterally affect domestic

dynamics is limited, and its interventions usually counterproductive.

The "pink tide" could be receding, but historic problems between Latin America and the U.S. will surely remain for some time. To address them most effectively, the U.S. should be willing to modify longstanding policies no longer in sync with the region's realities. From drug policy to a new trade policy and the environment, the gap between the rhetoric and reality of genuine partnership needs to be further reduced.

Despite these differences, Latin America stands out as a peaceful and democratic region in a world that is increasingly unstable and less propitious for U.S. engagement. With few exceptions, most democracies in the region are as strong as they have ever been. Judicial systems are investigating political and business elites and holding them accountable for the first time in recent memory. Vibrant civil societies are challenging incumbents and demanding better governance and more transparency.

To be sure, economies are under stress, but problems are relatively mild compared to previous crises, and much of the social progress of the commodity boom is likely to remain. The next U.S. administration would be wise to see the region in a global context and take full advantage of the opportunity. ∎

discussion questions

1. What does the future of Venezuela look like post-Maduro? Is there a case for fruitful U.S. intervention in the country?

2. In what ways is the "return of the right" narrative to describe the current trend in Latin American politics accurate? In what ways is it inaccurate?

3. Should the U.S. end the trade embargo against Cuba? How does the embargo inform U.S.-Latin American relations as a whole?

4. In your opinion, what is the single greatest area of opportunity for the incoming U.S. administration to improve relations with Latin America?

5. Is Chinese investment in Latin America a threat to U.S. interests? Or can the presence of all three parties engender economic and social progress in the hemisphere? UN votes

6. In both Latin America and the U.S., the appetite for globalization and trade has waned. How should the new U.S. administration approach economic relations? What types of policies are fit for the 21st century?

Don't forget: Ballots start on page 115!

suggested readings

Kuczynski, Pedro-Pablo and Williamson, John, eds., **After the Washington Consensus: Restarting Growth and Reform in Latin America**. Washington D.C.: Peterson Institute for International Economics, 2003. 325 pp. Leading Latin American economists address plausible economic policy agendas for the region after the failures of the 1990s. The work succeeds the Institute for International Economics' 1986 publication that championed Washington Consensus reforms.

O'Toole, Gavin, **Politics in Latin America (2nd ed.)**. New York: Routledge, 2010. 768 pp. This book delivers a comprehensive overview of politics in Latin America, including the region's role on the international stage.

Reid, Michael, "Obama and Latin America: A Promising Day in the Neighborhood." **Foreign Affairs**, vol. 94 no. 5, 2015. This article examines Obama administration policy in Latin America.

Roett, Riordan and Paz, Guadalupe, eds., **Latin America and the Asian Giants: Evolving Ties with China and India**. Washington

D.C.: Brookings Institution Press, 2016. 352 pp. This volume reviews Latin America's relationships with China and India, and their impact on regional politics and economics.

Smith, Peter H., **Democracy in Latin America: Political Change in Comparative Perspective**. Oxford: Oxford University Press, 2005. 400 pp. Smith recounts Latin America's trajectory toward democracy across the 20th century, joining historical and political science perspectives.

Sweig, Julia E., **Cuba: What Everyone Needs to Know**. Oxford: Oxford University Press, 2009. 304 pp. This guide provides an overview of Cuba's internal politics and its international relations.

Wise, Carol and Roett, Riordan, eds., **Post-Stabilization Politics in Latin America: Competition, Transition, Collapse**. Washington D.C.: Brookings Institution Press, 2003. 306 pp. The contributors to *Post-Stabilization Politics* look at the effects of market reforms on the domestic politics of six Latin American countries up to the year 2003.

To access web links to these readings, as well as links to additional, shorter readings and suggested web sites,

GO TO www.greatdecisions.org

and click on the topic under Resources, on the right-hand side of the page

Prospects for Afghanistan and Pakistan
by Austin Long

U.S. Army soldiers walk to their C-17 cargo plane for departure on May 11, 2013, at Bagram Air Base, Afghanistan. U.S. soldiers and marines were part of the NATO troop withdrawal from Afghanistan. (PHOTO BY ROBERT NICKELSBERG/GETTY IMAGES)

The new U.S. president will inherit involvement in a variety of conflicts, but none as long-running as Afghanistan. On October 7, 2016, the United States marked the end of the 15th year of virtually continuous military operations in Afghanistan following the attacks of September 11, 2001. For Afghans, the end of 2016 represents an even grimmer milestone: Their country has been beset by major internal conflict almost every year since 1978.

The U.S. invaded Afghanistan seeking to destroy al-Qaeda, the terrorist group responsible for the 9/11 attacks. At the time, al-Qaeda was being sheltered by the Taliban, which ruled much of Afghanistan. Neighboring Pakistan had been allied with the Taliban, but was forced to withdraw open support for the group on the insistence of the U.S. Throughout the decade and a half since 2001, Pakistan has continued to quietly support the Taliban's fight against the U.S. and against the new Afghan government, even while helping the U.S. combat al-Qaeda. The U.S. remains concerned about both the Taliban and al-Qaeda, while trying to manage relationships with Afghanistan and Pakistan.

Pakistan's security services have had significant success in fighting their own internal enemies, but the relationship with the U.S. has steadily worsened over Pakistani support to the Taliban in Afghanistan. Meanwhile, the Taliban is not without its own difficulties. It has internal divisions, and also faces challengers aligned with ISIS. It has nonetheless scored a variety of military successes.

The last *Great Decisions* article on Afghanistan in 2012

AUSTIN LONG *is an associate professor at the School of International and Public Affairs and a member of the Arnold A. Saltzman Institute of War and Peace Studies and the Harriman Institute for Russian, Eurasian, and East European Studies at Columbia University. He is also a non-resident senior fellow at the Foreign Policy Research Institute. Dr. Long is the author of* The Soul of Armies: Counterinsurgency Doctrine and Military Culture in the United States and United Kingdom *(Ithaca, NY: Cornell University Press, 2016). He received his B.S. from the Sam Nunn School of International Affairs at the Georgia Institute of Technology and his Ph.D. in political science from the Massachusetts Institute of Technology.*

described the beginnings of U.S. and allied withdrawal, with the planned end of combat operations set for December 2014. Since then, the situation in Afghanistan has grown significantly worse, forcing U.S. troops, and especially aircraft, back into the fight against the Taliban even as limited counterterrorism operations against al-Qaeda and its affiliates continue. The Afghan government remains divided between two major factions, further compounding the challenge of fighting the Taliban. This is the new U.S. administration's inheritance. ■

Afghanistan and Pakistan before 9/11

(Left) Afghanistan's King Muhammad Zahir Shah (L) shakes hands with Leonid Brezhnev, first secretary of the Soviet Union Communist Party, at the Kremlin on September 15, 1971, in Moscow, Russia. (PHOTO BY KEYSTONE-FRANCE/GAMMA-RAPHOVIA GETTY IMAGES) *(Right) Female students at the Polytechnical University in Kabul, circa 1975.* (PHOTO BY ZH. ANGELOV/HULTON ARCHIVE/GETTY IMAGES)

When the U.S. invaded Afghanistan in 2001, it was intervening in a conflict that was decades old. Many of the leaders on both sides of the present clash gained experience (or were born) in this earlier fighting, so some background is vital to understanding the current situation. Yet it is equally important to understand that Afghanistan was not always at war.

Before the 1970s, the country had experienced decades of peace under the rule of its king, Muhammad Zahir Shah. Zahir Shah was a cautious modernizer, seeking to develop his country while remaining wary of potential backlash from his traditional and tribal society. The country had major ethnic divisions, with the Pashtuns of the south and east being the largest and most dominant group. Pashtuns also made up a large portion of the population of western Pakistan, with many tribes on both sides of the border. Zahir Shah, like almost every ruler of Afghanistan before him, was Pashtun. Afghanistan was also home to Tajiks, the next largest ethnic group, and somewhat smaller groupings of Uzbeks and Hazaras (a people alleged to be descended from the soldiers of Genghis Khan), among others. These non-Pashtun groups were mainly concentrated in the north and west, with the capital, Kabul, acting as the one real melting pot of ethnicities.

Most of the development under Zahir Shah was done in Kabul, which was relatively cosmopolitan by the 1960s. Zahir Shah proclaimed a new constitution in 1964, making Afghanistan at least theoretically a constitutional monarchy, with elections for parliament. Yet in the vast hinterland of Afghanistan away from the capital relatively little changed, as rough terrain and the power of local leaders restricted the influence of the government. Zahir Shah was cautious in his reforms, recognizing that projection of his authority had limited reach across the mountains and valleys of rural Afghanistan.

Zahir Shah's caution made some Afghan elites in Kabul impatient, and in 1973, his cousin, Muhammad Daoud Khan, staged a bloodless coup while Zahir Shah was abroad. Daoud did not proclaim himself king; instead, he proclaimed himself president of the nascent Afghan republic. As president, he sought to further modernize the country, and particularly to strengthen its army, wary as he was of neighboring Iran and Pakistan. He also worried about the influence of the massive Soviet Union to the north, which supported the newly formed People's Democratic Party of Afghanistan (PDPA). Indeed, the PDPA, a Marxist-Leninist party bent on rapid modernization, overthrew Daoud in a coup in 1978 after he tried to arrest much of their leadership.

This coup installed Nur Muhammad Taraki, the leader of the Khalq

Before you read, download the companion **Glossary** that includes definitions and a guide to acronyms and abbreviations used in the article. Go to **www.greatdecisions.org** and select a topic in the Resources section on the right-hand side of the page.

(People) faction of the PDPA as president. Babrak Karmal, the leader of Parcham (Banner), the other main PDPA faction, was made deputy prime minister, though he had less power than the title implied. These factions diverged politically and ideologically, but they also had ethnic differences, with Parcham being more Tajik, and Khalq more Pashtun. The divisions between Pashtun and non-Pashtun would haunt the party for the next 15 years.

The PDPA quickly aligned with the Soviets and then began a dramatic modernization campaign, in particular focusing on socialist land reform, women's rights and decreasing the role of Islam. In the summer of 1978, all three of these issues provoked a violent response from the rural population on traditional tribal and religious grounds. The backlash soon spread to provincial cities. In March 1979, the western city of Herat rose in open revolt against the PDPA government, and Soviet advisers to the Afghan military in Herat were massacred. Another mutiny followed in April in the eastern city of Jalalabad. Even as it battled tribal and Islamic elements, Khalq began purging the government of Parcham members.

This situation was clearly unstable, a fact that the Soviets well understood, as did the U.S. The Carter administration approved limited and non-lethal support to the anti-Soviet rebels in the spring of 1979. At some point in the fall of that year, the Soviets began to discuss the possibility of intervention to replace the PDPA leadership. This discussion was driven by an internal Khalq upset: Taraki had been assassinated by his fellow Khalqist Hafizullah Amin. By December, the Soviets agreed to execute a coup. Plans had already been drawn up by Soviet advisers and observers in Afghanistan, so the coup was carried out only two weeks later. Amin was assassinated and replaced by Parcham's leader and former Deputy Prime Minister Babrak Karmal.

This intervention, rather than resolving the problems of the Afghan government, made things worse. The U.S. and Pakistan saw it as both a major threat and as an opportunity. On the one hand,

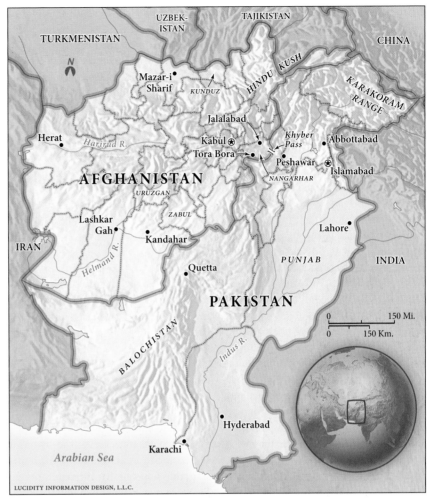

LUCIDITY INFORMATION DESIGN, L.L.C.

Pakistan was wary of Soviet troops on its border, while the U.S. worried that after Afghanistan the Soviets might expand their influence into the regional vacuum left by the fall of the Shah of Iran, a major U.S. ally. On the other hand, Afghans had traditionally been able to set many ethnic and tribal divisions aside to fight outside invaders: Supporting the rebels was a golden opportunity to damage the Soviets. Both the Carter and Reagan administrations approved significant increases in covert support to the rebels.

With this aid, the rebels, known by the Arabic term *mujahideen* (holy warriors), were able to fight the Soviets and their PDPA allies as guerillas, blending in with the local population and hiding in rugged terrain. The Soviets were no better prepared for guerilla war in Afghanistan than the U.S. Army was in Vietnam, but they began to improve over time. This led to another increase in covert aid to the mujahideen from the

U.S. and Pakistan, with the addition of Saudi Arabian funding.

The Saudis were flush with cash after the major upsurge in oil prices of the 1970s. The government was also eager to demonstrate its Islamic credentials to its population, at least some of whom believed the Saudi royal family were not worthy guardians of Islam's holy places. The House of Saud was clearly wary of the radicals in their midst, having faced the seizure by Saudi rebels of the holy site of Mecca in 1979. Supporting the mujahideen's fight against the atheist Soviets showed that the government was serious about Islam. The government also allowed (and tacitly encouraged) young men who might otherwise have rebelled against them to go fight in Afghanistan. Thousands of Saudis would flock to the war, including a young Osama bin Laden.

By the mid-1980s, the Soviets were weary of fighting in Afghanistan and began a slow withdrawal from the country.

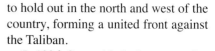
As they did, they sought to bolster the divided Afghan government: They replaced the scholarly Babrak Karmal with the PDPA intelligence chief, Muhammad Najibullah, while reforming and rearming the security forces. They also built up local militias of dubious loyalty to anything other than money. At the same time, fighting between factions of the mujahideen, always present, grew worse. In some cases, mujahideen factions would even cooperate with the Soviets and the PDPA to target their rivals.

After the Soviet withdrawal was completed in 1989, the PDPA government hung on with Soviet support until the collapse of the Soviet Union in 1991. After that, the PDPA only survived a few months: Many of the militia leaders that the Soviet Union had established defected to the mujahideen. By April 1992, the mujahideen and their new militia allies had ousted the government. Yet much of the mujahideen and militia factions were divided along the same ethnic lines that had bedeviled the PDPA. Forming a replacement government proved impossible. Even as the war between the PDPA and the mujahideen ended, the war between the mujahideen began.

This civil war would prove even more devastating than the one before it. Kabul, which had survived the Soviet-Afghan war with little damage, was shelled to ruins. With the Soviet Union gone, the U.S. lost interest in Afghanistan. The Paki-stanis did not. They supported Pashtun mujahideen against non-Pashtuns, seeking to ensure a friendly government in Afghanistan. After a few years of bloody war, though, the Pakistan grew disillusioned with these mujahideen commanders, and began to support a new movement, comprised of Pashtun students at Islamic schools that had been set up with Saudi support. This movement took its name from the Pashtun word for students: *taliban*.

The Taliban had originally formed sometime around 1994 under the leadership of Mullah Muhammad Omar. Hailing from Kandahar Province in southern Afghanistan, Mullah Omar had been educated in a Pakistani madrasa before returning to fight against the Soviets. According to an apocryphal story, the Taliban movement began when Omar led a small group of his followers to free two girls who had been kidnapped and raped by a local governor. After freeing the girls, the Taliban hanged the governor and began to mete out more such rough justice.

With Pakistani help, the Taliban seized territory in southern Afghanistan and then rapidly expanded north. By 1996, the Taliban had taken Kabul, imposing a harsh and austere version of Islamic law that was nonetheless welcomed by many Afghans after years of war and chaos. However, the non-Pashtun mujahideen commanders continued to hold out in the north and west of the country, forming a united front against the Taliban.

In 1996, Osama bin Laden returned to Afghanistan, having gone back to Saudi Arabia after the mujahideen triumph. In the years following the 1991 Gulf War, bin Laden had become increasingly hostile to both the Saudi government and the U.S. He had argued that the mujahideen model of victory against the Soviets could preempt the need for foreign troops in the war with Iraq. The Saudis rejected his offer and he was effectively banished to Sudan for speaking against the government. Upon returning to Afghanistan, he declared war on the U.S. while also helping the Taliban fight the United Front. Over the next five years, the Taliban seized ever more territory, and bin Laden's al-Qaeda (Arabic for "The Base") organization—a merger of his remaining followers from the holy war against the Soviets in Afghanistan with jihadist radicals from Egypt—launched several attacks against U.S. targets overseas (these included attacks on embassies in Africa in 1998, and on the U.S.S. *Cole* in 2000). By 2001, the United Front controlled only a few parts of Afghanistan. Bin Laden likely orchestrated the assassination of Ahmad Shah Massoud, the Front's de facto leader, on September 9, even as the 9/11 plotters finalized their preparations.

In parallel to the rise of the Taliban, the U.S. and Pakistan drifted apart. The two countries had already been aligned for decades, but the Afghan war against the Soviet Union and the PDPA had brought them into much closer alliance. At the same time, Pakistan was seeking to develop nuclear weapons, a cause for U.S. concern. This could be overlooked during the war, but once the Soviet Union collapsed, the U.S. began to examine Pakistan's nuclear ambitions more critically. Things came to a head after Pakistan's 1998 nuclear tests (in response to Indian nuclear tests): The U.S. sanctioned Pakistan, suspending arms sales and other economic transactions. As Pakistan confronted its much larger neighbor India in the late 1990s, Islamabad felt abandoned if not betrayed by the U.S. ∎

Soviet troops crossing the Soviet-Afghan border along the bridge over the Amudarya River near the town of Termez, Uzbekistan, during their withdrawal from Afghanistan, February 6, 1989. (PHOTO BY: SOVFOTO/UIG VIA GETTY IMAGES)

Enduring Freedom, 2001–14

After the 9/11 attacks, the United States demanded that the Taliban hand over Osama bin Laden and other key al-Qaeda leaders. The Taliban was unwilling, and Washington put pressure on Pakistan to convince the group, or, failing that, to cut support. The head of Pakistani intelligence, when told of U.S. demands by Deputy Secretary of State Richard Armitage, began to describe the long history of the war in Afghanistan. Armitage cut him off, forcefully stating: "History starts today."

This exchange encapsulates much of the tension between the U.S. and Pakistan after 9/11. Pakistan has been helpful with many U.S. counterterrorism operations, helping capture Khalid Sheikh Muhammad, the main 9/11 planner, and others. Yet as the events following the collapse of the Soviet Union demonstrated, the U.S. can always leave the region, while Pakistan will always be Afghanistan's neighbor: The U.S. wanted a fresh start in Afghanistan; Pakistan never left.

By early October 2001, it was clear that neither U.S. nor Pakistani efforts were going to convince the Taliban to hand over bin Laden. In this context, the U.S., along with some of its key allies, began military operations, dubbed Operation Enduring Freedom. These operations were both unconventional and effective. The CIA had maintained some ties to the non-Pashtun mujahideen commanders it supported in the 1980s, and now leveraged those ties to make a deal. The U.S. would provide money, supplies, special forces and air support to the United Front; the United Front would provide the bulk of the ground troops to launch an offensive against the Taliban. For the commanders of the United Front—on the verge of defeat or already in exile—the opportunity was impossible to pass up.

The combination of the U.S. and the United Front—now referred to as the Northern Alliance—was devastating to the Taliban. In just over a month, the group lost Kabul to the Front's advances, and in another month it lost its last major

U.S. 10th Mountain Division soldiers board a Chinook helicopter in the invasion of Afghanistan, 2001. (PHOTO BY UNIVERSAL HISTORY ARCHIVE/GETTY IMAGES)

stronghold, the southern city of Kandahar. Hamid Karzai, a Pashtun, was sworn in as interim president in December after a conference in Bonn set up a process for forming a new government.

The victory, though rapid and devastating, was not complete. Osama bin Laden had escaped into Pakistan after nearly being killed at a mountain fortress known as Tora Bora. Many senior Taliban leaders, including Mullah Omar, had also escaped into Pakistan. Still, in 2002 it was easy to believe that the war was essentially over and the only major task was to build a new Afghan democracy.

This challenge was monumental in itself, as the commanders of the Northern Alliance, who had provided the troops that won the war, had a major role in the interim government and began to set up patronage networks to reward their loyal supporters. Such networks were not unique to Afghanistan, but they did begin to create the same sort of factional divisions that had beset the PDPA. Key military commands and government offices were often distributed based much less on capability and much more on patronage. At the same time, corruption began to divert economic aid from the U.S. and

other countries from intended purposes.

Factional division and corruption meant that some Afghans gained much more from the new democratic government than others. Discontented Pashtuns provided fertile ground for Taliban recruiters, who began to return to communities in the south and east. Though it would take years to rebuild, the Taliban had the time and were convinced that the U.S., which after 2003 was increasingly distracted by the war in Iraq, would eventually leave. The U.S. and its allies kept very few troops in Afghanistan between 2002 and 2005. At the same time, efforts to build a new Afghan National Army and Afghan National Police proceeded slowly. There was thus only modest opposition to the Taliban's surreptitious return.

By 2005, it had become increasingly clear that the Taliban were developing a significant and renewed presence in the Pashtun areas of the east and south. It was lost on no one that these areas bordered Pakistan, where the Taliban leadership had re-formed in the city of Quetta. Officially, the Pakistani government could not find these leaders, but this was widely believed to be a rather thin fiction. Yet Pakistan had also alleg-

Afghan President Hamid Karzai is seen after a campaign speech about his five year plan if reelected, in Kabul, Afghanistan, on Aug 10, 2009. (RON HAVIV/VII/REDUX)

edly approved U.S. drone strikes against al-Qaeda and other terrorist leaders in the remote areas bordering Afghanistan. The United States thus faced a dilemma: To publicly accuse Pakistan of supporting the Taliban would likely end other Pakistani cooperation.

Pakistan also faced increasing Islamic militancy among its own Pashtun population. In the western tribal areas, resentment against the distant government in Islamabad was not new, but it grew stronger as militants from Afghanistan and elsewhere gathered there. A variety of smaller militant groups began to coalesce under an umbrella organization that became widely known as the Pakistani Taliban (to differentiate from the Afghan Taliban). The religious ideologies of the Afghan and the Pakistani Taliban were not radically different. Instead, the key division was on objectives, with the Afghan Taliban focused on driving the U.S. and its allies out of Afghanistan, and the Pakistani Taliban at least as focused on fighting the Pakistani government.

This further underscored the dichotomy within Pakistan: There was a tacit understanding in the Pakistani military and intelligence services that there were "good Taliban" (Afghan Taliban fighting only in Afghanistan) and "bad Taliban" (Pakistani Taliban fighting against the Pakistani government), though the distinction was often blurry to say the least. The "good Taliban" were allies—critical to ensuring that Afghanistan remain at least nominally under Pakistani control, and not aligned with India (the latter being the overwhelming security concern for the Pakistani military). In contrast, the "bad Taliban" fought the government and might even have been proxies of dreaded India.

In 2006, the U.S. and several key NATO allies began to launch operations against the resurgent Afghan Taliban, which was increasingly able to mount guerilla operations against the Afghan government and its international supporters. In southern Afghanistan, the allies took the lead, with the British and Danish in Helmand Province, the Australians and Dutch in Uruzgan, and the Canadians in Kandahar; the U.S. was at the helm in eastern Afghanistan. But many of the allies, and especially the U.S., had large numbers of troops committed to Iraq, so it was difficult to commit additional forces to Afghanistan. At the same time, the new Afghan National Army and Police remained relatively weak, hindered by corruption and factional divisions. Incompetent commanders were often replaced, and troops sometimes went unpaid, their salaries ending up in the pockets of others. It was little wonder desertion rates were relatively high for the rank-and-file Afghan soldier or policeman.

In 2009—after three years of guerilla warfare by the Taliban against the U.S., allies and the Afghan government—newly elected President Barack Obama ordered a review of U.S. Afghanistan strategy as one of his first acts. The review concluded that more resources and troops were needed for an effective campaign against the Taliban guerillas, though there was some difference among U.S. military and defense leaders about how many more and for how long they would be needed. The improvement in the security situation in Iraq meant that additional troops were available.

However, some U.S. leaders, allegedly including Vice President Joe Biden, were reluctant to commit large numbers of troops to a war that might drag on. For these leaders, the U.S. had lost sight of why it invaded Afghanistan in the first place. The objective had been getting bin Laden and al-Qaeda: Fighting the Taliban was necessary since the group would not turn him over, but it was not a goal. These leaders preferred an approach sometimes termed "counterterrorism plus," which would involve the withdrawal of most U.S. combat troops—other than special operations forces targeting terrorist leaders—with the remainder shifting to a supporting role for the Afghan National Army and Police.

The trepidation of committing large numbers of troops to support the Afghan government was underscored by the controversy surrounding the Afghan presidential election in 2009. Hamid Karzai—who had served as interim president since elected in 2004—now looked vulnerable to a challenge from Abdullah Abdullah, a Tajik associated with the Northern Alliance. After a first round of voting that saw widespread accusations of tampering, Abdullah and Karzai were supposed to have a run-off in November 2009. Abdullah eventually withdrew his name, believing the run-off would be rigged.

That same year, the Pakistani government also began to launch large and sustained offensives against the Pakistani Taliban. While the government had been fighting the Pakistani Taliban for years, it had not done so in such a sustained way, instead agreeing often to cease-fires and attempts at negotiation. Some in the U.S. hoped this change would be reflected by a new Pakistani attitude toward the Afghan Taliban.

It was against this backdrop that President Obama announced a compromise position in a speech at West Point in December 2009. He committed 30,000 additional U.S. troops on top of the 17,000 he sent shortly after taking office. This brought the total number of U.S. troops in Afghanistan to nearly 100,000, alongside roughly 40,000 allied troops. These forces were only committed through 2011, to be followed by a major U.S. withdrawal. The goal was to stabilize Afghanistan, just as a similar surge in troop numbers was believed to have done in Iraq. Simultaneously, the development of Afghan forces would be sped up so they could take over.

In 2010, these newly deployed troops launched offensives across Afghanistan, seizing territory that the Taliban held in the south and east. U.S. and allied casualties went up accordingly, and in the areas cleared by the U.S., the Afghan government was still hampered by corruption, patronage and factional divisions. The only Afghan leaders who did seem effective in fighting the Taliban increasingly resembled regional warlords and were implicated in corruption and even criminal activity, including the burgeoning opium trade. Indeed, it was sometimes difficult to tell whether fighting was actually about the Afghan government versus the Taliban, or if it was about local fights over the drug trade, corruption or the settling of old scores.

Opium production was not a new phenomenon in Afghanistan (*see sidebar on next page*), but between 2002 and 2009, the Afghan government and the U.S. had some success in slowing the growth of the trade. However, the more the U.S. relied on strongmen, such as the police chief of Kandahar Province, General Abdul Raziq, to fight the Taliban, the less it focused on the opium trade (and other forms of corruption). The Taliban, too, was able to fund itself in part through taxing opium and other illicit industries (such as illegal mining of precious stones or illegal harvesting of timber). This sometimes led to col-

lusion between government and Taliban officials in order to maximize revenue.

In 2011, despite being pushed out of many areas, the Taliban was still capable of putting up a tough fight in remote rural territory, and of conducting sophisticated terrorist attacks in Kabul. Nevertheless, a small number of U.S. troops were withdrawn in keeping with the president's timeline. It also became clear that Pakistan's government had not fundamentally altered its approach to the Taliban: Islamabad maintained the distinction between a good Afghan Taliban and a bad Pakistani branch.

The tension between the U.S. and Pakistan rose to new heights after the May 2011 raid on the Pakistani city of Abbottabad that killed Osama bin Laden. The Pakistanis were outraged that they had not been informed of the operation, and many in the U.S. were highly skeptical that bin Laden could have hidden in such a city without help from at least some part of the Pakistani government. In September, retiring Chairman of the Joint Chiefs of Staff Admiral Michael Mullen became the first senior U.S. official to bluntly and publicly accuse Pakistan of supporting some factions of the Taliban to launch terrorist attacks.

In 2012, the U.S. withdrawal ac-

celerated. All 33,000 troops deployed in the surge had left by the end of the year. The U.S. and Afghanistan also signed a Strategic Partnership Agreement to ensure that training and support for the Afghan National Army and Police would continue even after the withdrawal of U.S. combat forces. Yet the performance of these Afghan security forces indicated that they were still underdeveloped.

One sign of the weakness of the security forces was a dramatic rise in the number of so-called "insider attacks," in which members of the Afghan National Army or Police attacked U.S. troops. This phenomenon, which had been almost nonexistent before 2008, began to increase as U.S. troop numbers surged into Afghanistan in 2009. The number of insider attacks exploded over the next several years, and by 2012 had become so dramatic that they led to a temporary suspension of U.S.-Afghan joint operations. A series of preventive measures, including better screening of applicants to the army and police, combined with the accelerating drawdown, eventually reduced the phenomenon, but it remained a concern.

By 2013, much of the effort by U.S. troops was focused on withdrawal, which was a massive logistical chal-

U.S. President Barack Obama (C) poses with cadets after addressing the nation on Afghanistan at the United States Military Academy at West Point, NY, December 1, 2009. Obama said sending 30,000 more troops into Afghanistan is in the "vital national interest" of the United States. (JIM WATSON/AFP/GETTY IMAGES)

Opium in Afghanistan

The opium trade is not a new phenomenon in Afghanistan, but until the 1970s it was very limited. The kings of Afghanistan controlled the cultivation of opium poppies, and the remoteness of Afghanistan made other sources (e.g. the Golden Triangle of Southeast Asia, parts of Mexico) more attractive.

However, in the 1970s, three phenomena interacted to produce a surge in the Afghan opium trade. First, the increasing violence produced by the PDPA coup and subsequent war created opportunities for entrepreneurial warlords to cultivate opium poppies without state interference. Second, the development of infrastructure and the increasing capability of modern transport made getting Afghan opium to the world market much easier. Third, crackdowns on other sources of opium (such as Mexico) made Afghan opium more attractive, just as the world heroin demand surged.

The Afghan opium market expanded again after the collapse of the PDPA government. With the U.S.S.R. gone and U.S. interest in the region nearly zero, the former mujahideen and militia leaders scrambled for ways to fund their civil war. The opium trade was one of the few growth areas in the Afghan economy in the 1990s.

In contrast, one of the positive elements of the Taliban's rise to power was that it was both open to curtailing opium production and had an incentive to do so in terms of international recognition and aid. In 2000, the Taliban regime proclaimed a ban on opium production, calling it un-Islamic. This increased the group's stature with the international community and allowed it to press for development assistance, while also increasing the value of any opium stockpiles held by the Taliban or its allies. Although the ban was not total, it did lead to a major decline in production.

This ban was obviously short-lived, as the Taliban regime was driven from power in 2001. Following the U.S. invasion, opium cultivation once again began to boom, exploited as a source of revenue not only by the Taliban,

Afghan farmers harvest opium sap from a poppy field in Surkh Rod District, of Nangarhar province near Jalalabad in May 2015. (NOORULLAH SHIRZADA/AFP/GETTY IMAGES)

but also by corrupt Afghan government officials. Despite significant U.S. and allied investment in counternarcotics programs, cultivation continued to climb. Law enforcement, poppy eradication and programs to give Afghan farmers alternative livelihoods all failed to make a major dent. The business became so lucrative that previously unused areas of the southern Afghan desert were brought under cultivation.

Much of Afghan opium ends up as heroin destined for Europe and especially Russia, with Moscow viewing the growing heroin problem among its population as a major threat. This made counternarcotics in Afghanistan one of the only areas in which the U.S. and Russia were able to sustain cooperation as relations worsened. However, the war in Ukraine eventually strained even this unity, and in 2014 the U.S. added the head of the Russian Federal Drug Control Service to its list of sanctioned individuals.

In 2016, Afghan opium production continued to climb, in large part due to the ongoing weakness of the Afghan government. Afghanistan accounted for the vast majority of the estimated 4,800 tons of opium produced globally in 2016. Absent a major change in the political and economic environment, this pattern will continue indefinitely.

lenge. Bases had either to be prepared for turnover to the Afghans, or stripped of military equipment. Fewer and fewer U.S. troops, other than special operations forces, were directly involved in combat with the Taliban. Meanwhile, U.S. attention was drawn to conflicts elsewhere, as civil war broke out in Syria and security in Iraq massively deteriorated.

In parallel, the U.S. renewed emphasis on finding a negotiated settlement to the war. While very quiet discussions between the U.S., the Tali-

ban and the Afghan government had already begun, the talks (or at least the possibility of talks) became public in June 2013 when the Taliban opened a political office in Qatar. This office was somewhat controversial and was closed within a month, but it did indicate that all sides were at least potentially open to negotiation, even if agreement was far off.

Another set of negotiations, concerning the release of U.S. soldier Robert "Bowe" Bergdahl, culminated the following year. Bergdahl had been cap-

tured by the Taliban in 2009, but was freed in May 2014 after the U.S. agreed to release five Taliban detainees held at Guantanamo Bay. The five Taliban were handed over to the government of Qatar as part of an arrangement to keep them from returning to the battlefield. Bergdahl's release sparked controversy in the U.S., with some in Congress particularly aggrieved that they had been given very little notice of the prisoner exchange.

The U.S. drawdown continued in 2014, until finally in December of that year Operation Enduring Freedom, came to a close. This did not signal the end of U.S. military involvement in Afghanistan, which was renewed under the name Operation Freedom's Sentinel. The operation was intended to be much smaller than Enduring Freedom, employing about 10,000 U.S. troops focused almost exclusively on limited counterterrorism operations and training Afghan security forces. Even this limited contingent was to shrink further by the end of 2015.

Unfortunately, most of the problems plaguing the war over the previous decade remained. Most notably, the Afghan presidential election in 2014 was marred by the same divisions as the elections of 2009. This time, President Karzai was prevented by term limits from running again, so the election pitted Ashraf Ghani, a Pashtun former finance minister, against Abdullah Abdullah. After a lengthy audit process, Ghani was declared the winner, but rumors of a possible coup attempt were rife in Kabul. In order to keep the

Afghans wait in line on a rainy day to vote in the general elections, in Kabul, Afghanistan, April 5, 2014. Voting hours were extended nationwide due to longer-than-expected lines at polling places, and though widespread fears of the Taliban kept one in eight polling centers closed, no heavy attacks had taken place. (TYLER HICKS/THE NEW YORK TIMES/REDUX)

peace, and with U.S. encouragement, Ghani and Abdullah announced a power-sharing unity government in which Ghani would become president, but Abdullah would receive the new position of chief executive of the country.

Continuing problems in the Afghan security forces were also tragically underscored by an insider attack that killed a U.S. major general in August 2014—the first such senior officer killed by hostile fire overseas since Vietnam. ∎

Afghanistan after drawdown, 2015–16

Since the beginning of Operation Freedom's Sentinel, and its NATO counterpart, Resolute Support, security in Afghanistan has declined substantially. The Taliban wasted little time in seeking to test how well the Afghan National Army and Police would fight without large numbers of Western troops supporting them. In the south, they launched major offensives in Helmand Province, one of the largest opium producing regions. In the north, where the Taliban had long been weaker due to the relatively limited number of Pashtuns, they began to seize territory in the province of Kunduz.

In Helmand, the Taliban offensive gradually wore down the Afghan security forces in brutal fighting. By the end of the summer, the Taliban was in position to threaten the provincial capital of Lashkar Gah. Afghan government

troops continued to be afflicted by poor leadership and even worse logistical support—problems with roots in a political culture of patronage and corruption. Desertions were common in Helmand.

In Kunduz, the same sort of sustained fighting took place during this period, grinding down the Afghan security forces. In September 2015, government troops collapsed in the face of an attack on the provincial capital. Suddenly, and for the first time in nearly 14 years, the Taliban controlled a major city.

The military setbacks in 2015 were mirrored in continuing political friction between President Ghani and Chief Executive Abdullah. The unity government was to have shared senior ministerial positions, but many, including the crucial position of minister of defense, went unfilled over disagreements between the two factions. While

acting Defense Minister Muhammad Stanekzai, an ally of President Ghani, was widely seen as competent, the continued political disagreement limited his authority even as Afghan troops fought desperately.

The Taliban successes, particularly in Kunduz, led the Obama administration to expand the authority of U.S. forces to support Afghan military operations. The intent of the shift to Operation Freedom's Sentinel had been to greatly limit U.S. forces' involvement in combat. But U.S. and allied special operations forces were quickly dispatched to Kunduz and Helmand. They were not intended to participate directly in combat, but were nonetheless close to the front lines, helping direct airstrikes against the Taliban and advising Afghan ground commanders. The administration also decided to slow any further drawdown of U.S. forces for 2015, though it still planned to reduce the numbers by the end of 2016.

The situation in Helmand stabilized, with the government continuing to hold Lashkar Gah, but having lost control over much of the hinterland of the province, including many key opium-producing areas. In early October, Afghan troops, supported by the U.S., launched a counteroffensive to retake Kunduz city. After nearly two weeks of difficult conflict, they succeeded.

Yet amid this fighting, a U.S. gunship struck a hospital operated by the non-governmental organization Doctors Without Borders, killing dozens of civilians. This strike provoked accusations by some, including Doctors Without Borders, that the U.S. had committed a war crime. President Obama subsequently apologized and the U.S. military concluded that the strike had been an avoidable error, but was not intentional. The incident underscored the limits, in chaotic conditions, of even very precise U.S. air-power to minimize civilian casualties and collateral damage.

At the same time, U.S. and Afghan government relations with Pakistan remained tense. President Ghani set improved relations as a priority, but had made little progress. In April 2015, a

Pakistani court ruled that the former head of CIA operations in Pakistan should be tried for murder, for waging war against Pakistan, and for conspiracy and terrorism—charges stemming from an alleged 2009 drone strike in Pakistan. This marked a new low in U.S.-Pakistan relations, as it was widely believed that Pakistani intelligence had leaked the name of the CIA officer. Because there was no chance that the U.S. would extradite the officer, the criminal charges were seen as being largely political and symbolic.

Pakistan itself continued to face terrorist attacks from the Pakistani Taliban, even as many allege that government support for the Afghan Taliban continued. Unlike the Afghan security forces, the Pakistani security forces made substantial progress in their fight against the Pakistani Taliban in 2015, clearing many areas where the group had been overtly present. This progress was helped in part by the killing of the primary leader of the Pakistani Taliban, Hakimullah Mehsud, by an alleged U.S. drone strike near the end of 2013. His death led to factional infighting, which significantly weakened the group over the course of 2014–15. The outcome emphasized that even as relations were deeply strained, the U.S. and Pakistan could cooperate, and in some sense they

had to cooperate in order for each to achieve at least some of its objectives.

Mehsud was not the only leader who died in 2013. Apparently Mullah Omar had also died, of natural causes. This had been a closely held Taliban secret, though rumors circulated for years. In July 2015, the Afghan government finally believed it had reliable intelligence that Omar was indeed dead. Islamabad made a public announcement, which was subsequently confirmed by the Taliban. The Taliban soon named Mullah Akhtar Mansour—who had essentially been running the Taliban in Omar's name for years—as his successor. Yet not all factions agreed with this choice, and several groups of Taliban split off and began fighting against their former comrades, particularly in the southern province of Zabul.

Many of those disaffected with leadership change in the Taliban now had an alternative: The success of ISIS made it increasingly attractive. Former Taliban began, at least notionally, to pledge allegiance to ISIS, which referred to the Afghanistan-Pakistan region as Khorasan Province. For the first time, the Taliban had a potential major rival. The group began to launch fierce attacks on ISIS in the summer of 2015, concentrated in the eastern province of Nangarhar on the Pakistani border.

As 2016 began, the Obama administration, concerned at the rise of ISIS in Afghanistan, authorized the U.S. military to expand operations against the group. With U.S. support, the Afghan military launched a series of attacks in Nangarhar, which were successful enough to force ISIS fighters to flee to other provinces or across the border into Pakistan. The U.S.-Afghan efforts continued through the summer of 2016. The Taliban response to this offensive against its rival was mixed, with some reports of local cease-fires with ISIS, even as senior Taliban leaders continued to oppose the group. There were even reports of tacit cooperation between Afghan security forces and the Taliban against ISIS—an echo of the cooperation between the Soviets and mujahideen factions against other mujahideen in the 1980s.

Afghan army soldiers stand guard in front of a military vehicle in Kunduz, Afghanistan, Oct. 5, 2015. After five days of fierce fighting Afghan security forces evicted Taliban militants from the northern city. (XINHUA/AJMAL/ALAMY)

Refugees

Nearly four decades of almost continual war have produced millions of Afghan refugees scattered across the globe. After the Soviet intervention in 1979 and the violence that followed, Afghans of all ethnicities fled. Many ended up in Pakistan, where they filled refugee camps, with a somewhat smaller number fleeing to Iran. Others came to Europe and the U.S., leading to the formation of large Afghan communities in cities like New York and Washington, D.C.

After the collapse of the PDPA government, there was another wave of refugees, as areas like Kabul that had been relatively untouched by the previous war were now destroyed. Some ethnic groups, particularly the Hazaras, also faced ethnic cleansing and massacres, further pushing them to flee. The rise of the Taliban likewise propelled those opposed to them, especially non-Pashtuns, to seek escape. The Pakistani cities of Quetta and Peshawar swelled with refugees in this period.

After the initial U.S. invasion there was another small flux of refugees, but then a substantial number of Afghans either willingly returned from exile or were deported by the states that had been hosting them. This was particularly true of Iran, though as of 2016 there are still nearly a million registered Afghan refugees and their descendants there. Pakistan has likewise made it a priority to reduce the number of Afghan refugees it hosts, but still has more than 1.5 million registered. For comparison, the population of Afghanistan is estimated to be a little more than 32–33 million.

Since the end of Operation Enduring Freedom, a new wave of refugees has emerged, seeking not to flee just to Iran or Pakistan, but also to Europe and to a lesser extent the United States. While the flows of refugees from Syria dominate the headlines, the numbers of Afghan refugees seeking asylum in Europe have also boomed. One reason has been the Taliban offensives across Afghanistan, but another is declining economic opportunity. Apart from

Afghan refugees wait at a Voluntary Repatriation Center in Chamkani, Peshawar, Pakistan, on October 20, 2016, before returning to their country. According to the United Nations High Commissioner for Refugees (UNHCR) Representative in Pakistan, about 370,000 Afghan refugees have returned to their country. (PHOTO BY METIN AKTAS/ANADOLU AGENCY/GETTY IMAGES)

opium (*see sidebar*), the other growth area for the Afghan economy after 2001 was supporting U.S. and allied personnel and development projects, which created jobs ranging from trucking and construction to restaurants and tourism. As Western presence declined precipitously, these jobs disappeared, leaving many Afghans fluent in English (and other European languages) but with no economic prospects.

No matter what U.S. policies are pursued by the new administration, the increase in Afghan refugees is likely to continue until some negotiated settlement is reached to conclude the war. At best this is years away, so the U.S. and its allies should consider policies to deal with the refugee flow. The U.S. already has a small program that allows Afghans who worked for the U.S. government (such as interpreters) to seek special visas, but concerns about the potential for refugees to become radicalized and even commit acts of terror make expanding such programs politically challenging.

Informal talks between the Afghan government and the Taliban also resumed in 2015, again in Qatar. President Ghani was particularly interested in attempting to find a negotiated end to the war, but one of the main points of contention was the Taliban's demand that all foreign forces leave the country. Most of the Afghan government found this unacceptable. The talks were further disrupted by the revelation of Mullah Omar's death and the subsequent discord inside the Taliban.

Yet despite these attempts at talks, and the reports of limited cooperation against ISIS, the war continued. Both

sides launched offensives and counteroffensives across the country during the summer, with the Taliban continuing to make gains in Helmand Province, but having substantially less success in Kunduz and elsewhere. The Obama administration further loosened restrictions on U.S. participation in Afghan operations, allowing more troops to accompany Afghan units and to provide air support.

In May 2016, a U.S. drone strike killed the new Taliban leader Mullah Akhtar Mansour, who had officially led the group for less than a year. This strike was unusual as it took place in Balo-

chistan, an area of southwest Pakistan where no drone strikes had previously been reported. While Pakistan's public response was limited, the decision to strike does not seem to have been approved by the government, and likely added strain to relations with the U.S. Mansour was replaced by the less wellknown Mawlawi Hibatullah Akhundzada, a religious scholar previously involved in the Taliban's court system.

Even as the Taliban lost its second commander in three years, the leadership of the Afghan government was itself increasingly fractious. Abdullah felt sidelined by Ghani, and, in August

Al-Qaeda in the Indian Subcontinent

The death of Osama bin Laden in May 2011 was seen as the pinnacle of a decade-long campaign against the senior leadership of al-Qaeda. There is no doubt that this campaign greatly disrupted the organization. But al-Qaeda was still able to join with militants in other parts of the world to create "franchise"-like offshoots. These include al-Qaeda in the Islamic Maghreb (AQIM) operating in northern Africa, al- Qaeda in the Arabian Peninsula (AQAP) operating in Saudi Arabia and Yemen, and, until July 2016, the Nusra Front in Syria (having tried at that time to distance itself from al-Qaeda).

Yet perhaps most concerning is the rise of al-Qaeda in the Indian Subcontinent (AQIS) in 2014. In that year, Osama bin Laden's successor, Ayman al-Zawahiri, proclaimed that this organization had taken two years to create. It appears to have drawn together Islamic militants from a number of groups in India, Afghanistan and Pakistan (apparently including current or former members of groups such as Harakat-ul-Muhajideen, Harakat-ul-Jihad-al-Islami and Brigade 313, Jaish-e-Muhammad, and Lashkar-e-Jhangvi). According to an AQIS spokesman, the group "was formed by the gathering of several jihadi groups that have a long history in jihad and fighting ... so they united and came together and applied the directives of their beloved emir, Sheikh Ayman al Zawahiri, may Allah preserve him." AQIS seems to have garnered support from another Pakistani group, Lashkar e-Taiba (LeT), which in turn is believed to be supported by Pakistani intelligence. AQIS could number in the thousands, and appears to represent a significant expansion of al-Qaeda affiliated capability.

One of the chief worries about AQIS is that many members of the Pakistani security forces, including the military, have become increasingly radicalized in their interpretation of Islam. This has created numerous potential insider threats, wherein radicalized Pakistani government personnel support terrorist actions. One example of such an insider threat was the 2011 assassination of the governor of Pakistan's Punjab Province by his own bodyguard, who became a martyr to many radicals when he was executed in 2016. AQIS is believed to have exploited such insider connections when it attempted to seize a Pakistani warship in 2014.

The most worrying possible insider threat is to Pakistan's nuclear weapons and nuclear facilities. While Pakistan works hard to ensure the reliability of the personnel guarding its nuclear weapons, it is not impossible that a radicalized individual, or small group of individuals, could gain access. It is still unlikely that radicals could steal an entire weapon, but smuggling limited amounts of nuclear material out of facilities, while time consuming, might escape detection.

2016, publicly denounced him as unfit for the presidency. Still, the government did make progress on appointing key ministers: A defense minister and an intelligence director were confirmed in June, filling positions that had been officially vacant since the election in 2014.

Over the summer, the U.S. administration also announced that it intended to limit further drawdown of U.S. forces in 2016 to about 1,500 troops, leaving about 8,400 in place at the end of the year. Though smaller in number, these forces would be much more active participants in the war than envisioned at the beginning of Operation Freedom's Sentinel. Some analysts have noted that this force looks similar to the "counterterrorism plus" option that certain leaders wanted to pursue back in 2009. Regardless, the announcement effectively concluded President Obama's efforts to end substantial U.S. military involvement in Afghanistan, leaving it to his successor to decide the future of U.S. forces in the long running war. ∎

Which way ahead?

The new U.S. president faces hard choices about policy in Afghanistan, with essentially three major courses of action available. The first choice is at least politically the easiest and probably the default position: maintain the status quo. This would entail leaving roughly the same number of troops in place—perhaps a small increase, perhaps a small decrease—with the same authority to conduct counterterrorism operations and support Afghan troops in combat. It would also involve maintaining the same relationship with Pakistan—partly friend, partly foe.

This policy has two main advantages, apart from being relatively easy politically. First, it can likely be sustained indefinitely, as the costs in blood and treasure are low. The costs of Operation Freedom's Sentinel have been small compared to Operation Enduring Freedom, particularly in terms of casualties. Since the end of 2014, fewer than 40 U.S. troops have been killed in Afghanistan, compared to 499 in 2010, the peak year of casualties. All losses are tragic, but the cost here is relatively low, and has kept Afghanistan largely out of the spotlight of U.S. politics, especially compared to events in Iraq and Syria.

The second major advantage is that the status quo is likely to be enough to prevent a Taliban victory. While the Taliban will probably continue to advance in the south and east of Afghanistan—their traditional Pashtun strongholds—U.S. military support has curtailed Taliban advances in Kunduz and other parts of Afghanistan. The net result of this status quo policy would thus be a bloody stalemate.

Stalemate in this context would be a double-edged sword for the U.S. On the one hand, the Taliban is confronting dissension in its ranks, and many of its leaders are weary of a war that has kept them on the run for 15 years and ever more dependent on the whims of Pakistan. If the Taliban leadership believes it is confronting many more years of conflict without victory, it may compel them to serious negotiations.

On the other hand, the United States is also weary of war. Though Afghanistan is no longer the front-page news it was in 2012, maintaining the status quo may grow more untenable for the new administration, as Congress and the general public increasingly question U.S. presence there. The status quo may thus be an easy default for an administration in 2017, but by 2020, as the beginning of another decade of war in Afghanistan looms, it may become politically challenging.

U.S. relations with Pakistan will be important in determining whether the Taliban comes to the negotiating table in this first scenario. If relations are still very poor, the Pakistanis can use their influence with the Taliban to halt negotiations. They have done this before, arresting one senior Taliban leader in 2010 when he sought to open negotiations that the Pakistanis were unwilling to support. In contrast, if U.S.-Pakistan relations improve, Islamabad can put pressure on the Taliban to come to the table.

The second major course of action is a dramatic reversal of the drawdown, returning large numbers of U.S. troops to the battlefield in Afghanistan. This need not entail a return to the roughly 100,000 troops that were in Afghanistan in 2010, but would require at least 25,000 (about the level at the end of the George W. Bush administration). An increase of this size would ensure that U.S. troops could support Afghan forces on the battlefield in the south and east, halting and perhaps even reversing some of the Taliban gains in those regions.

The major advantage of this policy is that it would inflict significant losses on a Taliban already beset by internal challenges and the emergence of ISIS as a rival. Confronted with these losses, the Taliban might seek a quick negotiated end to the war. However, there may be real limits to the room for rapid negotia-

U.S. army and Afghan National Army (ANA) soldiers walk as NATO helicopters flies overhead at coalition force Forward Operating Base (FOB) Connelly in the Khogyani district in the eastern province of Nangarhar on August 13, 2015. (WAKIL KOHSAR/AFP/GETTY IMAGES)

tion given internal disputes. Moreover, as noted above, Pakistan would need to be willing to accept whatever settlement was negotiated, which is hardly a given.

The major drawback to this policy is that it is costlier than the status quo and may simply be politically indefensible. The appetite in the U.S. government—not to mention among the American public—for a major increase in troops is very low. While the emergence of al-Qaeda in the Indian Subcontinent (*see sidebar*) may provide sufficient rationale to overcome objections, this is far from guaranteed.

Additionally, a substantial increase in U.S. forces in Afghanistan would require an expansion of logistical support. Afghanistan is landlocked, so supplies would either have to come by air (increasingly difficult and costly as troop numbers grow) or land. Land routes to Afghanistan either lead through Iran (unlikely to allow U.S. access), Russia (once willing to support U.S. logistics in Afghanistan but unlikely now) or Pakistan, which would give Islamabad additional leverage.

The third and final major course of action is to further reduce U.S. troops with the goal of nearly total withdrawal by the end of the new administration's first term. The major advantage of this policy is that it brings the seemingly end-

less war in Afghanistan to a close for the U.S. (though not for Afghans). It would be less expensive than the status quo in terms of money and risk to U.S. troops. It would also allow the U.S. more freedom to choose how to deal with Pakistan, by reducing the need for Pakistani support in Afghanistan (though counterterrorism operations inside Pakistan would still require support).

However, the political cost of such a policy, if deliberately pursued from the outset of the new administration, may be high. President Obama faced substantial criticism for withdrawing U.S. troops from Iraq—criticism that redoubled as the security situation deteriorated. Indeed, the administration was forced to re-introduce troops to Iraq and to curtail its planned drawdown in Afghanistan. The new administration would likely face similar pressure or risk the accusation that it had "lost Afghanistan."

U.S. leaders thus face an almost no-win situation. If they seek to deliberately end involvement in Afghanistan, they will likely be criticized as too dovish. If they seek to escalate U.S. involvement, they will probably be accused of being foolishly hawkish. If they seek to maintain the status quo, they will face the least criticism in the short run, but may eventually be accused of perpetuating a nearly two-decade war with no end in sight. ∎

discussion questions

1. How should the U.S. proceed in Afghanistan? Should it maintain the current number of troops, dramatically reverse the drawdown, or withdraw completely within the next four years? Why is this the best course of action?

2. In what ways was the U.S./NATO "surge" into Afghanistan between 2009 and 2015 a success? In what ways did it fail?

3. Is it possible that Pakistan might cease to differentiate between "good" and "bad" Taliban, and instead cooperate with Afghanistan to defeat the group in the border region? What are incentives and disincentives for such a course of action?

4. In recent years, the U.S. has significantly cut military and economic aid to Pakistan, in the context of Islamabad's continued support for the Taliban in Afghanistan, and a shift in U.S. global priorities. What are the risks of reduced or deteriorated relations with Pakistan, and are they worth taking?

5. Some 15 years into the war in Afghanistan, what are the U.S.' goals there? What are the prospects for achieving them?

6. What are the prospects for settling the conflict between the Afghan government and the Taliban? What compromises would be involved in a long-term political solution?

Don't forget: Ballots start on page 115!

suggested readings

Abbas, Hassan, **The Taliban Revival: Violence and Extremism on the Pakistan-Afghanistan Frontier**. New Haven, CT: Yale University Press, 2014. 296 pp. Abbas grapples with the complexity of the Taliban revival in Afghanistan more than 15 years after the start of Operation Enduring Freedom.

Bergen, Peter L., **The Longest War: The Enduring Conflict between America and Al-Qaeda**. New York: Free Press, 2011. 496 pp. Bergan presents an authoritative account of the conflict between the U.S. and al-Qaeda, exploring history and strategy from both perspectives.

Haqqani, Husain, **Magnificent Delusions: Pakistan, the United States, and an Epic History of Misunderstanding**. New York: PublicAffairs, 2013. 423 pp. Haqqani, a former Pakistani ambassador to the U.S., recounts the often-fraught history of diplomacy between the two countries.

Katzman, Kenneth, "Afghanistan: Post-Taliban Governance, Security, and U.S. Policy." **Congressional Research Service**. Septem-

ber 26, 2016. 80 pp. Available free online: <http://www.fas.org/sgp/crs/row/RL30588.pdf>. Katzman presents a report of the current situation in Afghanistan and U.S. policy there.

"The Opium Economy in Afghanistan: An International Problem." **United Nations**, 2003. 226 pp. Available free online: <https://www.unodc.org/pdf/publications/afg_opium_economy_www.pdf>. This publication discusses Afghanistan's opium trade as a problem that can only be resolved through international efforts.

Rashid, Ahmed, **Taliban: Oil and Fundamentalism in Central (2nd ed.)**. New Haven, CT: Yale University Press, 2010. 344 pp. This book offers an extensive picture of the Taliban, and discusses Afghanistan as a center for modern Islamic fundamentalism.

Williams, Brian Glyn, **Afghanistan Declassified: A Guide to America's Longest War**. Philadelphia: University of Pennsylvania Press, 2011. 264 pp. This text has been revised since its initial publication by the U.S. Army. It provides a history and geography of Afghanistan, further informed by the author's personal travel experiences.

To access web links to these readings, as well as links to additional, shorter readings and suggested web sites,

GO TO www.greatdecisions.org

and click on the topic under Resources, on the right-hand side of the page

Nuclear security:
The enduring challenge of nuclear weapons

by Todd S. Sechser

U.S. Republican presidential candidate Donald Trump speaks during "Stop the Iran Deal" rally on the West Lawn of the Capitol in Washington D.C. Sept. 9, 2015. U.S. Republican presidential candidates Donald Trump and Ted Cruz called on lawmakers to boycott the Iran nuclear deal, warning of dire consequences if the agreement is implemented. (XINHUA/BAO DANDAN VIA GETTY IMAGES)

In July 2015, the United States, Iran, and five other world powers reached a landmark deal intended to prevent Iran from acquiring nuclear weapons. The product of years of diplomacy, this agreement offered Iran the promise of relief from crippling economic sanctions in exchange for constraining its ability to produce the raw material necessary for a nuclear weapon. The deal provoked impassioned reactions from both supporters and critics. U.S. Secretary of State John Kerry argued that the agreement represented "a hugely positive step" that would "make our citizens and our allies safer." By contrast, President-elect Donald Trump called the agreement "a disastrous deal," declaring that dismantling it would be his "number one priority" as President.

While the Iran deal continues to be a subject of intense debate, there is widespread agreement that nuclear proliferation poses a grave challenge to international security. In 1963, President John F. Kennedy called the spread of nuclear weapons "one of the greatest hazards which man faces." Since Kennedy's declaration, every U.S. president has made nuclear nonproliferation a chief foreign policy objective of their administration.

More than half a century later, nuclear nonproliferation continues to rank as one of the top foreign policy challenges faced by the United States. Questions persist about the nuclear deal with Iran, and North Korea continues to pursue a larger and more sophisticated nuclear arsenal. Moreover, the United States will face critical choices about its own nuclear arsenal in the coming administration. ∎

TODD S. SECHSER *is associate professor of politics at the University of Virginia, where he researches international security and the politics of nuclear weapons.*

SIGNATURE NONPROLIFERATION AND ARMS CONTROL ACHIEVEMENTS OF EACH U.S. PRESIDENT SINCE 1960

John F. Kennedy	Limited Nuclear Test Ban Treaty
Lyndon B. Johnson	Treaty on the Nonproliferation of Nuclear Weapons (NPT)
Richard Nixon	Threshold Test Ban Treaty
	Strategic Arms Limitation Treaty (SALT)
	Anti-Ballistic Missile Treaty
Gerald Ford	Nuclear Suppliers Group
Jimmy Carter	Nuclear Nonproliferation Act
Ronald Reagan	Intermediate-Range Nuclear Forces (INF) Treaty
	Missile Technology Control Regime
George H.W. Bush	Strategic Arms Reduction Treaty (START)
	Soviet Nuclear Threat Reduction Act
Bill Clinton	Plutonium Management and Disposition Agreement
	Iran Nonproliferation Act
	Agreed Framework with North Korea
George W. Bush	Strategic Offensive Reductions Treaty
	Proliferation Security Initiative
	Global Threat Reduction Initiative
Barack Obama	New START Treaty
	Joint Comprehensive Plan of Action (JCPOA)

Building and stopping the bomb

Nuclear weapons harness the energy of atomic fission to achieve their destructive power. At an atomic level, a nuclear explosion involves splitting the nucleus of one atom, which releases energy along with several other neutrons that, in turn, split neighboring atoms. Given enough fissionable material, this process triggers a chain reaction that releases a tremendous amount of energy—in the form of a nuclear explosion—in just one millionth of a second.

The power of nuclear explosions is so immense that they are measured by how many thousands—or millions—of tons of TNT would be required to create an equivalent explosion. For instance, the atomic bomb dropped on Hiroshima, Japan, in 1945 exploded with an energy equivalent to about 15 kilotons—that is, 15,000 tons—of TNT. But the United States and Soviet Union soon developed weapons that were vastly more powerful. During the Cold War, the most powerful nuclear weapon deployed by the United States carried an explosive yield of 25 million tons (megatons) of TNT. Soviet weapons were even more powerful. The largest thermonuclear weapon ever tested, a Soviet weapon known in the United States as "Tsar Bomba," created an explosion equivalent to 50 million tons of TNT—nearly 4,000 times more powerful than the atom-

ic bomb that destroyed Hiroshima. Today, the most powerful nuclear weapon in the U.S. arsenal, the B83 bomb, carries a maximum yield of 1.2 megatons.

All nuclear weapons rely on atomic fission. While the atomic weapons dropped on Japan in 1945 utilized strictly fission devices, however, modern thermonuclear weapons utilize fission as merely the first of two stages. In these weapons, a "primary" fission explosion triggers a much more powerful "secondary" device that relies on atomic fusion rather than fission. Because this process releases energy by fusing together hydrogen isotopes, thermonuclear weapons are often called "hydrogen bombs." These weapons can generate explosive power far more efficiently than pure fission weapons.

The most difficult step in building a nuclear weapon is not, however, constructing the bomb itself. The basics of nuclear weapons design are widely known, and easily available in unclassified literature. In fact, this has been the case for decades: more than 40 years ago, a former director of Lawrence Livermore Laboratory wrote that "the only difficult thing about making a fission bomb of some sort is the preparation of a supply of fissile material of adequate purity; the design of the bomb itself is relatively easy."

Rather, the most important hurdle for a government or organization with nuclear ambitions is obtaining the material necessary for a fission reaction. Paul Kerr, a nonproliferation analyst at the Congressional Research Service, notes that "obtaining fissile material is widely regarded as the most difficult task in building nuclear weapons." There are two such "fissile" materials: plutonium-239 (Pu-239) and uranium-235 (U-235). Both materials, in sufficient quantity, can sustain the chain reaction that characterizes nuclear fission. But both are difficult to obtain. Plutonium-239 does not exist in nature, and can only be obtained by extracting it out of spent uranium fuel from nuclear reactors. Uranium-235 is naturally occurring, but comprises less than 1% of natural uranium. To

---

! Before you read, download the companion **Glossary** that includes definitions and a guide to acronyms and abbreviations used in the article. Go to **www.greatdecisions.org** and select a topic in the Resources section on the right-hand side of the page.

obtain it in sufficiently pure quantities for a nuclear weapon, it must be separated from other uranium isotopes in a painstakingly process known as "enrichment."

The most effective way to prevent the spread of nuclear weapons therefore is to stop countries from acquiring the materials necessary to build them. Indeed, this is the basic organizing principle of the international nonproliferation regime. For example, the International Atomic Energy Agency (IAEA), which monitors compliance with nonproliferation agreements, does not actually monitor nuclear weapons programs or military facilities. Instead, it inspects civilian nuclear facilities, aiming to ensure that nuclear material is not diverted from civilian use to military programs. But the agency does not collect data relating to a country's progress toward building nuclear weapons themselves. In other words, accounting for nuclear materials takes precedence over monitoring their military application.

Preventing countries from acquiring the materials to build a nuclear weapon is challenging because those materials—or the ability to create them—are natural byproducts of civilian nuclear energy programs. Commercial nuclear reactors produce Pu-239 as part of the natural process of "burning" uranium fuel rods. The fuel rods themselves,

however, cannot be used in a nuclear weapon; the plutonium must be extracted through a complex chemical separation procedure known as reprocessing.

Uranium-235 is also inextricably connected to civilian energy programs because it is the primary fuel source for commercial nuclear reactors. In order to be usable in most nuclear reactors, uranium mined from the ground must be enriched so that it contains between 3% and 5% U-235. The process of enrichment removes some of the more prevalent isotope U-238, leaving a higher proportion of fissionable U-235. There are several techniques for enriching uranium, but the most common method involves transforming the uranium into a gas and feeding it into high-speed centrifuges. The spinning motion of the centrifuges—around 1,500 revolutions per second—separates the heavier isotopes from the lighter ones, allowing U-235 to be extracted in gradually higher concentrations. While the enrichment level required for a nuclear weapon is much higher than the level for a reactor—more than 90% U-235—this level of purity can be achieved using the very same facilities used to enrich nuclear fuel. The difference lies in the number of times the uranium is fed through the centrifuges, not the equipment used. In short, a country that has the abil-

ity to enrich fuel for a nuclear reactor also has the ability to obtain highly-enriched uranium for a nuclear bomb.

Just eight countries operate plutonium reprocessing facilities, only one of which (Japan) does not already possess nuclear weapons. Uranium enrichment capabilities are somewhat more common. Fourteen states operate such facilities, including six non-nuclear states: Argentina, Brazil, Iran, Japan, Germany and the Netherlands. The IAEA conducts regular monitoring and inspections of these facilities, ensuring that all nuclear material is accounted for and not diverted for other purposes.

The inherent tension between civilian nuclear energy and nuclear weapons has plagued nonproliferation efforts since the beginning of the nuclear age. The Treaty on the Nonproliferation of Nuclear Weapons (NPT), the backbone of the international nonproliferation regime, grants member states an "inalienable right" of access to "research, production and use of nuclear energy for peaceful purposes." Accordingly, a core mission of the IAEA is to facilitate the dissemination of nuclear technology to NPT members for civilian purposes, even though this technology could in principle be used to support a military weapons program. Yet this reflects the bargain at the heart of the

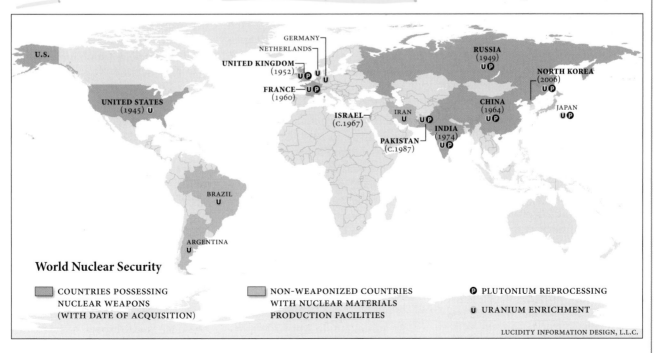

World Nuclear Security

COUNTRIES POSSESSING NUCLEAR WEAPONS (WITH DATE OF ACQUISITION)

NON-WEAPONIZED COUNTRIES WITH NUCLEAR MATERIALS PRODUCTION FACILITIES

P PLUTONIUM REPROCESSING

U URANIUM ENRICHMENT

LUCIDITY INFORMATION DESIGN, L.L.C.

treaty: in exchange for forswearing nuclear weapons, the world's nonnuclear states receive an assurance of access to civilian nuclear energy.

Yet the spread of nuclear weapons is by no means inevitable. President John F. Kennedy worried in 1963 that by 1970, there might be "ten nuclear powers instead of four, and by 1975, fifteen or twenty." His dire predictions have not come to pass: more than half a century after the Cuban missile crisis, just nine states possess nuclear

weapons. Four states have given them up (South Africa, Kazakhstan, Belarus and Ukraine), and several others terminated their programs before crossing the nuclear threshold, including Argentina, Brazil and Libya. Still more countries—perhaps numbering in the dozens—possess the scientific expertise and industrial wherewithal to produce a nuclear weapon if they wished, but have thus far declined to do so.

Still, the nonproliferation regime's record remains imperfect. Of great-

est concern are the four countries that remain outside the NPT: India, Israel, Pakistan and North Korea. All four have acquired nuclear weapons, the most recent of which—North Korea—conducted its first successful nuclear test just a decade ago. And Iran appeared to be on the cusp of acquiring enough nuclear material for a nuclear weapon when it signed the 2015 nonproliferation deal with the United States. Both countries will present the next U.S. president with difficult choices. ∎

Contrasting paths in nonproliferation

Iran

Iran's nuclear program dates back to the 1950s, when it signed its first nuclear cooperation agreement with the United States. Iran's first nuclear reactor, a small research reactor, was supplied by the United States in 1967. During the next decade, Iran launched an ambitious nuclear energy program, planning to build between ten and twenty nuclear reactors that would supply more than 20,000 megawatts of energy—enough to power New York City. Iran signed contracts to build nuclear reactors with several European companies, but these agreements were scuttled after the 1979 Iranian revolution.

Iran's nuclear ambitions, however, worried U.S. leaders even before the revolution. In the 1970s, as the United States was negotiating a provisional agreement for Iran to buy two nuclear reactors, a State Department official warned that these reactors could create a proliferation risk. He wrote that an "aggressive successor to the Shah might consider nuclear weapons the final item needed to establish Iran's complete military dominance of the region." In 1974, a U.S. National Intelligence Estimate argued that "there is no doubt... of the Shah's ambition to make Iran a power to be reckoned with. If he is alive in the mid-1980s," the report went on, "and if other countries have proceeded

with weapons development, we have no doubt that Iran will follow suit."

Since Iran's revolution, officials in the West have routinely offered dire projections about the inevitability of an Iranian nuclear bomb. In 1984, a West German intelligence report warned that Iran's nuclear weapons initiative was "entering its final stages" and would yield a bomb within two years. That same year, U.S. Senator Alan Cranston (D-CA) warned that Iran was seven years away from making a nuclear weapon. A decade later, in 1995, *The New York Times* quoted "senior American and Israeli officials" as saying that Iran might be "less than five years away from having an atomic bomb." U.S. General Anthony Zinni repeated the five-year forecast in 1998, and Israel's Defense Minister predicted in 2001 that an Iranian bomb was four years away. In 2013, Israeli Prime Minister Benjamin Netanyahu issued perhaps the most impassioned warning yet about Iran's nuclear ambitions, declaring that Iran was completing work on facilities that would put it merely weeks away from a nuclear weapons capability. After more than 30 years of these warnings, however, Iran has yet to obtain a nuclear weapon.

At the same time, Iran has made steady progress developing the ability to enrich uranium. In April 2006, Ira-

nian President Mahmoud Ahmadinejad announced that his country had, for the first time, successfully enriched uranium. At that time, Iran had installed roughly 300 centrifuges at its pilot uranium enrichment plant at Natanz, a facility 125 miles south of Tehran. By early 2009, that number had increased almost twentyfold, to nearly 6,000. And by 2015, the number of installed centrifuges had grown to more than 19,000—including 1,000 second-generation centrifuges that are five times more efficient than their predecessors.

The number of centrifuges is important because it dictates the speed at which Iran could enrich enough uranium for a nuclear weapon. According to the IAEA, a nuclear weapon requires roughly 27 kilograms of highly enriched uranium. In order to obtain this amount from natural uranium in a year's time, Iran would need about 5,000 of its first-generation centrifuges. With 18,000 first-generation centrifuges, it could produce the necessary amount in about three months. Adding an additional 1,000 advanced centrifuges would cut the timeframe for one nuclear weapon to about 11 weeks—or more than four nuclear weapons per year.

Iran maintains that it has a right to enrich uranium under the NPT—a claim the United States disputes—and Iranian leaders have always insisted that its enrichment capabilities are for peaceful purposes only. Indeed, Supreme Leader Ayatollah Khamenei apparently issued a religious edict that "the production, stockpiling, and use of nuclear weapons are forbidden under Islam and that the Islamic Republic of Iran shall never acquire these weapons." But following the revelation of secret Iranian nuclear facilities in 2002 and 2009, the United States, United Nations (UN) Security Council, and European Union imposed several rounds of harsh economic sanctions that targeted Iran's banks, petroleum exports, foreign assets, and ability to do business internationally.

The 2015 nuclear deal negotiated by the Obama administration offered Iran a way out from under these crippling sanctions. The Joint Comprehensive Plan of Action (JCPOA), as the deal is known, was signed by seven countries plus the European Union: Iran, the United States, Russia, France, China, Britain and Germany. Under the deal, Iran made five key commitments in exchange for the promise of partial relief from international sanctions. These commitments were structured to ensure that Iran remained at least one year away from enriching enough uranium to build a nuclear weapon, if it ever decided to do so.

Demonstrators form a human chain around the Natanz uranium enrichment facility during a rally in support Iran's nuclear program November 18, 2005, in Natanz, 350km south of Tehran, Iran. People were rallying in response to U.S. criticism of Iran's nuclear projects. (PHOTO BY MAJID/GETTY IMAGES)

- **Limits on centrifuges.** Iran agreed to reduce its number of operating centrifuges to about 5,000 (from the current level of 19,000) for a period of ten years. Those 5,000 centrifuges may only be first-generation machines, and may only be operated at a single enrichment facility at Natanz.
- **Limits on enrichment levels.** Iran is prohibited from enriching uranium beyond a maximum purity level of 3.67%—the level required for use in nuclear power plants—for a period of 15 years.
- **Limits on uranium stockpile.** At the time of the agreement, Iran possessed nearly 10,000 kilograms of low-enriched uranium—enough to make eight to ten nuclear weapons, according to the White House.

While low-enriched uranium cannot directly be used in a nuclear weapon, enriching it to a weapons-grade level would take much less time than starting from natural uranium. The agreement limits this stockpile to 300 kilograms.

- **Constraints on plutonium production.** Iran has been building a "heavy-water" nuclear reactor near the town of Arak, which could produce plutonium. The JCPOA commits Iran to redesigning the reactor so that it cannot produce weapons-grade plutonium, and prohibits Iran from conducting any plutonium reprocessing.
- **Inspections and monitoring.** To ensure Iran's compliance with these limitations, the agreement specifies a variety of monitoring and inspection provisions to be overseen by the IAEA. These provisions include IAEA monitoring of Iran's uranium mills, enrichment facilities, centrifuge manufacturing infrastructure, and other facilities.

In January 2016, the IAEA certified that Iran had met its key obligations under the JCPOA, including: shipping 98% of its low-enriched uranium to Russia, dismantling more than 12,000 centrifuges, and disabling the Arak re-

actor by pouring cement into its core. As stipulated by the agreement, the United States and European Union then lifted a variety of oil and financial sanctions on Iran. However, several U.S. sanctions that were not part of the agreement, including the U.S. trade embargo, remain in place.

Despite this apparent nonproliferation success story, President-elect Trump and many Congressional Republicans have been critical of the deal. During the recent presidential campaign, Mr. Trump maintained that the deal amounted to appeasement of a hostile foreign regime, and that Iran would ultimately renege. "They are going to have nuclear weapons," he argued after the deal was struck. "They are going to take over parts of the world that you wouldn't believe. And I think it's going to lead to nuclear holocaust." Mr. Trump's comments echoed those of Israeli Prime Minister Benjamin Netanyahu, who called the deal a "stunning, historic mistake."

Critics of the agreement cite several concerns. One concern is that Iran could construct—or may already possess—secret nuclear facilities that are not encompassed by the deal. Indeed, in both 2002 and 2009, Iran was revealed to be constructing secret facilities for uranium enrichment and plutonium

American Ambassador to the UN John Bolton speaks to the media at UN headquarters April 28, 2006, in New York City, after the International Atomic Energy Agency announced that Iran had successfully enriched uranium. (PHOTO BY SPENCER PLATT/GETTY IMAGES)

production. A second objection centers around the deal's timeframe: instead of committing Iran to permanent limits on its ability to enrich uranium, many of the agreement's key provisions expire after 15 years. Third, critics worry that the removal of economic sanctions and the return of $100 billion in assets under the agreement will strengthen Iran's economy and provide it with the resources to augment its nuclear program in the future. And most broadly, some have argued that the deal sends a signal of weakness to Iran, suggesting that the United States is not resolved to prevent it from acquiring nuclear weapons. John Bolton, who served as U.S. Ambassador to the UN under President George W. Bush, called the agreement "the worst act of appeasement in American history."

President-elect Trump has not specified exactly how he will approach the Iran deal. Some of Mr. Trump's key advisers are fierce critics of the deal, including Rep. Mike Pompeo (R-KS), his selection for director of the Central Intelligence Agency, who tweeted that "I look forward to rolling back this disastrous deal with the world's largest state sponsor of terrorism." In an op-ed in *USA Today*, Mr. Trump himself promised to renegotiate the agreement, though he did not say which provisions

he would seek to change. He will have the ability to unilaterally restore U.S. sanctions on Iran, which Iranian leaders have said they would treat as a breach of the agreement. If Iran withdraws from the deal, the United States could lose the ability to monitor its program through IAEA inspections. Moreover, the other parties to the agreement—including Russia and key European Union countries—have expressed little enthusiasm for returning to the negotiating table. Whether to risk alienating America's allies in Europe in exchange for a second bite at the apple is one of the first foreign policy decisions Mr. Trump will have to make.

North Korea

While Iran appears to have taken meaningful steps away from a nuclear weapon, the Democratic People's Republic of Korea—or North Korea—has moved decisively in the opposite direction under the leadership of "supreme leader" Kim Jong Un. After testing its first nuclear device in 2006, North Korea has carried out four more nuclear tests, including two in 2016. The last of these tests, in September 2016, was its largest to date, with an explosive yield greater than the atomic weapon dropped on Hiroshima in 1945. While the size of North Korea's nuclear arsenal is un-

known, estimates suggest that the country may have enough fissile material for one to two dozen weapons; in the next five years, that number could increase to between 50 and 100.

Efforts to prevent North Korea from obtaining nuclear weapons have failed repeatedly over the last two decades. In 1994, the Clinton administration reached a deal with North Korea known as the Agreed Framework, which called for North Korea to freeze its nuclear program in exchange for new nuclear reactors, fuel oil for heating and electricity, and a gradual normalization of relations with the United States. While North Korea complied with part of the agreement by halting plutonium production, it simultaneously launched a covert uranium enrichment program. When this program was discovered in 2002, the United States responded by terminating shipments of fuel oil, and North Korea announced its withdrawal from the NPT—the only country ever to do so.

Following North Korea's first nuclear test in 2006, the UN Security Council adopted a series of increasingly severe economic sanctions on North Korea, including arms and technology embargoes, luxury good bans, trade and financial restrictions and travel bans for key North Korean personnel. A number of other countries, including the United States and the European Union, have imposed their own sanctions over the last decade as well. Yet while these sanctions have damaged the North Korean economy, they have not stopped its nuclear program. Indeed, Jae Ku, director of the U.S.-Korea Institute at Johns Hopkins School of Advanced International Studies, argues that "no amount of sanctions will stop North Korea. Nuclear weapons are their sole survival strategy."

One reason economic sanctions have failed is that key countries—especially China—do not enforce them as vigorously as the United States would prefer. China is North Korea's most important ally and its largest trading partner, accounting for more than 70% of its trade volume. In 2014, trade between the two countries reached almost $7 billion. China recently opened a new high-speed rail line to North Korea, and established new shipping routes to boost its imports of North Korean coal. A key reason for China's reluctance to push Pyongyang harder is that it does not want to destabilize the North Korean regime. A collapse of the North Korean government could send hundreds of thousands of refugees across the border into China, an event that Chinese leaders desperately want to avoid. The effectiveness of economic sanctions therefore has been limited, as China attempts to balance its opposition to North Korea's nuclear program with its desire to preserve a stable North Korean regime.

For the incoming Trump administration, North Korea's nuclear program poses a variety of challenges. First, the new administration will have to decide what level of North Korean nuclear development—if any—is unacceptable. The North Korean government asserts that it has successfully tested a hydrogen bomb and that it can mount nuclear warheads on ballistic missiles. While experts are skeptical of those claims—and North Korea has provided no hard evidence to corroborate them—it seems clear that North Korea harbors ambitions to achieve these goals, and it has made significant progress developing long-range ballistic missiles over the last several years. The Trump administration will need to decide which technological milestones it is unwilling to let North Korea reach.

Once the new administration decides on its red lines, the next question is how to enforce them. Military force is one option. During the 1994 crisis, the United States considered—and rejected—an attack against North Korea's nuclear facilities. Presidents George W. Bush and Barack Obama likewise declined to use military force to stop North Korea's nuclear progress. One key reason is that a war against North Korea's 1.2 million-man army would be calamitous for South Korea, which would suffer devastating artillery—and possibly nuclear—attacks. East Asia experts Victor Cha and David Kang estimated that North Korea could fire 500,000 rounds of artillery

A woman in South Korea watches a television screen showing an image of Kim Jong Un, leader of North Korea, right, during a news broadcast about North Korea's nuclear test on Sept. 9, 2016. North Korea conducted its fifth nuclear test on the anniversary of the reclusive nation's founding. (PHOTOGRAPHER: SEONGJOON CHO/BLOOMBERG VIA GETTY IMAGES)

in the first *hour* of a conflict. Hundreds of thousands, and perhaps millions, could be killed. Moreover, China might elect to enter a war on the side of North Korea to prevent the country's collapse, as it did in 1950 during the Korean War.

But it is also possible that North Korea might back down in the face of a U.S. preemptive strike, especially if China or Russia were unwilling to come to its aid. Without outside assistance, the North Korean army would almost certainly be defeated by the smaller but more-sophisticated forces of the United States and South Korea. Anticipating this outcome, Kim Jong Un might call for Russia or China to help negotiate a face-saving resolution to the crisis rather than initiate a war that would almost certainly end in the collapse of his own regime. But North Korea's erratic behavior and bellicose rhetoric make it difficult to tell how it might react if attacked. A coercive strike would certainly be a tremendous gamble for the United States—with potentially catastrophic consequences if North Korea did not respond as planned.

If history is any guide, the next president is likely to have no more success ending North Korea's nuclear program than its predecessors. One alternative,

then, is to simply accept North Korea's nuclear status and rely on deterrence to contain the threat. Indeed, President Obama's Director of National Intelligence, James Clapper, argued in 2016 that convincing North Korea to give up its nuclear weapons peacefully is "probably a lost cause." If the next administration agrees that coercive diplomacy is unlikely to work, it could focus instead on reinforcing U.S. commitments to defend its allies in Northeast Asia.

During the presidential campaign, however, President-elect Trump appeared to lean in the opposite direction, suggesting that the United States might withdraw its military forces from South Korea and Japan and leave the two countries to develop their own nuclear weapons. "They have to protect themselves or they are going to have to pay us," he argued, prompting furious reactions from Japanese and South Korean leaders.

The challenge for the next administration therefore is how to contain the North Korean threat without provoking it, while simultaneously reassuring America's allies in Northeast Asia. The United States has now lived with a North Korean nuclear weapon for more than a decade. Whether it can continue to do so will be up to Mr. Trump. ∎

Nuclear weapons at home and abroad: U.S. options

Nuclear modernization debate

For decades, the United States has deployed its strategic nuclear weapons on three basic platforms: land-based intercontinental ballistic missiles (ICBMs), strategic bombers, and submarine-launched ballistic missiles (SLBMs). This collection of platforms is often called the "nuclear triad." Today, the United States deploys roughly 1,750 strategic weapons on these vehicles. By maintaining diversity in its nuclear arsenal, American leaders hope to minimize the possibility that an enemy could destroy the entire U.S. arsenal in a single attack. This principle is the cornerstone of nuclear deterrence.

But the U.S. nuclear triad is aging. For example, the country's 76 nuclear-capable B-52H bombers were produced in the early 1960s and are now decades older than the crews flying them. Its 450 Minuteman III ICBMs were last produced in 1977—40 years ago. The nuclear warheads themselves are beginning to gray as well: the United States has not produced a new nuclear warhead since the early 1990s, making the average age of a U.S. nuclear warhead nearly 30 years old, well past its intended lifespan of 20 to 25 years. Moreover, because of a voluntary national moratorium on nuclear testing, existing weapons cannot be tested to assess their reliability.

Beginning in 1993, the United States established the Stockpile Stewardship Program, a program intended to maintain the reliability and safety of U.S. nuclear warheads in the absence of nuclear testing. Under this initiative, the national laboratories conduct experiments, materials testing, and computer simulations to evaluate potential problems as the arsenal ages. They also implement Life Extension Programs designed to repair and replace thousands of high-precision components contained in nuclear warheads before they deteriorate. These programs have extended the life of existing nuclear warheads by up to thirty years beyond their original lifespan.

In response to concerns about the age and reliability of the U.S. nuclear triad, in 2014 the Obama administration embarked on a long-term effort to modernize the U.S. nuclear arsenal. These plans call for upgrading the U.S. warhead stockpile and either modernizing or replacing each leg of the triad.

But this modernization plan has its critics. One objection is to its cost: independent estimates put the cost of nuclear arsenal modernization at more than $1 trillion over the next 30 years. These costs include replacing the nation's ballistic missile submarines, building a new fleet of strategic bombers, buying new ICBMs, developing a new air-launched nuclear cruise missile, and refurbishing existing nuclear warheads. Sen. John McCain (R-AZ), chairman of the Senate Armed Services Committee, remarked dryly: "it's very, very, very expensive."

Other critics have observed that the Obama administration's modernization plans conflict with his commitment to pursue nuclear arms reductions. In 2009, shortly after taking office, President Obama delivered a widely publicized speech in Prague declaring that he intended to "reduce the role of nuclear weapons in our national security strategy." His vision appeared to take shape the following year, when the United States reached a nuclear arms reduction agreement with Russia known as "New START." Yet the modernization initiative suggests that deteriorating relations with Russia since 2010 have convinced the Obama administration to maintain a high priority on nuclear weapons.

U.S. nuclear modernization plans may also be in tension with international nonproliferation objectives. Article VI of the NPT stipulates that nuclear nations must "pursue negotiations in good faith on effective measures relating to cessation of the nuclear arms race at an early date and to nuclear disarmament." While the treaty provides no deadline for this obligation, some international observers have complained that the modernization program conveys the impression that the United States has no intention of meeting this commitment.

In light of these concerns, several questions face the incoming Trump administration. The new president will first have to decide whether to continue the nuclear modernization program launched by President Obama. Early indications suggest that he plans to do so: Mr. Trump complained during the 2016 presidential campaign that "our nuclear program has fallen way behind," and promised to "ensure our strategic nuclear triad is modernized to ensure it continues to be an effective deterrent."

Modernization plans, however, may confront budgetary realities. Jeffrey Lewis, a nuclear expert at the Monterey Institute of International Studies, argued that "there isn't enough money" to fund the entire modernization effort. If Congress indeed balks at the price tag, the Department of Defense will face difficult choices about which aspects of the plan to retain.

Budgetary concerns have prompted some analysts to suggest that the United States reconsider the need to maintain a complete nuclear triad. For example, nuclear experts from the Federation of American Scientists and the Natural Resources Defense Council argued that the United States should eliminate the sea-based leg of the triad, basing nuclear weapons solely on less-expensive ICBMs and bombers. In their view, this approach would maintain deterrence at an acceptable cost while also simplifying the nuclear command and control system. Others have suggested maintaining only the submarine leg of the triad, reasoning that submarines are more difficult to locate and destroy, and therefore more credible as a deterrent force. The Obama administration in 2013 reaffirmed its commitment to maintaining all three legs of the triad, but a new administration staring at a trillion-dollar modernization bill might reevaluate this position.

Nuclear weapons abroad

During the Cold War, the United States deployed nuclear weapons to at least 14 other countries. At the peak of these deployments during the 1970s, the number of U.S. nuclear weapons stationed abroad exceeded 7,000.

The primary purpose of deploying nuclear weapons abroad was to deter Soviet aggression. Beginning in the 1950s, U.S. leaders believed that the powerful Soviet military could be deterred only by a credible nuclear threat. The United States deployed nuclear weapons throughout Europe and the Mediterranean, beginning with nuclear gravity bombs delivered to French Morocco and Britain in 1954. These "non-strategic" nuclear weapons were thought to deter the Soviet Union because they created a credible risk that a conventional war in Europe would turn nuclear—even if inadvertently.

Today, the Soviet Union is long gone, but the United States maintains perhaps 200 nuclear gravity bombs in five NATO countries: Belgium, Germany, Italy, the Netherlands and Turkey. And official NATO policy continues to affirm the role of these weapons as a deterrent against potential aggressors.

Yet U.S. nuclear deployments in Europe recently have come under scrutiny. The failed July 2016 coup d'état in Turkey—where the United States stores its largest cache of NATO nuclear weapons—refocused attention on the risks of stationing nuclear weapons beyond U.S. borders. Incirlik Air Base, where these weapons are stored, was closed for 24 hours during the coup attempt, and electricity was cut off. The Turkish commander of the base was later arrested for collaborating with the coup plotters. Fortunately, the base witnessed no clashes between coup supporters and opponents, but the incident revived decades-old concerns about the security of U.S. nuclear weapons abroad.

Indeed, this was not the first time a

Incirlik Air Base in Turkey, where the U.S. stores its largest cache of nuclear weapons abroad. (PHOTO BY YUSUF KOYUN/ANADOLU AGENCY/GETTY IMAGES)

security breach occurred at a foreign installation storing U.S. nuclear weapons. In 2010, for example, peace activists made their way through two perimeter fences at a Belgian air base, entered a bunker containing nuclear weapons vaults, and wandered around for an hour before finally being apprehended by an unarmed guard. Incidents such as these have led former U.S. Sen. Sam Nunn (D-GA) to conclude that U.S. nuclear weapons abroad are "more of a security risk than asset to NATO."

In addition to citing security concerns, critics of these deployments argue that U.S. nuclear weapons in Europe no longer serve any military purpose. The Soviet threat to Western Europe disappeared a quarter-century ago, leaving the United States as the world's dominant conventional military power. The United States therefore no longer needs these nuclear weapons to compensate for conventional weakness. U.S. nuclear weapons in Turkey cannot even be used, since neither the United States nor Turkey has any aircraft at the Incirlik base capable of delivering them. According to former State Department official Richard Sokolsky and scholar Gordon Adams, "the military rationale for maintaining U.S. nuclear weapons in Europe has all but disappeared."

Even the historical deterrent value of U.S. nuclear deployments abroad has been disputed. A 2014 study conducted by Matthew Fuhrmann and Todd S. Sechser investigated nuclear deployments to 23 countries between 1950 and 2000, concluding that foreign-based nuclear weapons did not strengthen the deterrent effect of NATO and other alliances during this period. "While having a nuclear ally carries important security benefits," they write, "those benefits do not appear to be enhanced by hosting the ally's nuclear weapons."

The cost of maintaining nuclear weapons abroad has also become more salient in light of current debates about modernizing the U.S. arsenal. Former Defense Department officials Barry Blechman and Russell Rumbaugh have observed that the 200 or so weapons in Europe will add at least $8 billion to the cost of modernization: not only are the warheads themselves slated to be redesigned, but new aircraft will also need to be configured in order to carry them.

Yet the case for removing U.S. nuclear weapons from Europe is not entirely straightforward. Advocates of the weapons argue that they are important symbols of reassurance to NATO allies. Three former high-ranking national security officials—including two former national security advisers—argued that U.S. nuclear weapons in Europe are "fundamentally, political weapons." Their primary purpose, in this view, is not military, but symbolic: they serve as a visible reminder to both allies and adversaries of the U.S. commitment to defend NATO allies with every available tool. Withdrawing them could send an ominous message that this commitment has weakened, and perhaps create pressures for U.S. allies to obtain their own nuclear weapons. ■

discussion questions

1. Does the Iran nuclear deal make the region more stable? Is it a "good deal" for the U.S.? Why or why not?

2. What should U.S. policy be toward North Korea? How effective are sanctions? Should the U.S. have diplomatic relations with Pyongyang? Should Washington push for regime change?

3. The Obama administration advocated for a "nuclear free world." To what extent can the U.S. rely on other nuclear-armed states to work toward this goal?

4. How likely is it that terrorists might obtain a nuclear weapon, or the materials necessary to build one, today? Is the risk increasing or decreasing over the long term?

5. Should the U.S. continue to pursue nuclear modernization, as it did under the Obama administration? Should budgetary concerns outweigh arguments advocating the need for a nuclear triad?

6. Should the U.S. continue to deploy nuclear weapons beyond its borders? Are such deployments, in the words of Senator Sam Nunn, "more of a security risk than an asset to NATO" or not? Does their symbolic and political value outweigh such concerns?

Don't forget: Ballots start on page 115!

suggested readings

Cirincione, Joseph, Wolfsthal, Jon B. and Rajkumar, Miriam, **Deadly Arsenals: Nuclear, Biological, and Chemical Threats**. Washington, D.C.: Carnegie Endowment for International Peace, 2005. 490 pp. *Deadly Arsenals* is a useful guide to nuclear weapons programs and nonproliferation efforts around the world.

Gavin, Francis J., **Nuclear Statecraft: History and Strategy in America's Atomic Age**. Ithaca, NY.: Cornell University Press, 2012. 240 pp. Gavin covers the history of the role of nuclear weapons in U.S. foreign policy, including deterrence and nonproliferation strategy.

Roberts, Brad, **The Case for U.S. Nuclear Weapons in the 21st Century**. Palo Alto, CA.: Stanford University Press, 2016. 352 pp. Roberts, a former Pentagon official, argues against reducing the role of nuclear weapons in U.S. security strategy.

Schlosser, Eric, **Command and Control: Nuclear Weapons, the Damascus Accident, and the Illusion of Safety**. New York: Penguin Books, 2014. 656 pp. This book explores the history of America's management of its nuclear arsenal, recalling mishaps and near-catastrophes since the beginning of the nuclear age.

Sagan, Scott Douglas and Waltz, Kenneth N., **The Spread of Nuclear Weapons: An Enduring Debate (3rd ed.)**. New York: Norton, 2012. 288 pp. In this new edition of a classic International Relations text, two scholars discuss nuclear proliferation, examining today's most pressing issues and threats.

Sechser, Todd S. and Fuhrmann, Matthew, **Nuclear Weapons and Coercive Diplomacy**. New York: Cambridge University Press, 2016. 320 pp. This book provides an in-depth look at the history and effectiveness of nuclear threats in international diplomacy.

To access web links to these readings, as well as links to additional, shorter readings and suggested web sites,

GO TO www.greatdecisions.org

and click on the topic under Resources, on the right-hand side of the page

About the balloting process...

Dear Great Decisions Participants,

My name is Dr. Lauren Prather and I have been working with the Foreign Policy Association (FPA) for the last three years on the National Opinion Ballot (NOB). You have likely received emails from me about the NOB. A version of this letter appeared in last year's briefing book. We thought I might include it again this year to explain a bit my interest in assisting the FPA with fielding the NOB.

My research is primarily focused in international relations. I received my PhD in political science from Stanford University, where I worked with some of the top public opinion and international relations researchers in the field. I am now a faculty member at the School of Global Policy and Strategy at the University of California, San Diego (UCSD). My research interests are broadly revealed in the title of my dissertation: *Self-Interest, Group Interest, and Values: The Determinants of Mass Attitudes towards Foreign Aid in Donor Countries.*

As anyone who studies public opinion about foreign policy knows, one of the key difficulties is that the public is often uniformed or misinformed about the topics. This is where you come in! The Great Decisions participants are some of the most informed Americans about foreign policy issues, and the NOB is the perfect opportunity to voice those opinions.

The NOB is also one of the only public opinion surveys in the United States that attempts to gather the opinions of the educated public. Thus, it has great value to researchers and policymakers alike. Some of the questions in which researchers are interested include the following:

- Are the opinions of the educated public significantly different from those of the average American?
- How does public opinion about foreign policy change over time?
- How does public opinion on one foreign policy issue relate to public opinion on other foreign policy issues? For example, are people who support U.S. government policies to mitigate climate change more or less willing to support drilling in the Arctic?
- How do different segments of the population, men or women, liberals or conservatives, view foreign policy choices?

In order to answer these types of questions, the NOB needed to have certain attributes. We needed to have a way to organize the ballots by participant across all topics. That way, we know, for example, how participant #47 responded to the question about climate change mitigation and how he or she responded to the question about drilling, even if those were in different topics in the NOB.

Furthermore, in order to understand how public opinion has changed over time, we needed a way to measure #47's opinion on drilling in 2014 for example and a way to measure #47's opinion on drilling in 2015. When you signed on with your email address to enter the ballot the past few of years, you were assigned a random number (like #47). **Only** this number is connected to your responses and **never** your email address.

In fact, as a researcher, I must receive the approval of my Institutional Review Board by demonstrating that your data will be protected at all times, and that your responses will be both confidential and anonymous. I do this by only using secure computing networks and by storing your identifying information separately from your responses to the NOB. My work with the FPA has received approval from Stanford and now also from UCSD.

While I hope this provides some assurances about the security of your personal data, I understand that there have been some difficulties with simply going online to take the survey. Each year we continue to improve on these practices, but it is a learning process.

You will find the paper ballot in every briefing book in addition to directions for each topic on how to record your opinion online. You will be asked to use the unique hyperlink for each topic to record your response. Because we would still very much like to match your responses across topics, and to previous years if you have completed the ballot online, we will ask you to use your email address. Again, you will be given a random number or the number assigned to you in previous years; this, rather than your email address, will be matched to your responses.

If you have any questions or comments, I am always happy to respond via email at LPrather@ucsd.edu. To learn more about my research and teaching, you can visit my website at www.laurenprather.org.

I'll end where I should have begun: by thanking everyone who has participated in the NOB over the years. I have learned a tremendous amount about your foreign policy views and it has greatly informed my own research. In the future, I hope to communicate to the scholarly world and policy communities how the educated American public thinks about foreign policy.

Sincerely,

Lauren Prather

2017 National Opinion Ballot

First, we'd like to ask you for some information about your participation in the Great Decisions program. If you are not currently a Great Decisions program member, please skip to the "background" section in the next column.

How long have you participated in the Great Decisions program (i.e., attended one or more discussion sessions)?

- ☐ This is the first year I have participated.
- ☐ I participated in one previous year.
- ☑ I participated in more than one previous year.

How did you learn about the Great Decisions program?

- ☐ Word of mouth
- ☑ Local library
- ☐ Foreign Policy Association website
- ☐ Promotional brochure
- ☐ Other organization _____

Where does your Great Decisions group meet?

- ☐ Private home
- ☑ Library
- ☐ Community center
- ☐ Learning in retirement
- ☐ Other _____

How many hours, on average, do you spend reading one *Great Decisions* chapter?

- ☐ Less than 1 hour
- ☑ 1–2 hours
- ☐ 3–4 hours
- ☐ More than 4 hours

Would you say you have or have not changed your opinion in a fairly significant way as a result of taking part in the Great Decisions program?

- ☑ Have
- ☐ Have not
- ☐ Not sure

Background Section: Next, we'd like to ask you some information about your background.

How strongly do you agree or disagree with the following statement? Although the media often reports about national and international events and developments, this news is seldom as interesting as the things that happen directly in our own community and neighborhood.

- ☐ Agree strongly
- ☐ Agree somewhat
- ☐ Neither agree nor disagree
- ☑ Disagree somewhat
- ☐ Disagree strongly

Generally speaking, how interested are you in politics?

- ☐ Very much interested
- ☑ Somewhat interested
- ☐ Not too interested
- ☐ Not interested at all

Do you think it is best for the future of the U.S. if it takes an active role in world affairs or stays out of world affairs?

- ☑ Takes an active role in world affairs
- ☐ Stays out of world affairs

How often are you asked for your opinion on foreign policy?

- ☐ Often
- ☐ Sometimes
- ☑ Never

Have you been abroad during the last two years?

- ☐ Yes   ☑ No

Do you know, or are you learning, a foreign language?

- ☐ Yes   ☑ No

Do you have any close friends or family who live in other countries?

- ☐ Yes   ☑ No

Do you donate to any charities that help the poor in other countries?

- ☐ Yes
- ☒ No

Generally speaking, do you usually think of yourself as a Republican, a Democrat, an Independent, or something else?

- ☒ Republican
- ☐ Democrat
- ☐ Independent
- ☐ Other _____

What is your gender?

- ☐ Male
- ☒ Female

What race do you consider yourself?

- ☒ White/Caucasian
- ☐ Black/African-American
- ☐ Asian-American
- ☐ Native American
- ☐ Hispanic/Latino
- ☐ Other (please specify) _____

How important is religion in your life?

- ☐ Very important
- ☐ Somewhat important
- ☐ Not too important
- ☒ Not at all important

What is your age? _61_

Are you currently employed?

- ☐ Full-time employee
- ☐ Part time employee
- ☐ Self-employed
- ☐ Unemployed
- ☒ Retired
- ☐ Student
- ☐ Homemaker

What are the first three digits of your zip code? (This will allow us to do a state-by-state breakdown of results.)

_801_ _____ _____

Can you give us an estimate of your household income in 2015 before taxes?

- ☐ Below $30,000
- ☐ $30,000-$50,000
- ☐ $50,000-$75,000
- ☐ $75,000-$100,000
- ☐ $100,000-$150,000
- ☐ Over $150,000
- ☐ Not sure
- ☒ Prefer not to say

What is the highest level of education you have completed?

- ☐ Did not graduate from high school
- ☐ High school graduate
- ☐ Some college, but no degree (yet)
- ☐ 2-year college degree
- ☐ 4-year college degree
- ☐ Some postgraduate work, but no degree (yet)
- ☒ Postgraduate degree (MA, MBA, MD, JD, PhD, etc.)

Now we would like to ask you some ballot questions from previous years:

1. From 2001's "European integration: past, present and the future": In the foreseeable future, is integration in the European Union more likely to flourish, or to stagnate?

- ☐ Flourish
- ☒ Stagnate

2. From 2014's "Turkey's challenges": Generally speaking, do you think that Turkey's membership in the European Union would be…?

- ☐ A good thing
- ☒ A bad thing
- ☐ Neither good nor bad

3. From 2014's "China's foreign policy": In general, do you think Chinese trade policy toward the U.S. is fair or unfair?

- ☐ Fair
- ☒ Unfair

4. From 2008's "U.S.-China economic relations": Does the fact that a product is made in China affect your decision on whether or not to buy it? (*Check only one*)

- ❏ I buy products made in China
- ☑ I don't buy products made in China
- ❏ I don't care where the products I buy are made

5. From 2014's "China's foreign policy": How worried are you, if at all, that China could become a military threat to the U.S. in the future? Please say whether you are very worried, somewhat worried, not too worried, or not worried at all.

- ❏ Very worried
- ☑ Somewhat worried
- ❏ Not too worried
- ❏ Not worried at all

6. From 2012's "Oceans": The U.S. should ratify the UN Convention on the Law of the Sea.

- ❏ Yes
- ☑ No, the U.S.'s current status as a non-ratifying signatory is sufficient
- ❏ No, and the U.S. should not be a signatory to the treaty
- ❏ Not sure

7. From 2012's "Middle East realignment": The U.S. should reassess its relationships with semi-democratic allies such as Saudi Arabia and Bahrain.

- ❏ Strongly agree
- ❏ Agree
- ☑ Disagree
- ❏ Strongly disagree

8. From 2014's "Energy independence": Thinking about long-range foreign policy goals, how much priority do you think the U.S. government should give to reducing U.S. dependence on imported energy sources?

- ☑ Top priority
- ❏ Some priority
- ❏ No priority at all

9. From 2012's "Promoting democracy": The United States should actively promote democracy around the globe.
1. Strongly agree
- ❏ Agree
- ☑ Disagree
- ❏ Strongly disagree

10. From 2016's "The rise of ISIS": Which of the following statements about Islamic extremist groups like ISIS do you agree with more:

- ☑ We should use military strength to destroy Islamic extremist groups once and for all
- ❏ We should accept that we cannot destroy Islamic extremist groups by using military force

11. From 2008's "Latin America":
Do you think that Latin America should be a priority for the next U.S. administration?

- ❏ Yes
- ❏ No

12. From 2012's "Afghanistan and Iraq": In your opinion, what is the most compelling reason for a continued U.S. presence in Afghanistan?

- ❏ It is critical to thwart the Taliban and terrorist groups seeking sanctuary in Afghanistan
- ☑ Considering the strained nature of U.S.-Pakistani relations, Afghanistan is essential to curbing Pakistani extremists
- ❏ The U.S. has an obligation to assist the Afghan government in stabilizing the country
- ❏ Other

13. From 2006's "Sanctions and nonproliferation": To what degree do you feel that U.S./EU/UN economic sanctions against nuclear proliferators represent an effective policy tool for dealing with "rogue states" that pursue nuclear weapons?

- ❏ They represent the best option available
- ❏ They are not necessarily the best choice, but one of the only tools we have
- ❏ They have proven ineffective time and again and are a waste of time and political and diplomatic resources

Want to save money on postage? Enter your answers online at

www.fpa.org/ballot

Topic 1. The future of Europe

1. Have you engaged in any of the following activities related to "The future of Europe" topic? Mark all that you have done or mark none of the above.

- ☑ Read the article on Europe in the 2017 *Great Decisions* briefing book
- ☑ Discussed the article on Europe with a Great Decisions discussion group
- ☑ Discussed the article on Europe with friends and family
- ☑ Followed news related to Europe
- ☐ Taken a class in which you learned about issues related to Europe
- ☐ Have or had a job related to the European Union (EU) or United Kingdom (UK)
- ☐ Traveled to the EU or UK
- ☐ None of the above

2. How interested would you say you are in issues related to Europe?

- ☐ Very interested
- ☑ Somewhat interested
- ☐ Not too interested
- ☐ Not at all interested

3. In June 2016, the UK voted to leave the EU. What effect do you think "Brexit" will have on the special relationship between the U.S. and the UK? Will it improve relations between the U.S. and the UK, neither improve nor make relations worse, or make relations worse between the U.S. and the UK?

- ☑ Improve relations between the U.S. and the UK
- ☐ Neither improve nor make relations worse
- ☐ Make relations worse between the U.S. and the UK

4. Which of the following do you think poses the greatest challenge to the EU?

- ☐ Managing Britain's exit from the EU
- ☑ Immigration from non-EU countries
- ☐ Terrorist attacks inspired or directed by ISIS
- ☐ Russian actions in Crimea and Ukraine

5. Do you think the UK leaving the EU will help or hurt the U.S. economy?

- ☑ Help
- ☐ Hurt

6. Do you think the UK leaving the EU will help or hurt the economy of the UK?

- ☐ Help *Long Term*
- ☑ Hurt *Short Term*

7. Do you think the UK leaving the EU will help or hurt the economy of other European countries?

- ☐ Help
- ☑ Hurt

8. How much will the UK leaving the EU affect you personally?

- ☐ A great deal
- ☐ Somewhat
- ☑ Not too much
- ☐ Not at all

9. Was the vote by the UK to leave the EU an isolated referendum or part of a larger populist trend affecting other countries, including the U.S.?

- ☐ Isolated referendum
- ☑ Part of a larger trend

10. Would you like to share any other thoughts with us about the future of Europe? If so, please use the space below.

....

....

....

....

Topic 2. Trade, jobs and politics

1. Have you engaged in any of the following activities related to the "Trade, jobs and politics" topic? Mark all that you have done or mark none of the above.

- ☒ Read the article on trade and politics in the 2017 *Great Decisions* briefing book
- ❏ Discussed the article on trade and politics with a Great Decisions discussion group
- ❏ Discussed the article on trade and politics with friends and family
- ❏ Followed news related to trade and politics
- ❏ Taken a class in which you learned about issues related to trade and politics
- ❏ Have or had a job related to international trade
- ❏ Traveled to China
- ❏ None of the above

2. How interested would you say you are in issues related to trade and politics?

- ❏ Very interested
- ❏ Somewhat interested
- ❏ Not too interested
- ❏ Not at all interested

3. In general, do you think that free trade agreements between the U.S. and other countries have been a good thing or a bad thing for the United States?

- ❏ Good thing
- ❏ Bad thing

4. The United States has negotiated a free trade agreement with 11 countries in Asia and Latin America called the Trans-Pacific Partnership, or TPP. Do you think this trade agreement would be a good thing for our country or a bad thing?

- ❏ Good thing
- ❏ Bad thing

5. Do you think free trade agreements have definitely helped, probably helped, probably hurt, or definitely hurt the financial situation of you and your family?

- ❏ Definitely helped
- ❏ Probably helped
- ❏ Probably hurt
- ❏ Definitely hurt

6. How important were free trade agreements in your vote for president in 2016?

- ❏ Very important
- ❏ Somewhat important
- ❏ Not too important
- ❏ Not important at all

7. Do you think the United States should increase or decrease the amount of trade it conducts with the following countries?

7.1. Brazil
- ❏ Increase
- ❏ Decrease

7.2. China
- ❏ Increase
- ❏ Decrease

7.3. Canada
- ❏ Increase
- ❏ Decrease

7.4. Mexico
- ❏ Increase
- ❏ Decrease

7.5. United Kingdom
- ❏ Increase
- ❏ Decrease

8. Globalization is the increase of trade, communication, travel and other things among countries around the world. In general, has the United States gained more or lost more because of globalization?

- ❏ Gained more
- ❏ Lost more

9. Overall, would you say U.S. trade with other countries creates more jobs for the U.S., loses more jobs for the U.S., or does U.S. trade with other countries have no effect on U.S. jobs?

- ❏ Creates more jobs
- ❏ Loses more jobs
- ❏ Has no effect on jobs

10. How important is the trade deficit among all of American global priorities?

- ☐ Very important
- ☐ Somewhat important
- ☐ Not too important
- ☐ Not important at all

11. More than 20 years ago Congress passed the North American Free Trade Agreement (NAFTA) with Mexico and Canada. So far, would you say that NAFTA has had more of a positive impact on the nation's economy, had more of a negative impact on the nation's economy, or has not had much of an impact on the nation's economy?

- ☐ Positive impact
- ☐ Negative impact
- ☐ Not had much of an impact

12. Have free trade agreements between the U.S. and other countries been a good thing or a bad thing for American workers?

- ☐ Good thing
- ☐ Bad thing

13. Would you like to share any other thoughts with us about trade and politics? If so, please use the space below.

. . . .

. . . .

. . . .

. . . .

Topic 3. Conflict in the South China Sea

1. Have you engaged in any of the following activities related to the "Conflict in the South China Sea" topic? Mark all that you have done or mark none of the above.

- ☑ Read the article on the South China Sea in the 2017 *Great Decisions* briefing book
- ☑ Discussed the article on the South China Sea with a Great Decisions discussion group
- ☑ Discussed the article on the South China Sea with friends and family
- ☑ Followed news related to the South China Sea
- ☐ Taken a class in which you learned about issues related to the South China Sea
- ☐ Have or had a job related to China, the South China Sea, or other East Asian countries
- ☐ Traveled to China, the South China Sea, or other East Asian countries
- ☐ None of the above

2. How interested would you say you are in issues related to the South China Sea?

- ☐ Very interested
- ☑ Somewhat interested
- ☐ Not too interested
- ☐ Not at all interested

3. How big of a problem for the U.S. is the territorial dispute over the South China Sea? Do you think this is a very serious problem, somewhat serious, not too serious, or not a problem at all?

- ☑ Very serious
- ☐ Somewhat serious
- ☐ Not too serious
- ☐ Not a problem at all

4. Some people say that China is an expansionist power that is building up its military to enforce its claims to sovereignty in the South China Sea. Other people say that China is primarily a peaceful country that is more interested in economic growth than in military adventures. Which view is closer to your own?

- ☑ China is an expansionist power
- ☐ China is primarily a peaceful country

5. The International Tribunal for the Law of the Sea (ITLOS) recently ruled in favor of the Philippines in a dispute with China over territory in the South China Sea. Do you think the ruling will have significant impact, some impact, or no impact at all on future disputes in the South China Sea?

- ☐ It will have significant impact
- ☑ It will have some impact
- ☐ It will have no impact at all

6. In terms of America's relations in East Asia, what priority should the U.S. place on protecting freedom of navigation on the sea lanes between the U.S. and East Asia?

- ☒ High priority
- ❏ Medium priority
- ❏ Low priority
- ❏ No priority at all

7. In terms of reducing the national deficit, to what extent do you agree or disagree that the U.S. should reduce its Navy fleet?

- ❏ Agree strongly
- ❏ Agree somewhat
- ❏ Disagree somewhat
- ☒ Disagree strongly

8. If one of our allies in Asia, such as Japan, South Korea or the Philippines, gets into a serious military conflict with China, do you think we should or should not use military force to defend them?

- ☒ Should use military force to defend them
- ❏ Should not use military force to defend them

9. The United States has announced plans to commit more military resources to Asia. Indicate which comes closer to your view: This is a good thing because it could help maintain peace in the region, or this is a bad thing because it could lead to conflict with China.

- ☒ This is a good thing because it could help maintain peace in the region
- ❏ This is a bad thing because it could lead to conflict with China

10. Would you like to share any other thoughts with us about conflict in the South China Sea? If so, please use the space below.

. . . .

. . . .

. . . .

. . . .

. . . .

Topic 4. Saudi Arabia in transition

1. Have you engaged in any of the following activities related to the "Saudi Arabia in transition" topic? Mark all that you have done or mark none of the above.

- ☒ Read the article on Saudi Arabia in the 2017 *Great Decisions* briefing book
- ☒ Discussed the article on Saudi Arabia with a Great Decisions discussion group
- ☒ Discussed the article on Saudi Arabia with friends and family
- ☒ Followed news related to Saudi Arabia
- ❏ Taken a class in which you learned about issues related to Saudi Arabia
- ❏ Have or had a job related to Saudi Arabia
- ❏ Traveled to Saudi Arabia
- ❏ None of the above

2. How interested would you say you are in issues related to Saudi Arabia?

- ☒ Very interested
- ❏ Somewhat interested
- ❏ Not too interested
- ❏ Not at all interested

3. Do you feel that Saudi Arabia is a close ally of the United States, is friendly but not a close ally, is not friendly but is not an enemy, or is unfriendly and is an enemy of the United States?

- ☒ Close ally of the United States
- ❏ Friendly but not a close ally
- ❏ Not friendly but is not an enemy
- ❏ Unfriendly and is an enemy of the United States

4. Generally speaking, how much do you think the United States can trust Saudi Arabia: a great deal, a fair amount, not too much, or not at all?

- ☑ A great deal
- ☐ A fair amount
- ☐ Not too much
- ☐ Not at all

5. Over the next ten years, do you think Saudi Arabia will become more democratic, less democratic, or will it be about the same as it is now?

- ☑ More democratic
- ☐ Less democratic
- ☐ About the same

6. Do you think the government of Saudi Arabia respects the personal freedoms of its people or does not respect their personal freedoms?

- ☐ Respects personal freedoms
- ☑ Does not respect personal freedoms

7. To what extent do you approve or disapprove of Saudi Arabia's involvement in the war in Yemen?

- ☐ Approve strongly
- ☑ Approve somewhat
- ☐ Disapprove somewhat
- ☐ Disapprove strongly

8. To what extent do you approve or disapprove of the U.S. providing military assistance to Saudi Arabia in the war in Yemen?

- ☐ Approve strongly
- ☐ Approve somewhat
- ☑ Disapprove somewhat
- ☐ Disapprove strongly

9. How likely or unlikely do you think it is that we will see a war between Saudi Arabia and Iran in the Middle East?

- ☐ Very likely
- ☐ Somewhat likely
- ☑ Somewhat unlikely
- ☐ Very unlikely

10. Do you think the U.S. government should increase, decrease, or keep the same the amount of weapons and military equipment it trades with Saudi Arabia?

- ☐ Increase
- ☐ Decrease
- ☑ Keep the same

11. Would you like to share any other thoughts with us about Saudi Arabia in transition? If so, please use the space below.

. . . .

. . . .

. . . .

Topic 5. U.S. foreign policy and petroleum

1. Have you engaged in any of the following activities related to the "U.S. foreign policy and petroleum" topic? Mark all that you have done or mark none of the above.

- ☑ Read the article on U.S. foreign policy and petroleum in the 2017 *Great Decisions* briefing book
- ☑ Discussed the article on U.S. foreign policy and petroleum with a Great Decisions discussion group
- ☑ Discussed the article on U.S. foreign policy and petroleum with friends and family
- ☑ Followed news related to U.S. foreign policy and petroleum
- ☐ Taken a class in which you learned about issues related to U.S. foreign policy and petroleum
- ☐ Have or had a job related to U.S foreign policy and petroleum
- ☐ None of the above

2. How interested would you say you are in issues related to U.S. foreign policy and petroleum?

- ☑ Very interested
- ☐ Somewhat interested
- ☐ Not too interested
- ☐ Not at all interested

3. Right now, which one of the following do you think should be the more important priority for addressing the U.S. energy supply: developing alternative sources, such as wind, solar and hydrogen technology; expanding exploration and production of oil, coal and natural gas; or building more nuclear power plants?

- ☐ Developing alternative sources, such as wind, solar and hydrogen technology
- ☐ Expanding exploration and production of oil, coal and natural gas
- ☑ Building more nuclear power plants

4. To what extent do you favor or oppose the increased use of fracking to extract oil and natural gas from underground rock formations?

- ☑ Favor strongly
- ❑ Favor somewhat
- ❑ Oppose somewhat
- ❑ Oppose strongly

5. How threatening to U.S. national security do you think America's dependence on foreign oil is?

- ❑ Very threatening
- ❑ Somewhat threatening
- ☑ Not too threatening
- ❑ Not threatening at all

6. To address the country's energy needs, would you support or oppose action by the federal government to increase offshore oil and gas drilling?

- ❑ Support strongly
- ☑ Support somewhat
- ❑ Oppose somewhat
- ❑ Oppose strongly

7. To what extent do you support or oppose the federal government permitting gas prices to rise in order to decrease our reliance on oil for energy?

- ❑ Support strongly
- ❑ Support somewhat
- ❑ Oppose somewhat
- ☑ Oppose strongly

8. Many issues were discussed during the presidential campaign. Please indicate how much influence the candidates' positions on dependence on foreign oil had on your decision of who to vote for in 2016.

- ❑ A great deal of influence
- ☑ Some influence
- ❑ Not too much influence
- ❑ No influence at all

9. Would you like to share any other thoughts with us about U.S. foreign policy and petroleum? If so, please use the space below.

· ·

· ·

· ·

Topic 6. Latin America's political pendulum

1. Have you engaged in any of the following activities related to the "Latin America's political pendulum" topic? Mark all that you have done or mark none of the above.

- ❑ Read the article on Latin America in the 2017 *Great Decisions* briefing book
- ❑ Discussed the article on Latin America with a Great Decisions discussion group
- ❑ Discussed the article on Latin America with friends and family
- ❑ Followed news related to Latin America
- ❑ Taken a class in which you learned about issues related to Latin America
- ❑ Have or had a job related to Latin America
- ❑ Traveled to Latin America
- ❑ None of the above

2. How interested would you say you are in issues related to Latin America?

- ❑ Very interested
- ❑ Somewhat interested
- ❑ Not too interested
- ❑ Not at all interested

3. The United States has negotiated a free trade agreement with 11 countries in Asia and Latin America called the Trans-Pacific Partnership, or TPP. If TPP is <u>not</u> approved, to what extent would you support or oppose the United States negotiating a free trade agreement with just the Latin American countries in the deal?

- ❑ Support strongly
- ❑ Support somewhat
- ❑ Oppose somewhat
- ❑ Oppose strongly

4. To what extent do you approve or disapprove of the Supreme Court action which effectively blocked President Obama's executive order which would have provided work permits and prevented the deportation of nearly 4 million immigrants who have lived illegally in the U.S. since 2010 or earlier, have no criminal record, and are parents of children who are either U.S. citizens or lawful permanent residents?

- ❏ Approve strongly
- ❏ Approve somewhat
- ❏ Disapprove somewhat
- ❏ Disapprove strongly

5. To what extent do you support or oppose the United States government ending its trade embargo against Cuba?

- ❏ Support strongly
- ❏ Support somewhat
- ❏ Oppose somewhat
- ❏ Oppose strongly

6. Which of these do you think is most likely to happen in Venezuela?

- ❏ Venezuela will become a stable democracy in the next year or two
- ❏ Venezuela will become a stable democracy, but it will take longer than a year or two
- ❏ Venezuela will probably never become a stable democracy

7. In your view, is the temperature of U.S.-Latin America relations likely to get better, get worse, or remain about the same over the next five years?

- ❏ It will get better
- ❏ It will get worse
- ❏ It will remain about the same

8. Would you like to share any other thoughts with us about Latin America's political pendulum? If so, please use the space below.

. . . .

. . . .

. . . .

Topic 7. Prospects for Afghanistan and Pakistan

1. Have you engaged in any of the following activities related to the "Prospects for Afghanistan and Pakistan" topic? Mark all that you have done or mark none of the above.

- ☑ Read the article on Afghanistan and Pakistan in the 2017 *Great Decisions* briefing book
- ☑ Discussed the article on Afghanistan and Pakistan with a Great Decisions discussion group
- ☑ Discussed the article on Afghanistan and Pakistan with friends and family
- ☑ Followed news related to Afghanistan and Pakistan
- ❏ Taken a class in which you learned about issues related to Afghanistan and Pakistan
- ❏ Have or had a job related to Afghanistan and/or Pakistan
- ❏ Traveled to Afghanistan or Pakistan
- ❏ None of the above

2. How interested would you say you are in issues related to Afghanistan and Pakistan?

- ☑ Very interested
- ❏ Somewhat interested
- ❏ Not too interested
- ❏ Not at all interested

3. To what extent do you approve or disapprove of the way President Barack Obama has handled the war in Afghanistan?

- ❏ Approve strongly
- ☑ Approve somewhat
- ❏ Disapprove somewhat
- ❏ Disapprove strongly

4. In 2017, do you think things will be better or worse than they were in 2016 when it comes to the war in Afghanistan?

- ☑ Better
- ❏ Worse

5. How likely is it that Afghanistan can maintain a stable, democratic government once the U.S. has withdrawn all its troops?

- ❏ Very likely
- ❏ Somewhat likely
- ❏ Somewhat unlikely
- ☑ Very unlikely

6. How do you think history will judge the war in Afghanistan: complete success, more of a success than failure, more of a failure than success, or complete failure?

- ❏ Complete success
- ☑ More of a success than a failure
- ❏ More of a failure than a success
- ❏ Complete failure

7. President Barack Obama announced that the United States will delay withdrawing the remaining U.S. troops in Afghanistan, keeping about 9,800 troops in that country in 2016 and about 5,500 in 2017. Do you favor, oppose, or neither favor nor oppose this plan?

- ❏ Favor
- ❏ Neither favor nor oppose
- ☑ Oppose

8. How important is eliminating the opium trade to making Afghanistan a country that is stable enough to withstand the threat posed by the Taliban or other extremist groups?

- ☑ Very important
- ❏ Somewhat important
- ❏ Not too important
- ❏ Not important at all

9. Do you have a very favorable, somewhat favorable, somewhat unfavorable or very unfavorable opinion of Pakistan?

- ❏ Very favorable
- ❏ Somewhat favorable
- ❏ Somewhat unfavorable
- ☑ Very unfavorable

10. Do you have a very favorable, somewhat favorable, somewhat unfavorable or very unfavorable opinion of Afghanistan?

- ❏ Very favorable
- ☑ Somewhat favorable
- ❏ Somewhat unfavorable
- ❏ Very unfavorable

11. Do you approve or disapprove of the United States conducting missile strikes from pilotless aircraft, called "drones," to target extremists in countries such as Pakistan and Afghanistan?

- ☑ Approve strongly
- ❏ Approve somewhat
- ❏ Disapprove somewhat
- ❏ Disapprove strongly

12. Would you like to share any other thoughts with us about Latin America's political pendulum? If so, please use the space below.

. . . .

. . . .

. . . .

. . . .

Topic 8. Nuclear security

1. Have you engaged in any of the following activities related to the "Nuclear security" topic? Mark all that you have done or mark none of the above.

- ☑ Read the article on nuclear security in the 2017 *Great Decisions* briefing book
- ❏ Discussed the article on nuclear security with a Great Decisions discussion group
- ❏ Discussed the article on nuclear security with friends and family
- ❏ Followed news related to nuclear security
- ❏ Taken a class in which you learned about issues related to nuclear security
- ❏ Have or had a job related to nuclear security
- ❏ None of the above

2. How interested would you say you are in issues related to nuclear security?

- ❏ Very interested
- ☑ Somewhat interested
- ❏ Not too interested
- ❏ Not at all interested

3. Would you support or oppose the following countries acquiring nuclear weapons?

3.1. South Korea

- ☑ Support
- ❏ Oppose

3.2. Japan

- ☒ Support
- ❑ Oppose

3.3. Saudi Arabia

- ☒ Support
- ❑ Oppose

3.4. Germany

- ❑ Support
- ☒ Oppose

3.5. Canada

- ☒ Support
- ❑ Oppose

4. How important was U.S. nuclear security to your vote for president in 2016?

- ❑ Very important
- ❑ Somewhat important
- ❑ Not too important
- ☒ Not important at all

5. Do you think the world is more secure or less secure from nuclear threats than it was eight years ago, or has there been no change?

- ❑ The world is more secure from nuclear threats
- ☒ The world is less secure from nuclear threats
- ❑ The world is about as secure from nuclear threats as it was eight years ago

6. How likely do you think it is that the U.S. will experience a nuclear terrorist attack in the near future?

- ❑ Very likely
- ☒ Somewhat likely
- ❑ Not too likely
- ❑ Not likely at all

7. To what extent do you think that North Korea's nuclear program is a major threat, a minor threat or not a threat to the well being of the United States?

- ❑ Major threat
- ☒ Minor threat
- ❑ Not a threat

8. Last year the United States made an agreement with Iran that lifts sanctions for ten years in exchange for Iran curtailing its pursuit of a nuclear program over that time period. So far, do you think the Iran deal is making the United States safer or less safe?

- ☒ Safer
- ❑ Less safe

9. Last year the United States made an agreement with Iran that lifts sanctions for ten years in exchange for Iran curtailing its pursuit of a nuclear program over that time period. So far, do you think the Iran deal is making the *world* safer or less safe?

- ❑ Safer
- ❑ Less safe

10. To what extent do you support or oppose the Iran nuclear agreement?

- ❑ Support strongly
- Support somewhat
- ❑ Oppose somewhat
- ❑ Oppose strongly

11. Would you like to share any other thoughts with us about nuclear security? If so, please use the space below.

. . . .

. . . .

. . . .

. . . .

. . . .

Become a Member

For nearly a century, members of the Association have played key roles in government, think tanks, academia and the private sector.

Make a Donation

Your support helps the FOREIGN POLICY ASSOCIATION's programs dedicated to global affairs education.

As an active participant in the FPA's Great Decisions program, we encourage you to join the community today's foreign policy thought leaders.

Member—$250

Benefits:
- Free admission to all Associate events (includes member's family)
- Discounted admission for all other guests to Associate events
- Complimentary **GREAT DECISIONS** briefing book
- Complimentary issue of FPA's annual ***National Opinion Ballot Report***

Visit us online at

www.fpa.org/membership

Make a fully tax-deductible contribution to FPA's Annual Fund 2017.

To contribute to the Annual Fund 2017, visit us online at **www.fpa.org** or call the Membership Department at

(800) 628-5754 ext. 333

The generosity of donors who contribute $500 or more is acknowledged in FPA's *Annual Report.*

All financial contributions are tax-deductible to the fullest extent of the law under section 501 (c)(3) of the IRS code.

FPA also offers membership at the SPONSOR MEMBER and PATRON MEMBER levels. To learn more, visit us online at www.fpa.org/membership or call (800) 628-5754 ext. 333.

Return this form by mail to: Foreign Policy Association, 470 Park Avenue South, New York, N.Y. 10016. *Or fax to:* (212) 481-9275.

ORDER ONLINE: WWW.GREATDECISIONS.ORG

OR CALL (800) 477-5836

FOR MEMBERSHIP: WWW.FPA.ORG/MEMBERSHIP

❑ MR.   ❑ MRS.   ❑ MS.   ❑ DR.   ❑ PROF.

NAME _____

ADDRESS _____

_____ APT/FLOOR _____

CITY _____ STATE _____ ZIP _____

TEL _____

E-MAIL_____

❑ AMEX   ❑ VISA   ❑ MC   ❑ DISCOVER

❑ CHECK (ENCLOSED)

CHECKS SHOULD BE PAYABLE TO FOREIGN POLICY ASSOCIATION.

CARD NO.

SIGNATURE OF CARDHOLDER

EXP. DATE (MM/YY)

PRODUCT	QTY	PRICE	COST
GREAT DECISIONS 2017 Briefing Book (FPA31659)		$25	
SPECIAL OFFER TEN PACK SPECIAL GREAT DECISIONS 2017 (FPA31616) *Includes 10% discount		$225	
GREAT DECISIONS TELEVISION SERIES GD ON DVD 2017(FPA31660)		$40	
GREAT DECISIONS 2017 TEACHER'S PACKET (1 Briefing Book, 1 Teacher's Guide and 1 DVD (FPA 31662) E-MAIL: (REQUIRED) _____		$70	
GREAT DECISIONS CLASSROOM-PACKET (1 Teacher's Packet & 30 Briefing Books (FPA31663) E-MAIL: (REQUIRED) _____		$615	
MEMBERSHIP		$250	
ANNUAL FUND 2017 (ANY AMOUNT)			

SUBTOTAL $ _____

plus S & H* $ _____

TOTAL $ _____

For details and shipping charges, call FPA's Sales Department at (800) 477-5836.
Orders mailed to FPA without the shipping charge will be held.